THE POLITICS
OF
ILLUSION
AND
EMPIRE

THE POLITICS
OF
ILLUSION
AND
EMPIRE

German Occupation Policy
in the Soviet Union,
1942–1943

TIMOTHY PATRICK MULLIGAN

PRAEGER

New York
Westport, Connecticut
London

Copyright Acknowledgment

The author and publisher are grateful to the following for allowing the use of extracts from:

Louis P. Lochner (ed.), *The Goebbels Diaries, 1942–1943* (New York: Doubleday and Co., 1948). Reprinted by permission of the publisher.

Library of Congress Cataloging-in-Publication Data

Mulligan, Timothy.
    The politics of illusion and empire: German occupation policy in
the Soviet Union, 1942–1943 / Timothy Patrick Mulligan.
      p.   cm.
      Bibliography: p.
      Includes index.
      ISBN 0–275–92837–3 (alk. paper)
      1. World War, 1939–1945—Soviet Union.   2. Soviet Union—History—
German occupation, 1941–1944.   3. Military occupation.   I. Title.
D802.S75M85   1988
940.53′47—dc19   87–32702

Library of Congress Catalog Card Number: 87–32702
ISBN: 0–275–92837–3

First published in 1988

Praeger Publishers, One Madison Avenue, New York, NY 10010
A division of Greenwood Press, Inc.

Printed in the United States of America

The paper used in this book complies with the
Permanent Paper Standard issued by the National
Information Standards Organization (Z39.48–1984).

10 9 8 7 6 5 4 3 2 1

TO MY PARENTS

Q.: You mean, you had so developed your organization that the individual offices of individual persons carried out their own private wars against one another?

A.: That was the basic principle of the Third Reich.

—From an interrogation of
SS-*Brigadeführer* Otto
Ohlendorf, November 15, 1946

CONTENTS

ILLUSTRATIONS

ABBREVIATIONS

BHO   *Berg- und Hüttenwerksgesellschaft Ost*, Mining and Smelting Corporation East

BNS   *Belaruskaia Narodnaia Samapomach*, Belorussian 'Self-Help' Organization

EgM   *Ereignismeldungen UdSSR*, reports prepared by the RSHA on conditions in the occupied Soviet Union

FHO   *Fremde Heere Ost*, Foreign Armies East (intelligence branch of Army High Command)

FMS   Foreign Military Studies

GBA   *Generalbevollmächtiger für den Arbeitseinsatz*, Plenipotentiary General for the Allocation of Labor

Hiwis   *Hilfswillige*, "auxiliary volunteers," Russians serving as noncombatants in German units

HSC   Hitler's Secret Conversations

HSSPF   *Höherer SS- und Polizeiführer*, Senior SS and Police Commander

IVOVSS   *Istoriia Velikoi Otechestvennoi voiny Sovetskogo Soiuza, 1941–1945*, Soviet official history of the Great Patriotic War

KTB   *Kriegstagebuch*, war diary

La-Führer   *Landwirtschaftsführer*, agricultural leaders

NA   National Archives, Washington, DC

NCA   *Nazi Conspiracy and Aggression* (Washington, DC: Government Printing Office, 1946–1947)

NMT	*Trials of the War Criminals before the Nuernberg Military Tribunals under Control Council Law No. 10*, (Washington, DC: Government Printing Office, 1949–1954
NO, NG, NI, PS, NOKW, EC, OCC	Prefixes assigned to German documents collected by the Allied Powers during the Nürnberg war crimes trials
OD	*Ordnungsdienst*, Russian auxiliary police employed by the Germans
OKH	*Oberkommando des Heeres*, German Army High Command
OKW	*Oberkommando der Wehrmacht*, German Armed Forces High Command
OKW/WPr	*Oberkommando der Wehrmacht/Wehrmacht Propaganda*, Armed Forces Propaganda Division
OMi	*Ostministerium*, "Eastern Ministry," The Reich Ministry for the occupied eastern territories
OSS	Office of Strategic Services
OUN	*Organizatsiia Ukrains'kykh Natsionalistiv*, Organization of Ukrainian Nationalists
RG	Record Group (National Archives designation)
RKFDV	*Reichskommissar für die Festigung deutschen Volkstums*, Reich Commissioner for the Strengthening of Germandom
RM	*Reichsmarks* (German currency)
ROA	*Russkaia Osvoboditelnaia Armiia*, Russian Popular Army of Liberation
RONA	*Russkaia Osvoboditelnaia Narodnaia Armiia*, Russian Popular Army of Liberation
RNNA	*Russkaia Natsionalnaia Narodnaia Armiia*, Russian National People's Army
RSHA	*Reichssicherheitshauptamt*, Reich Central Security Office
SA	*Sturmabteilung*, "storm troopers"
SD	*Sicherheitsdienst*, Security Service of the SS
SS	*Schutzstaffel*, "Guard Echelon"
TMWC	*Trial of the Major War Criminals before the International Military Tribunal Nuremberg, 14 November 1945–1 October 1946* (Nürnberg: The International Military Tribunal, 1947–1949)
UPA	*Ukrainska Povstanska Armia*, Ukrainian Insurgent Army
VfZ	*Vierteljahreshefte für Zeitgeschichte*
Wi-Stab-Ost	*Wirtschaftsstab Ost*, Economic Staff East
YIVO	YIVO Institute for Jewish Research, New York, NY
ZHO	*Zentralhandelsgesellschaft Ost*, Central Trade Corporation East

PREFACE

An undertaking of this nature incurs many debts that cannot be repaid, only acknowledged. I am particularly indebted for the guidance and support of Dr. George O. Kent and the late Dr. Gordon Prange of the University of Maryland. Drs. John Sumida, Clifford Foust, John Lampe, and Tönu Parming read the manuscript and provided valuable suggestions and comments. Mr. Robert Wolfe and the reference staff of the National Archives contributed greatly in the identification of source materials. My research was also greatly facilitated by Messrs. Werner and Hagner of the Bundesarchiv, Koblenz; Mr. Meyer of the Bundesarchiv–Abt. Militärarchiv, Freiburg; Dr. Helmut Krausnick and the staff of the Institut für Zeitgeschichte, Munich; Dr. Daniel Simon of the Berlin Document Center; and Dr. Joseph Berg and Miss Fruma Mohrer of the YIVO Institute for Jewish Research, New York.

The following individuals contributed valuable information, comments and ideas to this project: Mr. Heino Taremae, Estonian Archives of the U.S., Inc.; Dr. Theodor Oberländer, Bonn; Dr. Leonid Mihalap, Old Dominion University; Dr. Heinrich Stammler, University of Kansas; Dr. Charles Burdick, San Jose State University; Dr. Sam Newland, University of Kansas; Dr. S.J. Lewis, U.S. Army General Staff College; Mr. Stan Ausky, Las Cruces, NM; Dr. Earl Ziemke, University of Georgia; Mr. Robin Cookson, National Archives; Dr. Ortwin Buchbender, Cologne; and Dr. David H. Kitterman, Northern Arizona University. I particularly wish to thank Mr. Gunter d'Alquen and his gracious family for their kindness and hospitality. Ms. Eva Krusten, Dr. Dane Hartgrove, and Dr. James Miller kindly assisted in translations of Estonian, Russian, and Italian language materials, respectively. Dana Carpio and Kay King typed the manuscript.

Finally I express my deepest gratitude to my wife Bonnie, not only for her assistance in the preparation of the index, but for putting up with so much for so long.

THE POLITICS
OF
ILLUSION
AND
EMPIRE

INTRODUCTION

On June 22, 1941 the German Army swept across the frontiers of Soviet Russia "to secure for the German people the land and soil to which they are entitled on this earth," as proclaimed in Adolf Hitler's *Mein Kampf*.[1] Forty-six months later Soviet forces stormed Berlin and ended the Nazi dream of empire as Hitler took his own life beneath the rubble. The intervening period marked a titanic struggle that altered the face of Europe and elevated the USSR to the status of global power. Yet this outcome hardly appeared inevitable to contemporaries or to post-war analysts, who believed either in Germany's superior military capability or in the Soviet Union's greater political vulnerability. Though the former was proven false by 1943, the latter view has persisted into the present.

Specifically, this concept holds that Germany missed the chance to capitalize on popular dissatisfaction with Josef Stalin's totalitarian regime. The leading Western scholar in this field has concluded that Germany "had a rare opportunity" to exploit the "many latent fissures in Soviet state and society," but "failed utterly to take advantage of this opportunity."[2] Nearly 30 years after this was written, another historian commented on Hitler's policies in Russia: "Yet there was here the possibility of a bloodless victory which was his for the asking. . . . All that was necessary was a soft hand and a soft word."[3]

Could it really have been so simple? The assumption of a missed German opportunity, despite its long history, raises issues that are often overlooked. First, the treatment of Soviet political disaffection under German occupation inevitably reflects ideological influences that are themselves a legacy of that conflict. Marxist historians deny the Soviet political system's susceptibility to German blandishments, and reject any interpretation of collaboration beyond that of opportunism or "bourgeois nationalism."[4] The majority of Western scholars who have studied this topic[5] produced their work in the early years of the cold war, when Germany's experiences were carefully scrutinized for possible operational use against the USSR. The perceived "lessons learned" moreover received mass distribution to the American public through such magazines as *Life*, where the advantages of "psychological fission" were extolled over the atomic bomb as a weapon against Moscow.[6]

More significant than ideological influences, however, the argument for a potentially "bloodless" victory by Hitler over Stalin ignores the many formidable problems that such a policy entailed. How could political discontent be effectively harnessed by an invading power? How could the aspirations of the minority nationalities be reconciled with anti-Stalinist Russian nationalism? How would a fighting force of nominal Soviet nationals be armed, organized and employed in combination with a foreign army? What were the intelligence risks involved, and the danger of redefection? Above all: How could German war aims be moderated within the framework of National Socialist ideology?

A significant number of German civil and military officials wrestled with precisely these questions during the Soviet-German conflict, when the answers had to be balanced against the multiple demands of a war for survival. The attitudes, efforts and limitations of these men during the critical period from the autumn of 1942 to the summer of 1943 provide the focus of this study.

The events have been partially recounted in memoirs, yet these are often self-serving and usually written without access to official records for verification.[7] More importantly, such works suffer from the limited perspective of one individual or one particular aspect of the subject, a distortion reinforced by the polycratic nature of the National Socialist regime and especially the chaotic structure of the German occupation administration in Russia.

Our priority moreover lies not with the "lessons for the West" of what might have been. Rather, we will examine the nature and extent of the envisioned reforms, the process by which they were proposed, disputed, implemented or rejected, and their relationship to the broader questions of German economic mobilization, military strategy, and diplomatic relations within the Axis coalition. Special attention will be given to the underlying assumptions—and illusions—among German policy-makers involved in the reform efforts. The question of continuity of German policies between the First and Second World Wars will also be considered.

An examination of this topic should benefit two areas of study. Above all, the attempts to reform German policies in Russia provide an invaluable insight into Germany's strategic dilemma at this crucial time, the adjustment of means and ends to confront increasingly superior resources in a multi-front war. The selection of the period from autumn 1942 to summer 1943 is not arbitrary as this nine-month interval of the most intensive reform activity coincides with the turning of the tide against Germany. On the Eastern Front, the gradual collapse of the 1942 summer offensive was followed by the Stalingrad catastrophe and a withdrawal of several hundred miles before the front could be restored; spring saw the final destruction of Axis forces in North Africa and the bloody retreat of Admiral Doenitz's U-boats from the North Atlantic. These hammer blows rocked the foundations of the Axis coalition, causing Germany's allies to broach the subject of a compromise peace.[8] Many German leaders also experienced a crisis of faith and began to cast about for alternatives to an all-or-nothing military decision. As in the winter of 1941, when the Blitzkrieg's collapse before Moscow resulted in increased pressure for changes in occupation policies, a significant number of German officials turned to *Ostpolitik* reform and rationalization as a political solution to Germany's deteriorating military situation. These efforts moreover affected many other areas of concern in the wake of Stalingrad: an intensified economic mobilization of natural resources and labor, the determination of future German military strategy, and the stability of the Axis coalition. The story of the reform of Germany's Eastern policy is a description of the crisis of the German war effort.

A second benefit of our study is the opportunity to examine a major policy debate among the National Socialist leadership. Far from its projected image as an efficient, monolithic totalitarian state, Nazi Germany represented a jungle of competing authorities and personal empires that handicapped any centralized direction of effort. Knowledge of these conditions has sparked a debate among historians as to Hitler's exact role in the determination of policy: Was the will of the führer all-important, or did policy emerge through the interaction of Hitler and the component institutions of his regime?[9] The attempted reform of occupation policy in Russia offers a case study for precisely this question. Of perhaps greater significance, the proposed reforms reveal much in the manner of perceptions and attitudes of their sponsors: perceptions and attitudes regarding the limitations of German power, the process of policy formulation under Hitler, and ultimately the capacity of National Socialism to reform itself. If we thereby gain a better understanding of how intelligent and humane men could serve a regime that has become synonymous with genocide, then this study will have served a useful purpose: for the power of illusion in the making of policy is a phenomenon limited neither to National Socialism nor to the past.

For the sake of clarity, some definitions of terms and source materials are necessary. *Ostpolitik* (literally, "Eastern policy") is used as a collective term for German occupation policy, war aims, and propaganda. Reliance on the words *reform* and *reformers* does not imply a value judgment of the motives or goals of those so described, but serves simply as convenient terminology for those attempts to alleviate conditions for the indigenous population or to concede powers, privileges, or material benefits to them.[10] For similar reasons, *collaborators* and *collaborationists* denote those who actively cooperated with German authorities in the occupied areas regardless of nationalist, ideological, or opportunist motivation. The transliteration of Russian names follows the Library of Congress system. A list of the abbreviations used in the text and footnotes precedes this introduction.

The records of the German occupation shared the fate of Germany herself—they were divided between East and West. Records maintained in the field offices of the numerous German authorities in Russia, and which were not destroyed by their retreating originators, fell into Soviet hands. Many of these were eventually turned over to the German Democratic Republic's Central State Archives,[11] but others remained in the custody of various Soviet state archives. Marxist historians have utilized these sources in both monographs and documentary publications,[12] but they remain unavailable to Western scholars. A wealth of agency headquarters records, however, were captured by the Western Allies at war's end. Exploited initially for use in the Nürnberg war crimes trials, the originals have nearly all been restituted to the German Federal Republic's *Bundesarchiv*, after many were microfilmed for deposit with the National Archives.[13] These records inevitably reflect a bias toward the perspective of Berlin, but it is precisely these views and perceptions of German officials that are under scrutiny here.

I have attempted to incorporate both topical and geographic treatment while maintaining a rough chronological narrative. Certain areas of the occupied Soviet Union, however, have been largely excluded because their particular administrative status removed them from the mainstream of *Ostpolitik*. These include Bialystok, annexed to German East Prussia; Bukovina, Bessarabia and Transnistria, occupied and administered by Rumania; Karelia, occupied by Finland; and the western Ukraine, attached to Hans Frank's *Generalgouvernement* of Poland as Galicia. The last has received some consideration, however, because of its relationship to occupation policy in the rest of the Ukraine.

NOTES

1. Adolf Hitler, *Mein Kampf*, trans. Ralph Manheim (Boston: Houghton Mifflin, 1943), p. 652.

2. Alexander Dallin, *German Rule in Russia 1941–1945: A Study of Occupation Policies* (New York: St. Martin's Press, 1957), pp. 674–75. Regarded as the best treatment of the subject, a revised edition (Boulder, Col.: Westview Press, 1981) included only six changes in the text and footnotes and a historiographical postscript summarizing the most recent literature.

3. Ronald Lewin, *Hitler's Mistakes* (New York: William Morrow and Company, 1984), pp. 127–128.

4. See, for example, V. Cherednichenko, *Collaborationists* (Kiev: Politvidav Ukraini, 1975), and Günter Rosenfeld, "Zur Entstehung des Programms der sogenannten 'Politischen Kriegführung' gegen die Sowjetunion und seinen Apologeten in dder Gegenwart," in *Der deutsche Imperialismus und der Zweite Weltkrieg*, Bd. III (Berlin: Rütten & Loening, 1962), pp. 163–70.

5. In addition to Dallin, a partial listing would include George Fischer, *Soviet Opposition to Stalin: A Case Study in World War II* (Cambridge, Mass.: Harvard University Press, 1952); Roman Ilnytzkyj, *Deutschland und die Ukraine 1943–1945; Tatsachen*

europäischen Ostpolitik (2 vols.) (Munich: Osteuropa-Institut, 1955); and John A. Armstrong, *Ukrainian Nationalism 1939–1945* (New York: Columbia University Press, 1955).

6. Wallace Carroll, "It takes a Russian to beat a Russian," *Life Magazine*, December 19, 1949, pp. 80–88, an article cited by Dallin nine times.

7. See, for example, Otto Bräutigam, *So hat es sich zugetragen* (Würzburg: Holzer Verlag, 1968); Peter Kleist, *Zwischen Hitler und Stalin* (Bonn: Athenäum-Verlag, 1950); Wilfried Strik-Strikfeldt, *Against Stalin and Hitler 1941–1945*, trans. by David Footman (New York: John Day Co., 1973); Hans von Herwarth with Frederick Starr, *Against Two Evils* (New York: Rawson Wade Publishers, Inc., 1981); and Reinhard Gehlen, *The Service: The Memoirs of General Reinhard Gehlen*, trans. by David Irving and intro. by George Baily (New York: The World Publishing Co., 1972).

8. See Jürgen Förster, *Stalingrad: Risse im Bündnis 1942/43* (Freiburg: Rombach Verlag, 1975), and F. W. Deakin, *The Brutal Friendship: Mussolini, Hitler and the Fall of Italian Fascism* (New York: Harper & Row, 1962).

9. See particularly Gerhard Hirschfeld and Lothar Kettenacker, eds., *Der "Führerstaat": Mythos und Realität. Studien zur Struktur und Politik des Dritten Reiches*, intro. by Wolfgang J. Mommsen (Stuttgart: Klett-Cotta, 1981), esp. pp. 23–40.

10. We shall also refrain from rendering judgment on German officials based on the phraseology of their memoranda (see, for example, Dallin, *German Rule*, pp. 536–37, 603–04, and Fischer, *Soviet Opposition*, pp. 9–14), as the use of Nazi rhetoric provided an effective vehicle for proposing change to the Nazi leadership.

11. See Helmut Lötzke and Hans-Stephan Brather, *Übersicht über die Bestände des deutschen Zentralarchivs Potsdam* (Berlin: Rütten & Loening, 1957).

12. Examples include: *Prestupnye Tseli-Prestupnye Sredstva: Dokumenty*, comp. Institut Marksizma-Leninizma Pri TsK KPSS (Moscow: Izdatel'stvo politicheskoi literatury, 1968); Norbert Müller, ed., *Deutsche Besatzungspolitik in der UdSSR* (Berlin and Cologne: Pahl-Rugenstein Verlag, 1980); and *Documents Accuse*, comp. B. Baranauskas and K. Ruksenas (Vilnius: "Gintaras," 1970).

13. The pertinent records, from the National Archives Collection of Seized Enemy Records, Record Group (RG) 242, have been microfilmed by the National Archives with the following designations:

T–77: German Armed Forces High Command (OKW)
T–78: German Army High Command (OKH)
T–81: Nazi Party and the Deutsches Ausland-Institut
T–84: Miscellaneous German Records Collection
T–120: German Foreign Ministry
T–175: Reichsführer-SS and Chief of the German Police
T–311: German Field Commands: Army Groups
T–312: German Field Commands: Armies
T–454: Reich Ministry for Occupied Eastern Territories
T–501: German Field Commands: Rear Areas, Occupied Territories and Others.

Subsequent citations to these records will follow the format: document identification, microcopy ("T-") number/roll number/frame numbers.

1

CREDOS OF ILLUSION

At the führer headquarters "Wolfsschanze" east of Rastenburg, East Prussia, the afternoon of July 16, 1941 showed a flurry of activity beyond even the usual bustle of staff officers attending to Adolf Hitler's orders. A stream of high-ranking dignitaries were greeted by Hitler with a simple lunch and beer in the *Führerbunker* before withdrawing to the conference room to discuss the meeting's purpose: dismembering the Soviet Union.[1]

For Hitler the moment represented the restoration of Germany's 1918 supremacy in Eastern Europe and an opportunity to consolidate that position through large-scale colonization, a theme he had stressed in speeches as early as 1919.[2] "And so we National Socialists," he wrote in *Mein Kampf*, "turn our gaze toward the land in the east. . . . If we speak of soil in Europe today, we can primarily have in mind only Russia and her vassal border states."[3] In an unpublished 1928 manuscript he drew an explicit lesson from the Great War:

The sole war aim that the monstrous bloodbath would have been worthy of [sic] could consist only in the assurance to German soldiers of so and so many hundred thousand square kilometers . . . German grenadiers really had not shed their blood so that Poles might acquire a state. . . .[4]

Four days after assuming the office of Reich chancellor, Hitler raised the prospects of a future conquest of *Lebensraum* in Eastern Europe to an informal gathering of senior German Army officers.[5]

The opportunity to realize this vision lay at the heart of Hitler's decision to attack Russia, though strategic factors also played a role.[6] By mid-July 1941, that goal appeared to be within Germany's grasp. The *Wehrmacht*'s spearheads had already covered more than half the distance to Moscow, capturing huge numbers of Soviet prisoners. General Franz Halder, chief of the German Army General Staff, believed the campaign won in the first 14 days; on July 14, Hitler shifted armaments production priorities in favor of Luftwaffe and Navy requirements for the renewed struggle against England. When Hitler received Japanese ambassador Hiroshi Oshima the next day he held out the prospect of an offensive alliance against the United States following the conclusion of the Soviet campaign. It was in this euphoria of global triumph that Hitler summoned his ministers to the "Wolfsschanze" on July 16, 1941.[7]

Attending this conference were Hitler, *Reichsleiter* Alfred Rosenberg, Chief of the Nazi party Chancellery Martin Bormann, Field Marshal Wilhelm Keitel (chief of the Armed Forces High Command), Chief of the Reich Chancellery Dr. Hans Lammers and later *Reichsmarschall* Hermann Goering, head of the Luftwaffe and the Four Year Plan. Hitler set the tone of the meeting with the comment, "We must make of the newly-acquired Eastern areas a Garden of Eden." In the course of a five-hour discussion he set forth his vision: The Crimea would be emptied of its inhabitants and resettled by German colonists, the Baltic states would be incorporated within the Reich, the Volga colony of ethnic Germans (*Volksdeutsche*) and the nickel-rich Kola Peninsula would be annexed, and Finland would be prepared for later federation with Germany. To administer the occupied territories Hitler designated Rosenberg as "Eastern Minister" and a host of Nazi party officials for specific areas; Goering, as head of the Four Year Plan, was made responsible for the economy and *Reichsführer*–SS Heinrich Himmler for police and security matters.[8]

The collapse of the *Blitzkrieg* over the next six months did not sway Hitler from his grandiose plans. On the evening of October 17, 1941 he outlined to his first Reich Minister for Armaments and Munitions, Dr. Fritz Todt, plans for building great highways to connect the Crimea, Caucasus, and other areas with Germany, in anticipation of 10 million settlers colonizing the East in the next 20 years.[9] In late January 1942, as his armies fought for survival, Hitler rationalized the losses suffered as "paid for several times over by our colonization in the East."[10]

Hitler's conviction reflected the power of eastern expansionism within German politics, and more specifically the unstable mixture of two rival ideologies as the rationale for German imperialism. The concept of *Lebensraum*, first publicized by the Pan-German League in the 1890s, proposed to save the small German farmer from the forces of modern industrial society through mass colonization of large parts of Eastern Europe, to be annexed in a future war. Ideologically, however, *Lebensraum* represented an attempt to build a broad national consensus that incorporated a variety of disparate political ideas and social groups within a radical conservative framework. Migrationary colonialism figured as a key element by displacing agrarian unrest as an internal problem to a foreign policy goal, thus allowing the small farmer and landed aristocrat to make common cause. In contrast, the ideology of *Weltpolitik* (literally, "world policy") developed around the same time as an endorsement of the more traditional forms of economic imperialism represented by German industrial and commercial circles, who looked to the government for support in the opening of foreign markets.[11]

The competing ideologies clashed openly in the war aims debates of 1914–18. *Lebensraum* considerations gained the advantage with the rise of General Erich Ludendorff in 1917, but even then German *Ostpolitik* remained a mixture of fantasy (e.g., colonization plans for the Caucasus) and pragmatism (cooperation with the Bolshevik government). That brief moment of supremacy in 1918, however, lingered in the minds of Nazi leaders, who planned to surpass that accomplishment. With a program of grandiose imperialism, National Socialism seemingly offered an integration of the rival ideologies in the future empire; that this integration was merely superficial would become evident in the policy debates of 1942–43.[12]

But for the bulk of the German people *Lebensraum* had little attraction. Hitler found that he could rely upon a heritage of ethnic prejudices and partially absorbed ideological indoctrination to imbue his campaign with the appropriate ruthlessness, but he could not appeal to a pioneer mentality among the German population.[13] The Propaganda Ministry, mindful of foreign reaction, specifically directed the German press on December 21, 1941 to refrain from the use of such terms as "colonies" or "colonial methods."[14] Rumors of compulsory settlement of German peasants in the occupied areas nevertheless circulated among the prospective colonists, who responded with a noticeable lack of enthusiasm.[15] A survey conducted in the summer of 1943 throughout the *Wehrmacht* of those interested in post-war resettlement in the Ukraine reportedly yielded only 237 applicants.[16] Hitler's colonial war aims in Russia signified a major break with the perceived interests of his public, as an opinion survey in Leipzig in June 1942 observed that the average citizen regarded the "New Order" in Europe as imperialism: "A concept of vast territorial acquisition is still far from the minds of most."[17]

Hitler apparently sensed this as well, for despite his frequent candor he did not completely share his vision with those charged with the task of realizing it. He informed all parties sufficiently to implicate them in his designs, yet deceived or misled those whose cooperation he needed but whose aims differed from his own. Whether calculated or improvised, this trait is nowhere more evident than in Hitler's choice for the position of Reich minister for the Occupied Eastern Territories.

Alfred Rosenberg entered his office with unique qualifications, for he straddled the *Ostpolitik* of two Germanies with the heritage of a personal familiarity with Russia. Born in Reval (now Tallinn) to an established middle-class Baltic German family, Rosenberg received his architectural degree in Moscow in time to volunteer for the German army of occupation in 1918.[18] One year later Rosenberg joined the infant National Socialist German Workers' Party and soon established himself as its philosopher with a torrent of literature on the theme of "Jewish Bolshevism."[19] His hatred of Communism was matched by his enmity for the Great Russians of Muscovy, the driving force behind Russian expansionism since the seventeenth century; his views on dismantling the Soviet Union derived from the lessons of Wilhelmine Germany's eastern policy. He proposed to arouse the minority nationalities of the Soviet Empire—White Russians, cossacks, the peoples of the Caucasus and especially the Ukrainians—against Muscovy and deflect the latter's ambitions toward Asia; as a permanent settlement he envisaged the Baltic states and "White Ruthenia" (White Russia) as a "Germanized protectorate" preparatory to eventual union with Germany, an independent Ukrainian state allied to the Reich, and a federated Caucasus with a German plenipotentiary.[20]

But by the time of BARBAROSSA, Rosenberg's star had long been on the wane. His once-significant influence on the development of Hitler's anti-Communist ideology ebbed steadily after 1930.[21] Contemporaries who acknowledged their philosophical debt to Rosenberg nevertheless considered him a man with an amazing predilection for the wrong decision.[22] An intellectual rigidity and a sensitive, introverted nature served him badly in the jungle world of Nazi power politics, where his rivals steadily undermined his authority.[23] Hitler himself ridiculed Rosenberg's ideological *magnum opus, The Myth of the Twentieth Century*, to his associates.[24]

Yet on April 20, 1941 Hitler appointed Rosenberg "Commissioner for the central consideration of Eastern European questions,"[25] a prelude to his subsequent nomination as Eastern minister. What can account for his selection? Rosenberg would later claim that Hitler agreed completely with his political conception of the East until the influence of Himmler and Bormann brought about a "radical" change in the führer, but this is unlikely.[26] As with the decision for BARBAROSSA itself, Hitler may have included strategic factors—in this case, an appeal to the minority nationalities—as part of his political program in the event of rough going at the beginning of the invasion. The early military victories then left him free to realize his maximum goals without regard for his nominal Eastern minister.

Hitler's prerogatives, however, were purchased at the cost of consistency in policy, particularly with regard to the Ukraine. During the pre-invasion planning, Rosenberg set as his goal "the establishment of a free Ukrainian state in the closest alliance with Germany."[27] More significantly, he transmitted his views as policy to those charged with its implementation. In late April 1941 Rosenberg conferred with the senior officers of the Armed Forces High Command (*Oberkommando der Wehrmacht*, or OKW), the Army High Command (*Oberkommando des Heeres*, or OKH) and even the navy on German political aims in the coming campaign, and with *Abwehr* chief Admiral Wilhelm Canaris he discussed the possible political use of *Abwehr* contacts within the USSR.[28] OKH subsequently issued directives to the army announcing the planned establishment of an independent Ukrainian state with its own administration under temporary German rule.[29]

Rosenberg drove home his thesis in a major speech delivered in Berlin two days before the invasion began. To an audience of senior military and Party officials (including Reinhard Heydrich), Rosenberg explained "the task of our policy . . . lies in the intelligent and firm recapture of the independence aspirations of all these (minority nationalities) and raising them to their destined level of political states. . . . " To restore Ukrainian national consciousness Rosenberg proposed the establishment of a Ukrainian university, reeducation in the native language, and eventually the founding of a political party.[30]

Hitler's disregard of Rosenberg's statements in the days preceding BARBA-ROSSA is understandable in view of the detailed diplomatic and military preparations that consumed the führer's time prior to the invasion. But in subsequent meetings, Hitler tolerated and even encouraged Rosenberg's ideas. At the afternoon conference of July 16, the Eastern minister reiterated his views regarding Ukrainian nationalism without objection by Hitler.[31] And at a conference of Hitler, Rosenberg, and Bormann on September 29, 1941, the führer appeared to openly endorse Rosenberg's views. Hitler approved a limited and gradual restoration of private farmland to Ukrainian and Russian peasants, and authorized the release of Soviet prisoners-of-war of Ukrainian origin. Hitler even implied eventual Ukrainian sovereignty: A conference participant recorded that, though the führer considered an independent Ukraine "out of the question for decades to come, he suggested a 25-year German protectorate over the region."[32]

But Hitler did not mean it. Ten days earlier he had revealed his true intentions in a conference with *Gauleiter* Erich Koch, newly appointed *Reichskommissar* (Reich commissioner) for the Ukraine. The notes kept by Dr. Werner Koeppen, Rosenberg's liaison officer at the *Führerhauptquartier*, are unequivocal:

Both the Führer and the *Reichskommissar* reject an independent Ukraine. . . . Besides, hardly anything will be left standing in Kiev. The Führer's inclination to destroy Russia's large cities as a prerequisite for the permanence of our power in Russia will be further consolidated by the *Reichskommissar*'s smashing of Ukrainian industry, in order to drive the proletariat back to the land.[33]

In thus deceiving Rosenberg, Hitler also misled all those who assumed the former's appointment signified power commensurate with his title. Only veterans of the Nazi political jungle like Propaganda Minister Joseph Goebbels perceived that Hitler intended Rosenberg's ministry "as a guiding and not an administrative instrument."[34]

This view is reflected in the inconsistency of *Ostministerium* staff selections. Several liberal *Weltpolitiker* occupied key positions: Dr. Otto Bräutigam, a career diplomat experienced in Soviet affairs and deputy chief of the Political Department;[35] a scholar once deemed unacceptable for his pro-Russian sentiments by

Rosenberg's own staff, Dr. Hans Koch, attached as liaison officer to Army Group South;[36] and Dr. Peter Kleist, a Foreign Ministry specialist assigned to OMi as head of the Political Department's Baltic section.[37] On the other hand, Dr. Erhard Wetzel transferred to Bräutigam's section from the Nazi party's Racial-Political Office as an ardent advocate of German colonization.[38]

In the autumn of 1941 Rosenberg finally grasped the reality of his situation, and capitulated totally to Hitler's program. To Hans Frank, *Generalgouverneur* of Poland, he conceded his abandonment of plans to build a Ukrainian state on October thirteenth. Seventeen days later he hosted an interagency conference on the future of occupied Russia, in which he faithfully repeated Hitler's grandiose colonization schemes. A Rosenberg directive of November nineteenth even defended the need for an "authoritarian" German rule of the Ukraine. Rosenberg's capitulation, however, would prove temporary as the military reversal before Moscow restored his faith in the Ukrainian solution.[39]

But if Hitler allowed Rosenberg to delude himself in policy matters, he blatantly lied to his military leaders as to the political goals of BARBAROSSA. Hitler had spoken openly of his *Lebensraum* goals to an earlier generation of *Wehrmacht* commanders in speeches of February 3, 1933 and February 28, 1934, only to meet a decidedly cool reaction; for the next several years he was much more guarded in his remarks.[40] Though by the end of 1940 many senior officers had retired or been purged, Hitler still did not trust his High Command. Instead he set the stage for Rosenberg by repeatedly outlining his war aims as, essentially, a return to the *Ostpolitik* of 1918. When Hitler first raised the idea of an attack on the USSR to his senior military leaders on July 22, 1940, he specified as his political objectives the establishment of a Ukrainian state and a federation of the Baltic states.[41] On December 5, 1940 he further advised the chiefs of OKH and OKW that after the Eastern campaign "new buffer states (Ukraine, White Russia, Lithuania, Latvia) will be erected while Rumania, Finland and the Government-General will be expanded."[42] Later, on March 3, 1941, Hitler revised OKW's "Special Instructions" to the BARBAROSSA directive to note that the Soviet area "must be split up into different states, each with their own government with whom we may then conclude peace. . . . Our task is to build up socialist states which will be dependent on us."[43]

The führer maintained these views in personal briefings as well. On March seventeenth Hitler divulged to Army Commander-in-Chief Field Marshal Walter von Brauchitsch, Halder, and their senior staff officers that his political goal was to create three "Kerensky republics" (a Baltic federation, White Russia, and the Pinsk-Ukraine region), while the Caucasus might be offered to Turkey to bind her to the Axis.[44] And on March 30, Hitler delivered a speech to over two hundred *Wehrmacht* officers at the Reich Chancellery, where he forecast the establishment of German protectorates over the Baltic states, the Ukraine, and White Russia, all of which would become "socialist states, but without their own intelligentsia."[45]

These stated objectives, however, were obscured by the larger message communicated by Hitler: to wage the coming campaign without regard for the laws of war. BARBAROSSA signified a war of annihilation, he explained, in which the Red Army could not be treated as fellow soldiers: Political commissars and Communist party functionaries were to be shot outright. Hitler thus appears to have employed a dual strategy toward his officers, appealing to their political conservatism in the use of radical (i.e., criminal) means to achieve conventional (and moderate) ends.[46]

It was, after all, only the swift and victorious conduct of the campaign that Hitler required of the army. Prior to BARBAROSSA Hitler specified that the occupied areas under German Army authority should be reduced to a minimum; military government would rapidly give way to civil administration, while special SS and police task forces (the *Einsatzgruppen*) would carry out security and "executive measures" even in the areas temporarily under army control.[47] With victory won, the army would be out of the picture.

The first months of BARBAROSSA seemed, indeed, to confirm all Hitler's expectations. Not only did the army win great victories, but the combination of Nazi ideology and the savage nature of combat on the Eastern Front elicited the responses Hitler desired. Army compliance with the infamous "Commissar Order," though not consistent, was far from insignificant.[48] Soviet partisan activity was countered by brutality and indiscriminate reprisals that facilitated cooperation with the mass murder of Jews by the *Einsatzgruppen*.[49] The deaths of 2 to 3 million Soviet prisoners-of-war in military custody may be attributed in part to the army's inability to care properly for unexpectedly huge numbers of captives with logistics limited to combat priorities, and in part to the disruption of food supplies due to German requisitions and Stalin's "scorched-earth" policy; but Nazi racist doctrine also played a major role, especially when reinforced by news of Soviet atrocities against German prisoners.[50]

The *Blitzkrieg*'s collapse before Moscow in December 1941, however, utterly and irrevocably altered the foundations of Hitler's plans. German military government in Russia became a fixture as the front stablized. As German planners grappled with the new requirements of a protracted, multi-front struggle against Britain, the United States, and the USSR, *Ostpolitik* began to be integrated with the overall German war effort. The need for increased armaments production compelled Hitler to revise his original plans and restore, rather than dismantle, the Soviet industrial economy in the occupied areas, and led to improved food rations for Soviet prisoners-of-war as an important labor supply.[51] More significantly, many military and civilian officials perceived the value of the occupied population's willing cooperation as an important political weapon. Throughout the winter of 1941–42 a stream of memoranda poured through German bureaucratic channels calling for a change in policy.[52]

Perhaps the most significant of these involved Field Marshal Walther von Reichenau, commanding the Sixth Army in the Ukraine. A talented and energetic officer who had been on close terms with Hitler before 1933, his National Socialist credentials were beyond doubt: throughout the 1941 campaign he sought to instill in his troops the ideological harshness stressed by Hitler, and worked closely with the *Einsatzgruppe* in his sector.[53] But by February 1942 Reichenau recognized the implications of the failed *Blitzkrieg* and urged a program of land reform, political autonomy and immediate food relief to win Ukrainian cooperation.[54]

This agitation did produce a number of reforms during the first half of 1942. Hitler surprised his agricultural specialists on February fifteenth by changing his mind and approving the "New Agrarian Order" that provided for gradual dissolution of collective farms.[55] In March the Rosenberg Ministry legalized the "self administrations" of Estonia, Latvia, and Lithuania that had been functioning since the beginning of the occupation.[56] Army protestations against the "Commissar Order," rejected by Hitler in late September 1941, persisted until the führer reversed himself and rescinded the order on May 6, 1942.[57] On June nineteenth Rosenberg issued a "Tolerance Edict" that formally recognized religious toleration in the occupied areas.[58] And despite Hitler's express orders to the contrary (reiterated as late as March 1942), the army steadily increased the military use of Soviet nationals until Hitler finally recognized their existence in August 1942.[59]

But the reform proposals of spring 1942 clouded the picture of *Ostpolitik* more than they revised it. Most of the reforms enacted were incomplete or gutted of substance from the start: Though they set a precedent, they did not lay the foundation for a redirection of policy. Their advocates exhibited no coordination of effort, nor any consensus as to the extent or ultimate goals of the initiatives they launched. The significance of these reforms lay not in what they accomplished, nor even the definition of issues in dispute, but in the exposure of the chaotic state of German eastern policy.

The best illustration of the confusion over policy making is the military's misperceptions of Hitler's role. Already deceived as to BARBAROSSA's political goals, army advocates of reform often exempted Hitler from responsibility for "excesses" committed, or even counted him on their side. Colonel Heinz Herre, a key reformer within OKH, revealed this attitude in his diary notes of 11 October 1942: "More and more the flaws (of *Ostpolitik*) become apparent. But the key question remains: how can the flaws be brought to the Führer's attention, so that he himself can redress them?" A month later, after preparing a lengthy critique of mistakes made, Herre pondered: "But *who* and *how* to present it to the Führer?"[60] Other German officers pinned the blame on Rosenberg: Even four years after the war, one veteran military government officer commented, "it is considered probable that Hitler viewed the Russian enigma through the eyes of a man like Rosenberg . . . Hitler's conceptions (were) partly caused by that charlatan Rosenberg, who was not dropped by Hitler until it was too late."[61] The idea that Hitler would correct abuses, a part of a broader political phenomenon described as "if the Führer only knew" syndrome,[62] cannot be overlooked in evaluating the reformers' efforts.

The führer, however, had neither abandoned nor postponed his colonization plans for the East, as he made clear in several remarks to guests at his Vinnitsa headquarters throughout the summer of 1942.[63] By this time the essential prerequisite for German colonization—the extermination of Soviet Jews in the occupied areas—was already far advanced.[64] By August 1942 Himmler's *Reichssicherheitshauptamt* (RSHA) had not only drafted a general settlement scheme for the future but had begun its first phase, the concentration of ethnic German inhabitants in organized communities in the northern Ukraine.[65] And before the end of the year the German Labor Front produced a detailed demographic study of the economic aspects of a resettlement of 5 million Germans into the new areas.[66]

Paradoxically, Hitler's decisions during this period further reinforced the particular illusions held by Rosenberg and the army. The Eastern minister, with renewed confidence in his program, passed July and August 1942 in conflict with *Reichskommissar* Koch over Ukrainian policy. In substance Hitler refused to resolve the disputes, yet Rosenberg won Hitler's paper assurance that he was "sole delegate of the Reich Government in matters of policy" concerning Soviet peoples.[67] And as the German Army advanced toward Stalingrad and the rich oilfields at Grozny in September 1942, OKH obtained Hitler's approval for a liberal occupation policy in the North Caucasus, one that encouraged self-government and prohibited the conscription of forced labor.[68]

Yet at the root of these illusions lay the most powerful illusion shared by all, the 1918 legacy of German power supreme in Eastern Europe, free to shape the region according to German needs and interests. As one of the sponsors of the agrarian reform later noted, "the view that the occupation of the Russian territories must be a permanent condition prevailed among all influential men in the military, and particularly among the civilian command in the military government. This thought had become so common a conviction it was not subject to discussion."[69] Such unspoken assumptions must be remembered in assessing the limitations of even the most liberal reforms considered in the occupied USSR.

Thus, as the second autumn of the Soviet-German war approached, the *Ostpolitik* of National Socialist Germany derived from three conceptions of political goals. Hitler's dream of colonial *Lebensraum* had already begun to be implemented; Rosenberg remained fixed on the role of the Ukraine and the minority nationalities; and army reformers grew increasingly involved in a program of general concessions to the Russian population. Based on a common vision of German domination in Eastern Europe, all suffered from varying degrees of self-delusion or deliberate deception. Rosenberg and the army, however, at least acknowledged some limitations to German power, while Hitler remained committed to an unqualified military victory. The policy conflict that ensued was rarely fought in the open but submerged in the personal feuds, jurisdictional disputes and jumbled responsibilities that characterized the structure of German occupation.

NOTES

1. Bräutigam, *So hat es*, pp. 330–39.

2. See Rudolph Binion, *Hitler Among the Germans* (New York: Elsevier Scientific, 1976), pp. 44–49, for a useful though overstated interpretation of Hitler's psychological debt to Imperial Germany's *Ostpolitik*. See also Binion's two articles in *History of Childhood Quarterly*, "Hitler's Concept of *Lebensraum*: The Psychological Basis," Vol. I, no. 2 (Fall 1973): 187–215, 249–58, and "Hitler Looks East," Vol. III, no. 1 (Summer 1975): 85–102.

3. Hitler, *Mein Kampf*, p. 654.

4. *Hitler's Secret Book*, intro. by Telford Taylor and trans. by Salvator Attanasio (New York: Grove Press, 1961), p. 78.

5. See Gerhard L. Weinberg, *The Foreign Policy of Hitler's Germany: Diplomatic Revolution in Europe, 1933–36* (Chicago: University of Chicago Press, 1970), pp. 26–27.

6. On the interaction of war aims and strategic considerations in BARBAROSSA, see Norman Rich, *Hitler's War Aims* (2 vols.) (New York: W.W. Norton, 1973–74), Vol. 1, pp. 204–22; the official history prepared by the Militärgeschichtliches Forschungsamt (MGFA), *Das deutsche Reich und der Zweite Weltkrieg*, Bd. 4: *Der Angriff auf die Sowjetunion* (Stuttgart: Deutsche Verlags-Anstalt, 1983), pp. 13–25 (Jürgen Förster's "Hitlers Entscheidung für den Krieg gegen die Sowjetunion"); and Andreas Hillgruber, *Hitler's Strategie. Politik und Kriegführung 1940–1941* (Frankfurt am Main: Bernard & Graefe Verlag für Wehrwesen, 1965), esp. pp. 207–42 and 352–77.

7. See Hillgruber, *Strategie*, pp. 536–41, and the same author's *Der Zenit des Zweiten Weltkrieges, Juli 1941* (Wiesbaden: Steiner, 1977), passim.

8. "Aktenvermerk," July 16, 1941, Doc. 221-L, *Trials of the Major War Criminals before the International Military Tribunal, 1947–1949* (42 vols.) (Nuremberg: International Military Tribunal, 1947–1949), Vol. XXXVIII, pp. 86–94 (hereafter cited as *TMWC*, followed by volume number in Roman numerals and page numbers in Arabic numerals).

9. Notes of Dr. Werner Koeppen (Rosenberg's liaison officer to Führer Headquarters), "Abendtafel 17.10.1941," T–84/387/809. See also "Aufzeichnung über die Chefbesprechung im Reichsministerium für die besetzten Ostgebiete am 30. Oktober 1941," on National Archives microcopy T–120, Records of the German Foreign Ministry, roll 2533, serial 5081, frames E292592–597 (hereafter cited in the format T–120/2533/5081/E292592–597).

10. *Hitler's Secret Conversations 1941–1944*, intro. by H.R. Trevor-Roper, trans. by Norman Cameron and R.H. Stevens (New York: Farrar, Strauss and Young, 1976 reprint), pp. 213–14 (entry for 28–29 January 1942) (henceforth cited *HSC*).

11. See the discussion of this in Woodruff D. Smith, *The Ideological Origins of Nazi Imperialism* (New York: Oxford University Press, 1986), pp. 52–111.

12. Smith, *Ideological Origins*, pp. 166–95, 232–58; Binion, *Hitler*, pp. 44–46, 114–18; on World War I *Ostpolitik*, compare Fritz Fischer, *Germany's Aims in the First World War* (New York: W.W. Norton, 1967), pp. 271–79, 346ff., and Winfried Baumgart, *Deutsche Ostpolitik 1918* (Vienna: R. Oldenbourg Verlag, 1966), pp. 60–92, 244–57, 300–11.

13. See Walter Laqueur, *Russia and Germany: A Century of Conflict* (Boston: Little, Brown, 1965), pp. 13–21, 28–38, 176–95.

14. Willi A. Boelcke, ed., *The Secret Conferences of Dr. Goebbels: The Nazi Propaganda War 1939–43*, trans. by Ewald Osers (New York: E.P. Dutton, 1970), p. 190.

15. See, for example, Interrogation C.S.D.I.C. (U.K.)/S.R.N. 1138, 5 October 1942, G–2 Division (MIS-Y Branch), Records of the War Department General and Special Staffs, Record Group (hereafter RG) 165, NA.

16. Bräutigam, *So hat es*, pp. 626–27.

17. See Marlis G. Steinert, *Hitler's War and the Germans*, ed. and trans. by Thomas E.J. DeWitt (Athens, OH: Ohio University Press, 1977), pp. 129–30, 154.

18. Alfred Rosenberg, *Letzte Aufzeichnungen. Ideale und Idole der nationalsozialistischen Revolution* (Göttingen: Plesse Verlag, 1955), pp. 13–15.

19. Laqueur, *Russia and Germany*, pp. 60–78.

20. Rosenberg's views are contained in a number of memoranda from April–May 1941 and published as Documents 1017-PS, 1019-PS, 1024-PS, 1028-PS, 1029-PS, 1039-PS, and 1056-PS, in *TMWC*, XXVI, 547–80, 584–609.

21. Laqueur, *Russia and Germany*, pp. 68–78.

22. Interview with Gunter d'Alquen (editor of the SS periodical *Das schwarze Korps* and commander of the *Waffen*-SS propaganda unit "Kurt Eggers"), May 26, 1984.

23. Joachim Fest, "Alfred Rosenberg—The Forgotten Disciple," in *The Face of the Third Reich*, trans. by Michael Bullock (New York: Pantheon Books, 1970), pp. 163–74.

24. *HSC*, pp. 342–45 (entry of April 11, 1942).

25. Führer decree, April 20, 1941, Document NG-2871, RG 238, NA.

26. Rosenberg, *Letzte Aufzeichnungen*, p. 208.

27. (Rosenberg), "Instruktion für einen Reichskommissar in der Ukraine," May 7, 1941, Document 1028-PS, *TMWC*, XXVI, 567–73.

28. (Rosenberg), "Bericht über die vorbereitende Arbeit in Fragen des osteuropäischen Raumes," June 28, 1941, Document 1039-PS, *TMWC*, XXVI, 584–92.

29. OKH/Gen.Qu./Qu.I, "Anordnungen über militärische Hoheitsrechte, Sicherung und Verwaltung im rückwärtigen Gebiet und Kriegsgefangenenwesen" (Ca. May 1941), file H 22/448, microfilm MR 1768, RG 242, NA.

30. "Rede des Reichsleiters A. Rosenberg vor der engsten Beteiligten an Ostproblem am 20. Juni 1941," reproduced as Document 1058-PS, *TMWC*, XXVI, 610–27.

31. "Aktenvermerk," Document 221-L, *TMWC*, XXXVIII, 89.

32. Notes of unidentified Foreign Ministry official, "Besetzte Ostgebiete," October 1, 1941, T–120/2533/5083/E292817–819.

33. Koeppen notes of September 19, 1941, T-84/387/770.

34. Joseph Goebbels, *The Goebbels Diaries, 1942–1943*, trans., ed., and intro. by Louis P. Lochner (New York: Doubleday, 1948), p. 267 (entry for March 2, 1943).

35. See the collection of Bräutigam memoranda, September 23, 1941–August 15, 1943, in folder "Wichtige Erlässe," ML 474, RG 242, NA.

36. See Hauptstelle Kulturpolitisches Archiv, "Prof. Dr. Hans Koch," February 20, 1940, file EAP 99/209, MR 287, RG 242, NA; Ilnytzkyj, *Deutschland und die Ukraine*, Bd. I, pp. 53–57.

37. Kleist, *Zwischen*, passim; untitled Kleist memorandum of October 24, 1941 in *Documents Accuse*, pp. 29–30.

38. See Helmut Heiber, "Der Generalplan Ost," *VfZ*, Bd. VI, no. 3 (July 1958), pp. 286–87.

39. Werner Präg and Wolfgang Jacobmeyer, eds., *Das Diensttagebuch des deutschen*

Generalgouverneurs in Polen 1939–1945 (Stuttgart: Deutsche Verlags-Anstalt, 1975), pp. 412–13; "Niederschrift über die Chefbesprechung am 30.10.1941 im Rm.f.d.b.O. über die Landesplanung im Ostraum," folder 566, ML 464, RG 242, NA; MGFA, *Deutsche Reich*, Bd. 4, p. 1077.

40. See the discussion in Robert J. O'Neill, *The German Army and the Nazi Party 1933–39*, (London: Corgi Books, Cassell & Company Ltd., 1966), pp. 178–95.

41. Halder's notes for July 22, 1940 in *Generaloberst Halder Kriegstagebuch* (3 vols.) (Stuttgart: W. Kohlhammer Verlag, 1962–1964), Bd. II, pp. 31–34.

42. Percy E. Schramm, et al., eds., *Kriegstagebuch des Oberkommandos der Wehrmacht (Wehrmachtführungsstab), 1940–1945* (4 vols. in 7 parts) (Frankfurt am Main: Bernard und Graefe Verlag für Wehrwesen, 1961–1965), Bd. I, pp. 203–55 (entry for December 5, 1940) (hereafter cited as *KTB/OKW*, followed by volume number in Roman numerals and page numbers in Arabic numerals).

43. *KTB/OKW*, I, 340–41 (entry of March 3, 1941); on the revised "Special Instructions," see Walter Warlimont, *Inside Hitler's Headquarters*, trans. by R.H. Barry (New York: Frederick A. Praeger, 1964), pp. 150–52.

44. See the notes of Walter Hewel, "Hitler/Ob.Kom.d.Heeres, Chef d. Generalstabes, General-Quartiermeister," March 18, 1941, T–120/738/1457/366480; and Halder, *Kriegstagebuch*, Bd. II, pp. 318–20.

45. Halder, *Kriegstagebuch*, Bd. II, pp. 335–37.

46. On the *Wehrmacht*'s acceptance of Nazi ideology for BARBAROSSA, see Manfred Messerschmidt, *Die Wehrmacht im NS-Staat: Zeit der Indoktrination* (Hamburg: R.V. Decker's Verlag, 1969), esp. pp. 394–416, and Jürgen Förster, "Programmatische Ziele gegenüber der Sowjetunion und Ihre Aufnahme im Deutschen Offizierkorps," *Deutsche Reich*, Bd. 4, pp. 18–25.

47. *KTB/OKW*, I, 341–42 (entry of March 3, 1941); and Helmut Krausnick and Hans-Heinrich Wilhelm, *Die Truppe des Weltanschauungskrieges: Die Einsatzgruppen der Sicherheitspolizei und des SD 1938–1942* (Stuttgart: Deutsche Verlags-Anstalt, 1981), pp. 116–41.

48. See Messerschmidt, *Wehrmacht*, pp. 390–407, and Krausnick, "Kommissarbefehl und 'Gerichtsbarkeitserlass Barbarossa' in neuer Sicht," *VfZ*, XXV, 4 (October 1977): 682–738.

49. See Edgar M. Howell, *The Soviet Partisan Movement 1941–1944* (Washington, DC: Department of the Army, 1956), pp. 52–60, 69–72, and Krausnick, *Weltanschauungskrieges*, pp. 217–23, 261–78.

50. On *Wehrmacht* culpability, see Christian Streit, *Keine Kameraden: Die Wehrmacht und die sowjetischen Kriegsgefangenen 1941–1945* (Stuttgart: Deutsche Verlags-Anstalt, 1978); the numbers involved are disputed. A study that would correlate prisoner mortality to the German logistical situation in 1941 is badly needed. On the killing of German wounded and prisoners, see Alfred M. deZayas, *Die Wehrmacht-Untersuchungsstelle: Deutsche Ermittlungen über alliierte Völkerrechtsverletzungen im Zweiten Weltkrieg* (Munich: Universitas/Langen-Müller, 1980), pp. 273–90, 304–06.

51. Robert J. Gibbons, "Soviet Industry and the German War Effort, 1939–1945" (unpublished Ph.D. dissertation, Yale University, 1972), pp. 132–65; and Streit, *Keine Kameraden*, pp. 191ff.

52. Dallin, *German Rule*, pp. 331n., 519–21; Ortwin Buchbender, *Das tönende Erz: Deutsche Propaganda gegen die Rote Armee im Zweiten Weltkrieg* (Stuttgart: Seewald Verlag), pp. 129–33.

53. On Reichenau's career and politics, see Karl Dietrich Bracher, Wolfgang Sauer and Gerhard Schulz, *Die nationalsozialistische Machtergreifung* (Cologne: Westdeutscher Verlag, 1962), pp. 710–15; on Reichenau and BARBAROSSA, see Krausnick and Wilhelm, *Weltanschauungskrieges*, pp. 219–21, 230–31, 243, 258–61.

54. See Reichenau's "Denkschrift über notwendige Sofortmassnahmen in den besetzten Ostgebieten, insbesondere in der Ukraine," February 8, 1942, Document 1684-PS.

55. See Karl Brandt, Otto Schiller and Franz Ahlgrimm, *Management of Agriculture and Food in the German-Occupied and Other Areas of Fortress Europe* (Stanford, CA: Stanford University Press, 1953), pp. 93–100, 665–70.

56. Seppo Myllyniemi, *Die Neuordnung der baltischen Länder 1941–1944; Zum nationalsozialistischen Inhalt der deutschen Besatzungspolitik* (Helsinki: Vammalan Kirjapaino Oy, 1973), pp. 112–20.

57. Messerschmidt, *Wehrmacht*, pp. 405–07.

58. Harvey Fireside, *Icon and Swastika: The Russian Orthodox Church under Nazi and Soviet Control* (Cambridge, MA: Harvard University Press, 1971), pp. 83–87.

59. The earliest police and security units composed of Baltic nationals date from August 1941; the first formations of Russians in German service were organized on October 6, 1941, though the unauthorized use of Russian *Hilfswillige* (noncombat auxiliaries) probably predates this: see MGFA, *Das deutsche Reich*, Bd. 4, pp. 1058–62, and Joachim Hoffmann, *Die Ostlegionen 1941–1943* (Freiburg: Verlag Rombach, 1976), pp. 17–25.

60. Heinz Danko Herre, "Auszüge aus meinem Tagebuch 1942" (entries for October 11, and November 18,), ZS 406/IV, 1–3, in the Institut für Zeitgeschichte, Munich (hereafter cited as the Herre diary, IfZ). See also Heinz Höhne and Hermann Zolling, *The General Was a Spy*, intro. by Hugh Trevor-Roper, Bantam Books (New York: Coward, McCann & Geoghegan, 1972), pp. 39–41.

61. Alfred Toppe, "German Military Government," FMS Mss. No. P-033 (Historical Division, U.S. Army, Europe, 1949), pp. 61–62.

62. Ian Kershaw, "The Führer Image and Political Integration: The Popular Conception of Hitler in Bavaria during the Third Reich" in Hirschfeld and Kettendacker, eds., *Führerstaat*, esp. pp. 140–42.

63. See *HSC*, pp. 572–79 (entries of August 5–6 and 8, 1942).

64. See Andreas Hillgruber, "Die 'Endlösung' und das deutsche Ostimperium als Kernstück des rassenideologischen Programms des Nationalsozialismus," *VfZ*, XX, 2 (April 1972): 133–53.

65. See Heiber, "Generalplan Ost," pp. 280–325, and Ingeborg Fleischhauer, *Das Dritte Reich und die Deutschen in der Sowjetunion* (Stuttgart: Deutsche Verlags-Anstalt, 1983), pp. 170–90.

66. Arbeitswissenschaftliches Institut der deutschen Arbeitsfront, "Die Erschliessung der Rohstoff- und Landwirtschaft des Ostens: Problematisches und Grundsätzliches," January 1943, microfilm ML 474, RG 242, NA.

67. See Gerald Reitlinger, *The House Built on Sand: The Conflicts of German Policy in Russia 1939–1945* (New York: Viking, 1960), pp. 198–202.

68. See Dallin, *German Rule*, pp. 238–41.

69. Brandt et al., *Management*, p. 67.

2

EMPIRE OF CHAOS

In an after-dinner remark in late March 1942 Hitler drew a lesson from the internal conflicts of the medieval Holy Roman Empire: "The policy of the Reich can be successful only if it is characterized by unity of action."[1] In this, at least, he was an accurate prophet.

Debates over *Ostpolitik* would be fought within the confines of a contorted and swollen framework of occupation. The requirements imposed by conflicting priorities—the conduct of military operations, the administration of an occupied population exceeding 60 million, and the first stages of colonization—all but precluded the development of either a coherent policy or a coordinated administrative apparatus. Worse, the immediate and anticipated tasks in the East generated a host of authorities who, in their scramble to stake claims in the future "Garden of Eden," carried with their baggage all the political rivalries, personal feuds, and ambition endemic to National Socialist politics. As a result, policy debates entered an arena of competing organizations and individuals where the decisive factor lay less with the issue than in the alignment of forces in support or opposition.

The führer's Decree of July 17, 1941 created the *Reichsministerium für die besetzten Ostgebiete* (Reich Ministry for the Occupied Eastern Territories), more commonly known as the *Ostministerium* (Eastern Ministry, often abbreviated as *OMi*), as the civil administration for the newly acquired areas of the Soviet Union. The decree provided for the transfer of control from military to civil jurisdiction and the organization of these areas into *Reichskommissariate* (Reich commissariats) and thereunder by general regions or commissariats (*General-*

bezirke or *Generalkommissariate*) divided into district areas (*Kreisgebiete*). Alfred Rosenberg was named head of the new ministry.[2]

While the decree apparently defined the Eastern minister's authority in several of its provisions, other sections limited Rosenberg's power and preserved Hitler's supremacy in crucial areas of policy. Article III of the decree maintained the independent prerogatives of Hermann Goering (as commissioner of the Four Year Plan) and *Reichsführer* Heinrich Himmler. While Rosenberg could select officials in the civil administration up to the level of *Hauptkommissar* (for a group of district areas administered collectively), Hitler retained the power of appointment for the heads of the Reich commissariats and the general regions. Finally, Hitler made explicit his own right of arbitration: "In differences of opinion which cannot be settled by direct negotiations, my decision is to be obtained. . . . "[3]

To assist him in implementing his program, Rosenberg selected as his deputy Dr. Alfred Meyer, *Gauleiter* (Nazi party regional chief) of Westphalia, a "true National Socialist" in Rosenberg's eyes but a curious choice to Otto Bräutigam, who later recalled of Meyer: "He understood nothing, but absolutely nothing, of Eastern problems."[4] Headquartered in the former Soviet embassy in Berlin, the new ministry's three main departments (policy, administration, economics) and about thirty subdivisions were staffed by about 635 professionals drawn from various backgrounds and, in part, borrowed from other ministries.[5] The diversity of political views among *OMi* officials has already been described, but many also moreover shared their *OMi* duties with positions held in rival organizations. These "personal unions," a regular feature of the Nazi political landscape, offered advantages in coordination of policies but implanted conflicts of bureaucratic loyalty.[6]

To fill the lower echelons of German civil administration in the field, Rosenberg relied upon the SA (*Sturmabteilung*, "storm troopers") and the products of the Nazi party's political training schools, the *Ordensjunker*.[7] Rosenberg hoped to fashion these into an *Ostführer Korps* ("Eastern leadership corps") clad in field gray uniforms similar to those of the *Goldfasanen* ("golden pheasants") after the mustard-brown tunics forced upon them by a surplus of cloth for the German Labor Front.[8] The SA leadership particularly welcomed the opportunity to regain its lost powers: by summer 1942 in *Generalkommissariat* "White Russia" SA men comprised 90 percent of all German civil officials.[9] SA hopes of institutionalizing their position in occupied Russia even aroused the concern of the SS.[10]

A lasting impression of the civil administration, reflected in the wordplay "too much administration" (*Zivilverwaltung–Zuvielverwaltung*), lay in its bloated numbers, especially in the Baltic states: the city of Riga alone supported between 10 and 12 thousand occupation officials.[11] The bulk of these worked for the swarm of economic and military logistical authorities that descended on the occupied areas. Throughout the Baltic states at the beginning of 1944, the *Reichskommissariat Ostland* employed 2235 German personnel.[12] In the Ukraine,

Reichskommissar Koch reduced his own staff of over 800 to 252 by February 1943, although most of these simply transferred to other parts of the occupation apparatus.[13] The lower levels of the civil administration were staffed by Party appointees with no more qualifications than a six-month training course, compelling the Germans ultimately to depend on local inhabitants to supervise the daily routine of life under occupation.[14]

Actual governing power in the areas under civil administration rested with the Reich commissioner (*Reichskommissar*), whose appointments were reserved to Hitler. To further limit Rosenberg's authority Hitler specified that *OMi* should not interfere in the "details of administration," a directive that Rosenberg refused to publicize in his ministry.[15] "When I came to selecting our Commissars for the occupied Eastern territories," Hitler later recalled, "I kept on coming back to the names of my old *Gauleiters*; Lohse and Koch leapt straight to my mind."[16] Thus, at the beginning of September 1941, *Gauleiter* of Schleswig-Holstein Hinrich Lohse assumed the concurrent post of *Reichskommissar Ostland* for the Baltic states and "White Russia" in Riga; Erich Koch, *Gauleiter* of East Prussia, added to his title the office of *Reichskommissar* for the Ukraine, based in Rowné.[17]

Hitler's selection of Koch over Rosenberg's objections and the subsequent discussions between führer and *Reichskommissar* revealed their unanimity of views in Ukrainian policy. Indeed, Koch knew he was destined for a major post in occupied Russia a full month before BARBAROSSA.[18] Koch wasted little time after his installation in propounding *Untermensch* ("subhuman") theories in the treatment of Slavs;[19] ironically, his background did not match his rhetoric as *Reichskommissar*. A member of the Nazi party's left wing in the 1920s, Koch had made no secret of his pro-Soviet sympathies, which earned him Rosenberg's hostility long before BARBAROSSA.[20] The news of his appointment to the Ukraine was initially welcomed at führer headquarters as "the most suitable choice and a second Stalin," but within days military leaders were arguing bitterly with him.[21] Koch apparently took little interest in the routine administration of his *Reichskommissariat*, passing most of his time in his East Prussian capital of Königsberg while the economic authorities and SS enjoyed a free hand in the Ukraine.[22] When Rosenberg intervened to redirect this policy, however, Koch could be roused to a passionate defense of his prerogatives.

In many respects Lohse offered a complete contrast to Koch. Always on good terms with Rosenberg, he shared the latter's views on the future incorporation of the Baltic states into the Reich.[23] And unlike his counterpart, Lohse immersed himself in the administration of his satrapy with a passion for regulation that subordinates found myopic against the larger issues of policy.[24] This would result in conflict during the 1942–43 period, and as with Koch, an issue of policy reform became entangled with the question of a *Reichskommissar*'s authority.

Though nominally a part of *Reichskommissariat Ostland*, the *Generalkommissariat "Weissruthenien"* (literally "White Ruthenia" or "White Russia," actually comprising much of Belorussia) operated almost independently under the direction of Commissioner-General Wilhelm Kube, former *Gauleiter* of Kur-

mark. During the spring of 1943 Kube engaged the SS in a unique struggle, one
that more properly belongs to the history of the Holocaust than to *Ostpolitik*.[25]
As his district contained a large number of Soviet partisans, however, Kube
would play a role in the attempted reform of antipartisan policy.

The German Army's misperceptions of Hitler's ultimate objectives in the
USSR have already been noted. This, together with the shock of Stalingrad,
facilitated the army's support of a pragmatic and moderate occupation policy.
A number of specific factors, however, also contributed to the army's disposition
in favor of reform. The first of these concerned the extensive contacts and
cooperation with Soviet nationals by the military. After several years' close
liaison with Ukrainian nationalists, and at the beginning of BARBAROSSA, the
Abwehr outfitted Ukrainian combat formations to spearhead the invasion.[26] Russian emigrés, despite Hitler's ban, found employment as interpreters and advisers, especially in the area of military government.[27]

Above all, the reliance on hundreds of thousands of former Soviet soldiers
serving in German units as noncombatant auxiliaries (*Hilfswillige*, here shortened
to *Hiwis*) and armed security and police units established a unique form of
collaboration in combat.[28]

The same factor assumed greater significance in the field of military government, where a skeletal German administration required the cooperation of local
community leaders. Army Group Center alone employed 60,000 Russian civilians in local administration in summer 1943, as well as over 56,000 in the
Organization Todt and 35,000 with the military railroads.[29] Preoccupied with
the immediate and specific needs of the army, *Kommandanturen* (military government offices) left the population to its own devices in restoring the functions
of civilian society. Representatives of the local intelligentsia and former Soviet
officials dominated the native administration, which often simply restored the
Soviet pattern of organization.[30]

Another factor involved outright political opposition to Hitler within the army,
a development reflected in the plots against Hitler in 1938 and 1939–40.[31] The
misperceptions of the führer's role in *Ostpolitik* still applied to many, but some
officers grasped the implications and began to draw conclusions. The most active
of these groups comprised Colonel Henning von Tresckow, Colonel Rudolf von
Gersdorff and Lieutenant Fabian von Schlabrendorff, all staff officers with the
headquarters of Army Group Center. These men, led by Tresckow, supported
Ostpolitik reform but based their opposition on the criminal actions associated
with BARBAROSSA from the start; they sought reform through a coup d'état,
culminating in two unsuccessful attempts to assassinate Hitler in March 1943.[32]

Less decisive at this stage, yet more directly involved in *Ostpolitik*, were such
officers at OKH headquarters as Quartermaster-General of the Army Eduard
Wagner and Major Claus Schenk von Stauffenberg, then serving in the organization branch. They and their associates opposed existing policies and com-
prehended the leadership's responsibility for them, but stopped short of opposing
the regime; the 1942–43 episode of *Ostpolitik* reform served as a way station to

Map 1
Administration of the Occupied USSR, November 1942

GERMAN-OCCUPIED USSR, 1942-43

Tallinn

Novgorod

Riga

Moscow

Kaunas

Vitebsk

Smolensk

GERMANY

Minsk

Mogilev

Bryansk

Orel

General-
Gouvernement

Luzk

Kursk

Rowne

Zhitomir

Lvov

Kiev

Kharkov

HUNGARY

Dnepropetrovsk

Nikolajev

Odessa

RUMANIA

Simferopol

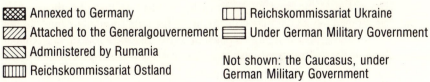

Annexed to Germany

Reichskommissariat Ukraine

Attached to the Generalgouvernement

Under German Military Government

Administered by Rumania

Reichskommissariat Ostland

Not shown: the Caucasus, under
German Military Government

the road of July 20, 1944.[33] Admiral Canaris, chief of the *Abwehr*, occupies a more ambiguous position: though neither a leader of the resistance nor principally interested in *Ostpolitik*, he nevertheless worked about the periphery of policy on behalf of reform.[34]

The military's ability to influence *Ostpolitik* derived from three areas of policy. Military government, the most important, controlled the lives of roughly 20 million occupied civilians.[35] Second, the army's establishment of regular combat units of Soviet nationals, designated *Osttruppen* ("Eastern troops"), represented a significant reversal of Nazi policy, to which Hitler had acquiesced but never accepted. Both military government and the *Osttruppen* also constituted part of the more general aspect of policy that may be termed *political warfare*. This could be defined as the combination of concessions, promises and propaganda designed to pacify the occupied population, offer tangible goals to the Russians fighting on the German side and win over the enemy across the front lines.[36] In launching reform initiatives here, the military battled both internal and external foes in the culmination of the 1942–43 reform period, the Vlasov movement.

SS ambitions in occupied Russia were reflected in the comment of one senior SS officer in Berlin: "The East belongs to the SS!"[37] Originally entrusted with police and security responsibilities, the role of the SS expanded tremendously in virtually every aspect of *Ostpolitik*. Yet this growth came at the cost of ideological consistency, as a number of influential SS officers broke with Nazi doctrine and supported changes in *Ostpolitik*.

For the execution of their original tasks, the SS employed its far-ranging authority to establish an extensive police apparatus. In the areas under civil administration, Senior SS and Police Commanders (*Höherer SS- und Polizei-führer*, abbreviated HSSPF) were assigned to each *Reichskommissariat* and lesser police officials to the level of the *Kreisgebiet*. The HSSPF were responsible for "all racial and political questions" in these areas, as well as coordination with other authorities.[38] Together with the *Einsatzgruppen* operating in the military government areas, the HSSPF and their subordinates combed through the occupied population to eliminate Communists, political opponents, Soviet agents, criminals, "asocial" elements, and above all the Jews.[39] In August 1942 the führer expanded these powers when he designated Himmler "the central authority for the collection and evaluation of all information concerning actions against bandits," with "sole responsibility for combating banditry in the Reich Commissars' territories."[40] The SS thus assumed a major role in the pacification of occupied Russia, employing 15,000 German personnel and over 238,000 native police in the *Reichskommissariate* alone by the end of 1942.[41]

The heavy losses incurred by *Waffen*-SS (Armed-SS) units on the Eastern Front discouraged native German enlistments in the elite formations, but did not dissuade Himmler from a major expansion and reorganization of his combat arm.[42] *Waffen*-SS and other SS officers who gained a healthy respect for the fighting qualities of the Russian soldier sought to overcome Himmler's prejudice against the use of eastern nationals, and with some success: by altering the racial standards Himmler extended his recruiting to include East European *Volks-deutsche*, natives of the Baltic states and even the Ukrainians, and more than doubled the size of the *Waffen*-SS from December 1942 to July 1943.[43] This not only involved the SS in the general question of eastern troops but demonstrated Himmler's own willingness—albeit reluctant—to sacrifice ideals to reality, a key to understanding the later SS role in *Ostpolitik*.

That Himmler basically shared Hitler's views toward the East cannot be doubted. In his capacity as 'Reich commissioner for the strengthening of Germandom' (*Reichskommissar für die Festigung deutschen Volkstums*, or RKFDV), Himmler initiated the colonization process in occupied Russia before the end of 1941, in yet another policy area stripped from the *Ostministerium*.[44] In May 1942 one of Himmler's subordinates prepared a "General Plan East" for the resettlement of millions of Germans at strategic locations throughout occupied Russia over a 20-year period.[45] Even as Himmler reconsidered his *Waffen*-SS recruiting policies, he initiated the initial colonization phase, the concentration of Russian *Volksdeutsche* in strategic, agriculturally fertile strongpoints: By the end of 1942 at least 43,000 *Volksdeutsche* had been settled in three strongpoint villages between Zhitomir and Vinnitsa in the northwestern Ukraine.[46]

Himmler sought to consolidate the SS's position in the East by venturing into the field of economic enterprise. By mid-November 1942 the SS Economic and Administrative Department (*Wirtschafts-Verwaltungshauptamt*, or WVHA) and the Race and Resettlement Department (*Rasse- und Siedlungshauptamt*, or RuSHA) jointly administered at least 90 agricultural estates throughout occupied Russia; the 600,000 hectares (nearly 1.5 million acres) of farmland supplied food to *Waffen*-SS units and supported about 700 wounded SS veterans as prototypic "SS-peasants" in the East.[47] Himmler also obtained from *Reichskommissar* Koch in 1942 the mining rights to a quartz quarry outside Zhitomir, and in early 1943 established colonial plantations to cultivate natural rubber from the *kok-saghyz* plants native to Russia.[48]

Among the many SS departments involved in the East, none occupied a more ambiguous position than the *Sicherheitsdienst* ("Security Service," abbreviated SD). Primarily concerned with political intelligence, the SD played a significant role in the murderous activities of the *Einsatzgruppen* and the later "sweeps" of opponents in the *Reichskommissariate*.[49] This intelligence function, however, also required closer contacts with, and a greater understanding of, the occupied population. Duplicating the operations of the *Abwehr*, SS-*Brigadeführer* Walter Schellenberg's Foreign Intelligence Section relied upon its Russian agents to infiltrate the Soviet rear areas and partisan bands, and even formed an antipartisan combat brigade from its pool of Russian operatives.[50] Intelligence within German-occupied territories fell under the *Inland-* (internal) SD, under SS-*Brigadeführer* Otto Ohlendorf. The former commander of an *Einsatzgruppe* that killed 90,000 in the Ukraine, Ohlendorf was a puritanical National Socialist whose candid assessments of German public opinion antagonized many Nazi party officials.[51] In the occupied Soviet Union, Ohlendorf's offices regularly reported with equal frankness the state of morale among the occupied population.[52] Both Schellenberg and Ohlendorf played accompanying roles in the 1942–43 reform efforts.

With impeccable ideological credentials, a diversity of viewpoints and an appetite for power, Himmler's SS occupied a position of unique advantage during the reform period. *Ostpolitik* reformers in the SS enjoyed much more freedom of action than their counterparts in the military and civil administrations, while Himmler's empire could expand or consolidate its position in the East either by reform or by its defeat.

German economic authorities confronted an embarassment of riches in the wake of BARBAROSSA's early successes: the German-occupied areas at the end of 1941 included 63 percent of the USSR's coal production, 68 percent of pig iron, 58 percent of steel and 38 percent of grain production.[53] In their haste to exploit these resources, German economic agencies scrambled into the East with considerable exertion of effort but little attempt at coordination. The *Blitzkrieg*'s collapse imposed changes but did not establish a comprehensive program, and by the time of Stalingrad, economic policy was entangled among the profits of immediate exploitation, the long-term demands of economic warfare and the political benefits of agrarian reform.

Original plans, based on the assumption of a rapid victory, avoided major changes in the Soviet economic administration system to maximize exploitation, particularly of foodstuffs, as quickly as possible.[54] In Berlin, *Reichsmarschall* Goering, as Commissioner of the Four Year Plan, chaired the *Wirtschaftsführungsstab Ost* (Economic Command Staff East), composed of representatives from Wehrmacht economic agencies and pertinent Reich ministries. Subordinate to this organization, but the actual executive authority in occupied Russia, was the Economic Staff East (*Wirtschaftsstab Ost*, or *Wi-Stab-Ost*) under General Wilhelm Schubert, and later General Otto Stapf. Six departments managed the different sectors of economic activity: military management, agriculture, industry, troop requirements and transportation, forestry, and labor. The last five offices were duplicated at the level of the *Wirtschaftsinspektion* (economic inspection), one of which was attached to each army group in Russia.

These in turn broke down into 23 military economic commands operating with the rear area headquarters of the individual armies. In an attempt to ensure a coordinated effort, *Wi-Stab-Ost* was attached directly to the OKW's Economics and Armaments Department (*Wi-Rü-Amt*), while the device of the "personal union" combined the civilian duties of such officials as Hans-Joachim Riecke (undersecretary of agriculture in the Reich Food Ministry) with command positions in *Wi-Stab-Ost* (chief of the Agriculture Department). For staffing the new offices the army appointed civilian specialists to officer-grade positions and temporary rank.[55]

The bulk of the latter served as agricultural specialists (*Landwirtschaftsführer* or *La-Führer*) installed at the *raion* level in the countryside, where each might be responsible for 10 to 15 *kolkhozy* (collective farms). This system, which operated in both the military government and civil administration areas, employed over 14,000 *La-Führer* at its height. Their task was greatly handicapped by the retention of the unpopular collectives, and by a harvest devastated by wartime disruption and Stalin's "scorched earth" measures. Initially commited to an unaltered adoption of the collective farms, agrarian policy sought in early 1942 to balance practical concessions to Russian peasants against maximum production for Germany with the "New Agrarian Order." The nature and extent of this agrarian reform became the heritage of the 1942–43 period.[56]

Except for *Wi-Stab-Ost*'s agricultural system, no unified economic control existed between the military government and civil administration areas. The "Economic Department" Rosenberg established within the Eastern Ministry wielded no power, and Rosenberg wasted the limited opportunities afforded him.[57] The coordination of policy was instead sacrificed to the principle that "the highest economic production could be expected only on the well-tested basis of private economy."[58] Supported by the Reich Economics Ministry, private enterprise secured a prominent place in both the agricultural and industrial sectors of the occupied economy through participation in government-sponsored monopoly corporations.[59] In agriculture, the Central Trade Corporation East (*Zentralhandelsgesellschaft Ost*, or ZHO) engaged many private firms in the collection, processing and storage of agricultural produce, as well as the importing of farm supplies and the exporting of farm products; the ZHO's Supervisory Board consisted largely of representatives from the private sector. Not subject to *Wi-Stab-Ost*, the ZHO operated in both the civil and military areas, employing over 6600 Germans and 518,000 Russians at the height of its activities in the summer of 1943.[60]

The exploitation of raw materials offered large corporations the opportunity to assume control of Soviet industrial facilities as "trustees" (*Treuhändern*). The Mining and Smelting Corporation East (*Berg- und Hüttenwerksgesellschaft Ost* or BHO), whose executive board included steel magnate Alfried Krupp, exercised monopoly rights for the mining and steel industries in occupied Russia and granted trusteeship to Krupp firms for specific steel works.[61] The Continental Oil Corporation, financed in part by Germany's four leading oil companies and I.G. Farben, obtained a 99-year lease for the exclusive rights of extraction, processing and sales of all oil in occupied areas, including those under Rumanian occupation.[62] Other monopoly corporations governed the textile, fur and cigarette industries, while I.G. Farben capitalized on its previous chemical interests to procure trusteeship of the Estonian phosphate industry.[63]

Germany's economic requirements for a protracted, multifront war further complicated the situation in the East by introducing two new authorities in 1942. The first aimed at a mass utilization of Soviet workers as a labor force in the German economy as Hitler commissioned *Gauleiter* Fritz Sauckel "Plenipotentiary General for the Allocation of Labor" (*Generalbevollmächtigter für den Arbeitseinsatz*, or GBA) on March 21, 1942. Though many Russians initially volunteered for labor service in Germany, the huge numbers sought by Sauckel could be obtained only by force; the workers thus procured, termed *Ostarbeiter*

(Eastern workers), were shipped like cattle to German factories, there to endure atrocious living conditions and low wages as manual laborers. The treatment of the *Ostarbeiter*, and the more general question of the use of Russian labor, became new issues of *Ostpolitik* in the autumn of 1942, as Sauckel prepared to intensify his manhunts.[64]

Slightly less significant was Hitler's appointment of Reich Minister for Armaments and Munitions Albert Speer as "Inspector General for Water and Energy in the newly occupied Eastern territories" on June 9, 1942. In addition to responsibility for construction and transportation, this gave Speer control of the important armaments industries of the Ukraine. Speer's concern with boosting armaments production would involve him with the interests of German heavy industry and Sauckel's slave-labor practices.[65]

To the dramatis personae of *Ostpolitik* must be added those figures and organizations removed from the complex web of policy making in the East but whose presence contributed to the reform issues of 1942–43. Some sortied into particular areas of policy, others worked behind the scenes; most served as potential allies or foes to the protagonists of *Ostpolitik* reform. All, however, played roles that cannot be overlooked.

Foremost among these was Martin Bormann, Hitler's private secretary and head of the Nazi party office after Rudolf Hess' ill-advised journey to Britain. With the power accruing from his Party office and his proximity to the führer, "the Brown Eminence" rose to one of the most powerful positions in the Reich. Bormann could, if he so desired, seize upon Hitler's after-dinner musings and issue them the next morning as policy directives. He shared Hitler's and Koch's views of the Ukraine and seconded the *Reichskommissar* in his duel with Rosenberg in the spring of 1943.[66]

Joseph Goebbels had been an enemy of Rosenberg's since the mid-1920s and had carried out his own psychological warfare against the Soviet Union through his *Anti-Komintern* office since 1933.[67] Goebbels' Ministry of Public Enlightenment and Propaganda therefore assumed an active interest in the conduct of political warfare in the East, where its minister continually sought to expand his own authority at Rosenberg's expense.[68]

The German Foreign Ministry under Joachim von Ribbentrop remained on the periphery of eastern policy for the duration. The once-proud ministry maintained liaison officers with each of the German Army groups, both Reich Commissariats, and Rosenberg's headquarters in Berlin; these and several Soviet specialists on the Wilhelmstrasse kept a close watch on conditions in the East and often participated in reform efforts. Hitler, however, specifically excluded Ribbentrop from any major role in *Ostpolitik*, though this did not deter the foreign minister from occasional, unsuccessful forays into the field. Relations between the two ministers were very poor, crippling any cooperation on key issues.[69]

Lastly, mention should be made of a heterogeneous group who left an indelible mark on eastern policy. These were the minor officials of all the various civil and rear-area military authorities, and the numerous train of enterprising restauranteurs, barbers, and hairdressers who followed in their wake. They justly earned the epithet applied to their counterparts in another time and another country, "carpetbaggers." Many enjoyed bloated salaries as a consequence of working in a theater of operations: a typist employed by the ZHO, for example, might earn several times the monthly salary of a *Wehrmacht* lieutenant.[70] Moreover, German officials created a brisk trade in the black market as they bartered household commodities and clothing from the Reich to local inhabitants for fresh eggs, butter, meats, furs, and liquor, which would then be mailed home to relatives in Germany. By summer of 1943 such practices had led to the *Reichskommissariat* Ukraine's informal designation as "the flea market of the Reich." Preoccupied with their profits, these proconsuls of empire remained oblivious to the impressions they left with the inhabitants and to the debates over *Ostpolitik* reform, though their conduct shaped much of the character of the German occupation.[71]

In a diary entry in May 1943, Goebbels commented on the "absolute lack of unity" in *Ostpolitik* and concluded: "Our Eastern policy lacks a clear basis. Everybody does what he likes."[72]

This observation precisely identifies the chief characteristic of German *Ostpolitik*. Berliner wits quickly dubbed Rosenberg's agency the "*Cha-ostministerium*" ("Ministry of Chaos").[73] Considering Germany's simultaneous pursuit of incompatible goals and the characteristic multiplication of rival National Socialist authorities, a more appropriate label for the whole might have been "Chaostpolitik." Those who wished to reform policy were left to grope through a dimly lit labyrinth where none could agree on the proper path but all realized they were running out of time.

NOTES

1. *HSC*, p. 309 (entry for March 31, 1942).

2. "Erlass des Führers über die Verwaltung der neu besetzten Ostgebiete, vom 17. Juli 1941," Document 1997-PS, *TMWC*, XXIX, 235–37.

3. Ibid.

4. Rosenberg, *Letzte Aufzeichnungen*, pp. 147–49, Bräutigam, *So hat es*, p. 307.

5. See the discussions in Dallin, *German Rule*, pp. 84–89, Reitlinger, *House*, pp. 138–40, and Bräutigam, *Überblick*, pp. 24–28. Statistics are provided in the original document, "Nachweisung über die im RMfdbO vorhandenen Beamten und Angestellten," n.d., Report No. XL–12675, Record Group 226, Records of the Office of Strategic Services (OSS), National Archives (hereafter cited as RG 226, NA).

6. See Bräutigam, *Überblick*, pp. 10, 26–29, and the more positive assessment (in the economic field) by Brandt et al., *Management*, p. 80.

7. See Dietrich Orlow, *The History of the Nazi Party: 1933–1945* (Pittsburgh: University of Pittsburgh, 1973), pp. 188–91, 384–92 and Bräutigam, *Überblick*, pp. 24–26.

8. "Construction and Administration, Minutes of a discussion with Reichsleiter Rosenberg, June 21, 1941," Doc. 1034-PS, *Nazi Conspiracy and Aggression* (Washington,

DC: Government Printing Office, 1947); (8 vols. and Supplements A and B), Vol. III, pp. 693–95 (hereafter cited as *NCA*).

9. Generalkommissar Kube, "Arbeiten für die Wehrertüchtigung der Deutschen in Weissruthenien," August 11, 1942, T-454/21/600.

10. See the SA memorandum, "Denkschrift zur Bildung eines 'Aufbaudienstes' aus Fremdstämmigen in den besetzten Ostgebieten," September 26, 1942, T-175/128/2654676-697; the letters of Gottlob Berger to Himmler, November 21, 1942, and Himmler to Lammers, November 30, 1942, T-175/128/2654674-75; and Heinz Höhne, *The Order of the Death's Head: The Story of Hitler's SS*, trans. by Richard Barry (New York: Coward-McCann, Inc., 1970), pp. 417–18.

11. See, e.g., Kleist, *Zwischen*, pp. 161–62; the figure for Riga is taken from Rosenberg's "Vermerk über eine Unterredung mit dem Führer im Führer-Hauptquartier am 8.5.42," Document PS-1520, *TMWC*, XXVII, 285.

12. Myllyniemi, *Neuordnung*, pp. 92–93.

13. Koch to Rosenberg, March 16, 1943, Document PS–192, *TMWC*, XXV, 256–57.

14. See Jaan Pennar, "Selbstverwaltung in den während des zweiten Weltkrieges besetzten Gebieten der Sowjetunion," *Sowjet Studien*, Nr. 12 (August 1962): 50–78, and OSS R&A No. 2500.8, "German Military Government Over Europe: Ostland and the Ukraine" (April 18, 1945), pp. 54–58.

15. Robert Herzog, *Grundzüge der deutschen Besatzungsverwaltung in den ost-und südosteuropäischen Landern während des zweiten Weltkrieges* (Tübingen: Institut für Besatzungsfragen, 1955), pp. 100–1.

16. *HSC*, p. 373 (entry for an unspecified date in May, 1942).

17. Orlow, *Nazi Party*, pp. 388–89.

18. Joseph Goebbels, *The Goebbels Diaries: 1939–1941*, trans. and ed. by Fred Taylor, foreword by John Keegan, Penguin Books (New York: G.P. Putnam's Sons, 1983), pp. 378–79 (entry for May 23, 1941).

19. See Jürgen Thorwald, *The Illusion: Soviet Soldiers in Hitler's Armies*, trans. by Richard and Clara Winston (New York: Harcourt Brace Jovanovich, 1975), pp. 21–23.

20. Gerald Reitlinger, "Last of the War Criminals: The Mystery of Erich Koch," *Commentary*, XXVII, 1 (January 1959): 30–42.

21. Koeppen notes of September 19 and 22, 1941, T-84/387/771, 783-84.

22. Reitlinger estimates that Koch spent no more than six months in the Ukraine ("Last," p. 35).

23. Myllyniemi, *Neuordnung*, pp. 55–57, 116–17; Rosenberg, *Letzte Aufzeichnungen*, pp. 154–56.

24. See, e.g., Kleist, *Zwischen*, pp. 159–64.

25. See Helmut Heiber, "Aus den Akten des Gauleiters Kube," *VfZ*, IV, 1 (January 1956): 67–77.

26. See Heinz Höhne, *Canaris*, trans. by J. Maxwell Brownjohn (New York: Doubleday & Company, Inc., 1979), pp. 316–21, 357–60, 459–63; Ilnytzkyj, *Deutschland*, Vol. II, pp. 139–42, 95–200; and Cherednichenko, *Collaborationists*, pp. 5ff.

27. See the excellent wartime study "Abschlussbericht über die Tätigkeit der Militärverwaltung im Operationsgebiet des Ostens," n.a., n.d. (probably 1944), file H. Geb. A 75156/1, on T-501/34/868ff., esp. frame 898.

28. See the discussion in Chapter 11, below.

29. Statistischer Arbeitsausschuss der Wi In Mitte, "Statistischer Bericht Nr. 1," July 30, 1943, T-77/1100/893-96.

30. Vladimir Pozdnyakov, "National Instinct and Governmental Institutions under German Occupation in Western Russia," FMS Ms. No. P-123 (Historical Division, U.S. Army, Europe, 1951), pp. 1–5, 11–22; Oleg Anisimov, *The German Occupation in Northern Russia During World War II: Political and Administrative Aspects* (New York: Research Program on the U.S.S.R., Study No. 56, 1954), pp. 2–19.

31. See Peter Hoffmann, *The History of the German Resistance 1933–1945*, trans. by Richard Barry (Cambridge, MA: The MIT Press, 1977), pp. 69ff.

32. Ibid., pp. 264–89; see also Bodo Scheurig, *Henning von Tresckow: Eine Biographie* (Oldenberg: Stalling Verlag, 1973), pp. 154–57.

33. See Herre's notes of his discussions with Stauffenberg and Schmidt von Altenstadt in the autumn of 1942, in ZS 406/III, pp. 49–50, 53–58, IfZ; Joachim Kramarz, *Stauffenberg*, trans. by R.H. Barry (New York: Macmillan, 1967), pp. 96–112.

34. The case against Canaris as a resistance figure is made by Höhne, *Canaris*, passim; yet he did undertake some action to moderate occupation policies (correspondence of Dr. Theodor Oberländer with author, February 14, and April 22, 1983); see also below, Chapter 3.

35. Herzog, *Grundzüge*, p. 28. See also Chapter 9, below.

36. Many of the works already cited deal with this theme in some form, but the most systematic is probably Paul W. Blackstock, "Covert Political Warfare: The Failure of German Political Warfare in Russia, 1941–1945" (unpublished Ph.D. dissertation, American University, 1954).

37. Statement of SS-Gruppenführer Otto Hofmann, quoted in Heiber, "Generalplan Ost," p. 284.

38. See Hans Buchheim's essay in Helmut Krausnick, et al., *Anatomy of the SS State*, intro. by Elizabeth Wiskemann and trans. by Richard Barry, Marian Jackson and Dorthy Long (New York: Walker, 1968), pp. 213–41.

39. See Raul Hilberg, *The Destruction of the European Jews* (Chicago: Quadrangle Books, 1961), pp. 177–256, and Krausnick and Wilhelm, *Weltanschauungskrieges*, pp. 243–54.

40. "Führer Directive No. 46," August 18, 1942, in H.R. Trevor-Roper (ed.), *Blitzkrieg to Defeat: Hitler's War Directives 1939–1945* (New York: Holt, Rinehart & Winston, 1964), p. 133.

41. Hilberg, *Destruction*, pp. 243–44.

42. See George H. Stein, *The Waffen-SS* (Ithaca, NY: Cornell University Press, 1966), pp. 177, 204–07, and Höhne, *Order*, pp. 472–75.

43. See Höhne, *Order*, pp. 501–05; and Stein, *Waffen-SS*, pp. 173ff.; see also, below, Chapter 11.

44. Bräutigam, *Überblick*, p. 11.

45. Heiber, "Der Generalplan Ost," *VfZ*, VI, 3 (July 1958): 281–325, and "Nachtrag zu der Dokumentation 'Generalplan Ost'," *VfZ*, VIII, 1 (January 1960): 119.

46. RKFDV, "Tätigkeitsbericht (Stand Ende 1942)," on T-175/194/2732994-996.

47. SS-Gruppenführer Hofmann to Hauptmann Lubkowitz, November 14, 1942, Document NO-4107, RG 238, NA; and Enno Georg, *Die wirtschaftlichen Unternehmungen der SS* (Schriftenreihe der Vierteljahreshefte für Zeitgeschichte; Stuttgart: Deutsche Verlags-Anstalt, 1963), pp. 99–101.

48. Albert Speer, *Infiltration*, trans. by Joachim Neugroschel (New York: Macmillan, 1981), pp. 185–93.

49. See Krausnick, *Anatomy*, pp. 166–87; Hilberg, *Destruction*, pp. 181ff.

50. Testimony of Walter Schellenberg in *Trials of the War Criminals Before the Nuremberg Military Tribunals Under Control Council Law No. 10* (15 vols.) (Washington, DC: Government Printing Office, 1949–1954), Vol. XIII, pp. 551–96 (hereafter *NMT*, followed by volume number in Roman numerals and page numbers in Arabic numerals); Walter Schellenberg, *The Labyrinth: The Memoirs of Walter Schellenberg* (New York: Harper and Bros., 1956), pp. 264–72; Alexander Dallin and Ralph S. Mavrogordato, "Rodionov: A Case-Study in Wartime Redefection," *The American Slavic and East European Review*, Vol. XVIII, no. 1 (February 1959): 25–33.

51. *NMT*, IV, 223–312, and Höhne, *Order*, pp. 422–27.

52. The weekly SD *Meldungen aus den besetzten Ostgebieten* (hereafter SD *Meldungen*), on T-175/235-236/2724328ff., provide valuable information on conditions in the occupied USSR from May 1942–May 1943.

53. N.A. Voznesensky, *Soviet Economy during the Second World War* (New York: International Publishers, 1949), p. 38.

54. The most complete set of economic directives, prepared by the *Wirtschaftsführungsstab Ost*, was known as *Grüne Mappe* ("Green Folder," more commonly referred to as the "Grüne Esel" or "Green Jackass"); its third edition appeared in September 1942 (Document EC-347, RG 238, NA). The "maximum exploitation" directives appear on pp. 16-18.

55. Brandt, *Management*, pp. 72–82, Bräutigam, *Überblick*, pp. 8–10. A draft history of the *Wi-Stab-Ost* was prepared in February 1944 but was broken up for use during the Nuremberg trials and is now located as Documents EC-38 (Weizsaecker Case Prosecution Exhibit 1059), 3013-PS, and 3013-PS (Weizsaecker Case Prosecution Exhibit 1060), RG 238, NA.

56. Brandt, *Management*, pp. 81–83, 92–93 Bräutigam, *Überblick*, pp. 33a–35; and below, Chapter 7.

57. Gibbons, "Allgemeine Richtlinien," pp. 252–61.

58. Testimony of State Secretary Dr. Paul Körner, *NMT*, XIII, 907. On private industry's involvement in *Ostpolitik*, see Rolf-Dieter Müller, "Die Rolle der Industrie in Hitlers Ostimperium," in *Militärgeschichte: Probleme-Thesen-Wege*, comp. by Militärgeschichtliches Forschungsamt (Stuttgart: Deutsche Verlags-Anstalt, 1982), pp. 383–406.

59. See Berthold Gerber, *Staatliche Wirtschaftslenkung in den besetzten und annektierten Ostgebieten während des Zweiten Weltkrieges unter besonderer Berücksichtigung der treuhänderischen Verwaltung von Unternehmungen und der Ostgesellschaften* (Tübingen: Institut für Besatzungsfragen, 1959), esp. pp. 113ff.

60. Brandt, *Management*, pp. 84–88; and Vera Köller, "Zur Rolle der 'Zentralhandelsgesellschaft Ost' . . . ," in Kommission der Historiker der DDR und der UdSSR, *Der deutsche Imperialismus und der Zweite Weltkrieg*, Bd. IV (5 vols.) (Berlin: Rütten & Loening, 1961–62), pp. 23–42.

61. See Matthias Riedel, *Eisen und Kohle für das Dritte Reich* (Göttingen: Musterschmidt, 1973), pp. 305–37; and testimony and documents in the Krupp Case, *NMT*, IX, 1471–82.

62. See Gerber, *Wirtschaftslenkung*, pp. 118–20.

63. Bräutigam, *Überblick*, p. 48; Gerber, *Wirtschaftslenkung*, pp. 116ff.; Roswitha

Czollek, "Estnische Phosphate im Griff der IG Farbenindustrie AG," *Jahrbuch für Wirtschaftsgeschichte*, 1966, Teil 4, pp. 201–14.

64. An excellent study of Sauckel's labor policies is Edward L. Homze, *Foreign Labor in Nazi Germany* (Princeton, NJ: Princeton University Press, 1967).

65. On Speer's powers in the East, see Bräutigam, *Überblick*, p. 12, and below, Chapter 8.

66. See Fest, *Face*, pp. 186–201, and Dallin, *German Rule*, pp. 141–42, 456–57.

67. See Laqueur, *Russia and Germany*, pp. 150–53, 176ff.

68. See Goebbels, *Diaries*, pp. 201–261, 266–69; and Buchbender, *Tönende Erz*, pp. 33–54.

69. See Dallin, *German Rule*, pp. 40–42, 133–37, and Bräutigam, *Überblick*, p. 28.

70. Ostministerium/Hauptabteilung Politik, "Vermerk," 11 July 1942, file EAP 99/1068 (not microfilmed), RG 242.

71. See especially "Bericht A über Zustände in der Ukraine auf Grund der Prüfung der 'Deutschen Dienstpost' Ukraine d.h. der Privatpost der im Reichskommissariat eingesetzten deutschen Firmen und ihrer Angestellten aus Richtung Ukraine nach dem Reichsgebiet," July 10, 1943, T-175/33/2542127-132, and Dr. Kinkelin to Lohse, March 8, 1943, T-454/89/437.

72. Goebbels, *Diaries*, p. 364 (entry of May 10, 1943).

73. Kleist, *Zwischen*, p. 148.

3

A QUESTION OF THE ALLIANCE: FOREIGN PRESSURE FOR *OSTPOLITIK* REFORM

Before turning to the internal policy debates over *Ostpolitik*, it is necessary to consider the pressure for reform within the Axis coalition. The shock waves from Stalingrad spread far beyond the circles of German military and civil officials to touch the very heart of the Axis coalition. Germany's allies and satellite states quickly perceived the implications of the defeat and began casting about for political alternatives to avert military defeat. Most common among these was the idea of a separate peace with either the Western Allies or the Soviet Union, but the reform of German occupation policy in Russia also occurred to several powers as a potential remedy for the military setbacks on the Eastern Front.[1] The intercession of these powers on behalf of a more moderate *Ostpolitik* reveals both the recognition of German mistakes in the treatment of occupied peoples and the importance attached to rectifying them by Germany's friends; and for those Germans interested in reform, it offered the advantage of diplomatic leverage.

A positive example of this was already evident in Turkey's influence on German policy in the Caucasus, whose inhabitants shared many ethnic and religious ties with their southern neighbors. Turkish attitudes figured prominently among the deliberations of German policy-makers regarding the Caucasus and contributed to the relatively moderate occupation policies in that area.[2] The Turks themselves did not hesitate to make their own views known to the German government. In August 1942, both Secretary General of the Ministry of Foreign Affairs Numan Menemencioglu and Minister President Sükrü Saracoglu approached German Ambassador Franz von Papen with proposals for granting autonomy to Turkic minorities in the occupied areas. They suggested that a "lasting solution to the Russian problem" required the construction of several new states from the minority nationalities, closely linked to Germany.[3] This concept simply reiterated the principles of *Ostpolitik* established in 1918 and endorsed by Alfred Rosenberg. Ribbentrop's sharp retort of September twelfth, however, demonstrated the limits of Turkish influence on German policy and Hitler's disinterest in political concessions.[4]

A similar situation existed at the opposite end of the Eastern Front, where the occupied Estonians shared linguistic and historical connections with Finland. That state moreover enjoyed the status of "brother-in-arms" with Germany, and when the Finns pressed for reforms in occupied Estonia during the autumn and winter of 1942–43, Germany was hardly in a position to refuse advice. By this time the Estonian issue was already a sensitive issue in Finnish-German relations. Hitler's failure to restore Estonian independence by December 1941 had provoked widespread criticism among Finnish military and government circles.[5] The Finnish government's celebration of Estonian independence day on February 24, 1942 and accompanying radio broadcasts in the Estonian language conversely angered the Germans, whose ineffective attempts to prohibit listening to these broadcasts undoubtedly marked the first time that civilians were jailed for listening to Allied rather than enemy broadcasts.[6] Public opinion in Finland shared this concern, as reflected in press and radio agitation for the restoration of full independence to Estonia.[7]

President Risto Ryti initially resisted such pressures, acknowledging in May 1942 that Estonia's future status could not be debated in the middle of the war.[8] By autumn, however, that position had begun to change. On October 13, Toivo Kivimäki, Finland's ambassador in Berlin, raised the topic of possible methods Germany might use to win over the occupied peoples in the occupied USSR.[9] Ryti himself followed this up two weeks later when he met with the German ambassador in Helsinki, Wipert von Blücher, and raised the need for voluntary cooperation from the occupied areas, inquiring directly as to the extent of autonomy permitted Estonia and the Ukraine.[10]

These early efforts appeared to have paid off when Ribbentrop solicited Kivimäki's views on encouraging indigenous cooperation.[11] The Finnish ambassador responded on November eleventh with a proposal for the establishment of individual satellite states for each of the non-Russian minorities—a familiar refrain, and one favorably received by the attending Foreign Ministry officials.[12] As Kivimäki had cushioned his suggestions as "unofficial and personal," however, Ribbentrop merely accepted them without comment.[13]

The severe German defeats of early 1943 greatly influenced Finnish attitudes toward the war. According to Marshal Gustaf Mannerheim, commander-in-chief of Finland's armed forces, the country's leaders agreed on February third that the war had reached a turning point and that Finland must use the first opportunity to withdraw from the conflict. Accordingly the Finnish government disavowed any territorial aggrandizement and dropped all claims to Eastern Karelia.[14] With this revised outlook, the Finns returned to the Estonian question through the use of unorthodox as well as standard diplomatic channels. Ambassador Kivimäki, aware of the German mobilization of the Baltic states for military service, contacted the Foreign Ministry with an offer of Finnish assistance, including the use of Estonian emigrés.[15] On January twenty-seventh the aged Pehr Svinhufvud, former president and ultra-Finnish nationalist, conferred with the German ambassador on the possible union between Finland and Estonia, an idea popular among many Finns.[16] The most important new overture, however, came from Marshal Mannerheim. The Finnish commander dispatched General Östermann, recognized as a good friend of Germany's in the Finnish Army, to the German military attaché in Helsinki to plead Estonia's case on February fourteenth: citing Kivimäki's abortive diplomatic efforts, Mannerheim appealed to the German Army for Estonia's independence as a potential source of military manpower against the Soviets. Mannerheim stressed that restoration of independence to the three Baltic states would produce at least ten divisions.[17]

But Ribbentrop terminated the discussion with a curt note to the Finnish government: "We fought not for Estonia's sovereignty but for Estonia's salvation."[18] Ribbentrop further advised Blücher to avoid discussions regarding Estonia and "this problem, which represents such a small segment of our great struggle against Bolshevism."[19]

The problem remained but gradually faded into the shadow of larger events. For the remaining year of her partnership with Germany, Finland continued to intercede on Estonia's behalf, though the Estonian language broadcasts from Finland ceased in June 1943.[20] What had changed was the basic orientation of Finnish foreign policy. Following his re-election in February 1943 Ryti replaced the pro-German Rolf Witting with the more neutral Carl Ramsey as foreign minister, whose primary task became Finland's disengagement from the Axis in search of a separate peace. Even as the internal German debate over Estonia and the Baltic states intensified—as will be seen—the strongest external force for reform turned to the more urgent business of survival.

At the other end of Europe, Spain was more than a "friendly" neutral toward Germany. The regime of *Caudillo* Francisco Franco owed Hitler much for his support during the Spanish Civil War, a debt partially repaid by the commitment of the hard-fighting "Blue Division" on the northern sector of the Eastern Front. But December 1942 marked a strain in the relations between the two powers when Hitler and his advisers redrafted earlier contingency plans for a pre-emptive occupation of the Iberian peninsula. Franco got wind of these plans and made known his intention to resist such a move.[21] The individual dispatched by Hitler to assess the situation also established—apparently deliberately—the link between Spain and *Ostpolitik* reform.

Admiral Wilhelm Canaris, chief of the German Secret Service (*Abwehr*), remains an enigmatic figure whose actions and attitudes are wrapped in legend and conjecture.[22] As in other areas of policy, he played his role in the reform of occupation policy offstage. When Hitler sent the *Abwehr* chief to his beloved Spain to ascertain Franco's willingness and capacity to resist invasion, Canaris appears literally to have rewritten the script on behalf of Spanish neutrality and reform in the East.

In Madrid Canaris met with Spanish Foreign Minister Francisco Jordana on December 8, 1942. Canaris afterwards wired to Berlin that Spain would defend her neutrality against any invasion, but might consider intervention on the Axis side pending the fulfillment of several conditions, one of which required "publication of German peace aims on the future of Europe, including Norway, Belgium, France, Poland, the Baltic States and the Ukraine." In fact, Canaris had composed this report hours before he met with Jordana.[23]

This issue resurfaced on March 12, 1943, when Spanish Air Minister Juan Vigon, a friend of Canaris' since 1928, conferred with the German air attaché in Madrid on the general war situation. In the course of an hour Vigon detailed his own thoughts regarding "necessary political measures" for the war's future conduct, including these blunt remarks:

[Vigon's] view is that Germany must abandon the notion of the annexing occupied areas in the East as "protectorates" or "Generalgovernments." Germany must rather *create independent national states in the occupied Eastern areas* [original emphasis], which rule and defend themselves and belong only to Germany's sphere of influence . . . .[24]

Spain's efforts on behalf of reform in the East apparently ended with Vigon's conversation. That they were limited and not sustained is not surprising in view of the lack of any direct Spanish interests in the issue; that they occurred at all attests to the international dimension of Germany's problem, and very likely to Canaris' influence.

If any power could empathize with Germany's plight vis-à-vis the Soviet Union, the most appropriate choice would be Japan, which occupied an analagous position toward China. Like its European ally, Japan had committed the bulk of its army along a farflung frontier in a land mass which simultaneously represented a theater of operations, an occupied territory, and the object of long-range imperial goals. The difference lay in the protracted stalemate that had left each exhausted combatant in control of half a country. This condition contributed to a greater reliance by the Japanese on collaborationist regimes, an experience later extended to most of Japanese-occupied Southeast Asia.[25]

Ironically, at exactly the same time that German officials were considering the advantages of a more liberal and humane *Ostpolitik*, the Japanese government was reevaluating its own policies in Asia in precisely the same light. One year after Pearl Harbor, Japan's leaders recognized the need to readjust their grand strategy in the face of the growing Allied counter-offensive in the Southwest Pacific. On December 21, 1942 they announced the "great departure" in policy toward China, strengthening the collaborationist regime of Wang Ching-wei in Nanking in return for a declaration of war against the United States and Great Britain. Though results in popular Chinese support never fulfilled expectations, throughout 1943 Japan increasingly yielded direct supervision of domestic affairs

in occupied China to Nanking officials.[26] Japan extended the principle of con-
ciliation to other occupied territories. In January 1943 Prime Minister Hideki
Tojo announced to the Japanese Diet that Burma and the Philippines would be
granted formal independence before year's end, a pledge redeemed respectively
on August 1 and October 14, 1943. On June 16, 1943 Tojo promised to increase
political participation and self-government in Indonesia.[27]

Thus convinced of the discovery of a self-cure to the maladies of occupation,
the Japanese prescribed the same treatment for their German allies. They based
their diagnosis on several well-placed intelligence sources. As Japan was not at
war with the Soviet Union, it maintained an embassy in the provisional Soviet
capital of Kuibyshev, with access to information on Soviet domestic and foreign
policy. Moreover, the Japanese maintained considerable intelligence activities
throughout the German-occupied Soviet areas, to an extent that alarmed the
leader of the Russian emigré community in Warsaw over Japanese intentions.[28]
An espionage network operating in the Ukraine reported to the Japanese embassy
in Sofia in June 1943 on the lack of clarity in German agrarian policy, the
absence of a national goal offered to the Ukrainians, and the great dissatisfaction
of the population with German civil authorities.[29]

Japanese concerns over *Ostpolitik* led to critical exchanges between the Allies
in February 1943. Ribbentrop discovered that the Japanese ambassador in An-
kara, Sho Kurihara, had openly and strongly criticized German policies in Russia
in his reports to Tokyo, and directed Papen to speak with him and correct this
"false impression."[30] Papen carried out these instructions, but his counterpart
remained unconvinced. Kurihara needed only to pull out a map from a German
journal illustrating Germany's annexationist aims in the East to make his point,
adding that the German failure to establish a collaborationist Russian government
only strengthened the Soviets.[31] This view was shared by Ambassador Hiroshi
Oshima in Berlin. As his country's representative to Germany, Oshima confronted a daunting task in the spring of 1943. An admirer of Hitler's, thoroughly
acquainted with and welcome among Berlin's government circles,[32] Oshima
needed every advantage in trying to coordinate an Axis grand strategy. Mamoru
Shigemitsu, the author of Japan's "new China" course who assumed the post
of foreign minister in April 1943, instructed Oshima to press Hitler on the need
for a combined strategy, particularly Japan's preference for concentrating on the
Americans and British first. Oshima had not only to convince Hitler of the need
for combined strategic planning, he also had to try to influence the führer to
disengage from the Soviet front, at a time when Hitler sought to coax Japan into
war with Russia.[33]

Japan's efforts to moderate *Ostpolitik* must be placed within this broader
context of the attempt to establish a common strategy for coalition warfare. But
if a secondary aspect, it assumed significance as a consequence of Hitler's
determination to renew the effort against the Soviet Union. When he met with
Oshima on April 18, 1943, Ribbentrop rejected the notion of separate peace
with Russia and urged Japan to join in a decisive offensive against the Soviets;

Oshima countered by pointing to the need for an effective propaganda in Russia through a subversion program aimed at the minority nationalities.[34] A few days later Oshima expanded this argument in a meeting with Hitler himself, urging the adoption of a political strategy based on the emancipation of the Soviet Union's minority nationalities. Hitler simply replied that the best strategy remained a military offensive, and that the danger of such political schemes entailed "directly opposite results" to those intended.[35]

Meanwhile the Japanese government held up its own end in pressuring German representatives in Tokyo. When, on May fifth, German ambassador Heinrich Stahmer assured Shigemitsu of the decisive success of the upcoming summer offensive in Russia, the Japanese foreign minister interrupted him and asked if Germany were not repeating the same mistake she had committed twice before.[36] Less than two weeks later Shigemitsu took advantage of the publicity attending the discovery of the Katyn Forest murders to propose the establishment of a collaborationist Polish state.[37] Also that month Shigemitsu treated envoy Eugen Ott and a party of German officials to a tour of occupied Southeast Asia which apparently had the desired effect: Ott complimented a Japanese official in Saigon on the empire's "excellent job in the administration of the southern occupied areas [where] she had gradually been increasing her popularity . . . in contrast to the German occupied areas in Europe . . . ."[38]

Oshima continued his efforts into the summer of 1943. When he next met Ribbentrop on May nineteenth, Oshima spoke more forcefully and directly concerning the East: "You cannot quell a people by force of arms alone . . . I think you should lose no time in giving guarantees of independence to the Ukraine and the three Baltic nations." Once again, Ribbentrop rejected the proposal.[39] Oshima nevertheless believed a change in policy was indicated by shifts in propaganda. A speech by Goebbels on June fifth which called for a policy of European socialism based on voluntary cooperation was enthusiastically received by Shigemitsu as "a marked advance" of "unlimited significance."[40] On June twenty-eighth Oshima reported at length on reformist editorials of the German press, and concluded, "I would say that there is a general tendency in Germany to temper down its attitude toward Russia and a desire to benevolently develop the occupied territory."[41]

In reality, Oshima had failed in his mission. This stemmed neither from lack of effort nor the validity of his criticism, as even Goebbels acknowledged.[42] The failure resulted from Hitler's disinterest and from the chaotic power structure that obscured the determination of policy. Oshima in 1943 could not discern, much less influence, German strategy in Russia: When Hitler committed Germany's strategic reserves in the abortive "Zitadelle" offensive of July fifth, the German Foreign Ministry assured the anxious Oshima that this "was not the real thing."[43] When the Japanese envoy later met with Hitler and Himmler, he must have realized the truth as he listened to the führer's categoric rejection of a compromise peace and Himmler's dismissal of any significant political concessions to the occupied population.[44]

For Italy, too, the spring of 1943 marked a critical period of reevaluation, and like Japan it looked to a compromise peace with the Soviet Union and a concentrated effort against Britain and the United States. These were the proposals presented by Benito Mussolini to Hitler at Klessheim Castle near Salzburg in early April 1943.[45] During the initial sessions of the conference, Italian Foreign Undersecretary Guiseppe Bastianini suggested to Ribbentrop a propaganda measure to counteract the Allies' Atlantic Charter. Bastianini proposed a "European Charter" to bind all occupied Europe and the satellite states into a political bloc around Germany and Italy, with guarantees of independence to small nations and respect of the nationality principle. But Ribbentrop rejected the idea out of hand, citing the unreliability of small states and the obstacle they represented to total war mobilization.[46]

Ribbentrop's rebuff foreshadowed the outcome of the subsequent discussions between Hitler and Mussolini. The senior but weaker Axis leader listened as all of his proposals were refused: The Eastern Front remained Germany's first priority, a separate peace with Stalin was impossible, a "European Charter" at best premature. Ironically, and as a tribute to the force of Hitler's personality, Mussolini departed the Klessheim conference defeated in his aims but renewed and confident of victory. Three months later his government collapsed.[47]

The question of *Ostpolitik* reform permits few conclusions with respect to the Axis coalition, as by itself the issue never rose beyond secondary significance. Together with the more important proposal of a separate peace with the USSR, however, it represents the search for a political alternative to a steadily deteriorating military situation. Hitler's rejection of the counsel of his allies cannot have improved Axis relations, but without Stalingrad it was unimportant. The proposals themselves, and their repudiation by Hitler, illustrate the provisional nature of the Axis alliance as each state advocated policies to further its own exclusive interests, with little room for compromise. If Hitler's obstinacy confirms his own pursuit of the chimera of a military victory to realize his grandiose war aims, his allies' proposals reveal a similar indulgence of self-deception: Italy could not make the Eastern Front disappear by the magic of a separate peace, and Japan's political concessions to her occupied territories could not ultimately salvage her position in East Asia.

Yet for those Germans hoping to reform occupation policy in the East, the attempted interventions by friendly powers nevertheless constitute a lost opportunity. The reformers were largely unable to capitalize on a favorable international situation to mobilize additional pressure, as in Estonia, where a major debate characterized occupation policy and a coordinated plan of action between German and Finnish officials might have accomplished more. This failure highlights the role of Foreign Minister Ribbentrop. Notwithstanding his later flirtation with the Vlasov Movement, the former champagne salesman did nothing more than parrot his master's voice throughout this period. Canaris' contacts in Spain demonstrate the possibilities of linking internal reforms to foreign pressure, but Ribbentrop's disinterest restricted the reformers to official channels.

NOTES

1. See Förster, *Risse im Bündnis*, passim.

2. See Patrik von zur Mühlen, *Zwischen Hakenkreuz und Sowjetstern. Der Nationalismus der sowjetischen Orientvölkern im Zweiten Weltkrieg* (Düsseldorf: Droste Verlag, 1971), pp. 44–81.

3. Papen to the Foreign Ministry, August 26 and 27, 1942, in *Akten zur deutschen auswärtigen Politik 1918–1945, Serie E: 1941–1945: Band III, Juni bis September 1942* (Göttingen: Vandenhoeck & Ruprecht, 1974), pp. 399–402, 411–14 (hereafter *ADAP*, E: III, 399–402, 411–14).

4. Sonnleithner to Hewel, September 12, 1942, *ADAP*, E: III, 486–87.

5. "Finland, Germany and the War" (December 1941), Office of Strategic Services Research and Analysis Branch (hereafter OSS R & A) report no. 11384, RG 226, NA.

6. Ungern-Sternberg to the Foreign Ministry, March 21, 1942, in *ADAP*, E: II, 105–07; RSHA, *Ereignismeldungen UdSSR* (hereafter *EgM*) Nr. 156, T-175/234/2723640, 2723665–666; and SD *Meldungen* Nr. 9, T-175/235/2724454–456.

7. See, for example, RSHA, *EgM* Nr. 175, T-175/235/2723940; SD *Meldungen* Nr. 36, T-175/236/2725335–338; and SD *Meldungen* Nr. T-175/236/2725651–657.

8. Memorandum by Ernst Woermann, May 20, 1942, T-120/748/1243/33725–726.

9. Memorandum by Ernst von Weizsaecker, October 13, 1942, T-120/244/275/178345.

10. Blücher to the Foreign Ministry, October 27, 1942, in *ADAP*, E: IV, 182–83.

11. See Weizsaecker's memorandum of November 23, 1942, T-120/244/275/178245–46.

12. Ibid.; Kivimäki's memorandum is summarized in Werner von Tippelskirch, November 17, 1942, T-120/593/B20/B004358–360.

13. Note by Sonnleithner, November 25, 1942, T-120/244/275/178350.

14. Carl Gustaf Mannerheim, *The Memoirs of Marshal Mannerheim*, trans. by Eric Lewenhaupt (New York: E. P. Dutton, 1954), p. 460; Leon Lundin, *Finland in the Second World War*, (Bloomington, IN: Indiana University Press, 1957), pp. 127–43.

15. Weizsaecker memorandum, February 15, 1943, T-120/247/290/183405.

16. See Blücher's memoirs, *Gesandter zwischen Diktatur und Demokratie; Erinnerungen aus dem Jahren 1935–1944* (Wiesbaden: Limes Verlag, 1951), pp. 102–4, 320–21.

17. See Blücher to the Foreign Ministry, February 14, 1943, T-120/279/406/214714–715, and the report of the German naval attaché to Finland to the Naval High Command, February 16, 1943, on microcopy T-1022, Records of the German Navy, 1850–1945, roll 2935, file PG 48787 (hereafter T-1022/2953/PG 48787).

18. Ribbentrop to Blücher, February 22, 1943, *ADAP*, E: V, 272.

19. Blücher to Ribbentrop, February 26, 1943, and Ribbentrop to Blücher, March 1, 1943, T-120/279/406/214718–720.

20. Lundin, *Finland*, pp. 168–71.

21. See Charles B. Burdick, *Germany's Military Strategy and Spain in World War II* (Syracuse, NY: Syracuse University Press, 1968), pp. 166ff.

22. See: Karl Heinz Abshagen, *Canaris*, trans. by A. H. Broderick (London: Hutch-

inson, 1956); Höhne, *Canaris*; and Andre Brissaud, *Canaris: Le "petit amiral" prince de l'espionage allemand (1887–1945)* (Paris: Librairie Academique Perrin, 1970).

23. See Brissaud, *Canaris,* pp. 596–99.

24. Deutsche Botschaft in Spanien/Der Luftattaché, "Ansicht des spanischen Luftfahrtministers über die voraussichtliche Entwicklung der Kriegslage und sich aus ihr ergebene politische Zwecksmässigkeiten, " March 15, 1943, T-1022/3284/PG 31747; on Canaris and Vigon, see Höhne, *Canaris*, pp. 106, 233, 424ff.

25. See John H. Boyle, *China and Japan at War 1937–1945: The Politics of Collaboration* (Stanford, CA: Stanford University Press, 1972), and Akira Iriye, ed., *The Chinese and the Japanese: Essays in Political and Cultural Interactions* (Princeton, NJ: Princeton University Press, 1980), pp. 254ff.

26. Boyle, *China and Japan*, pp. 308–10.

27. Willard H. Elsbree, *Japan's Role in Southeast Asian Nationalist Movements, 1940–45* (Cambridge, MA: Harvard University Press, 1953), pp. 47–52, 84–98.

28. Note by Foreign Ministry official Strecker, April 6, 1943, file EAP 99/498, MR 336, RG 242, NA.

29. See, for example, the intercepted Japanese diplomatic messages from Sofia to Tokyo, June 14, 1943, and Tokyo to the Kuibyshev legation, June 18, 1943, SRDJ 38703–706, Records of the National Security Agency, Record Group 457, National Archives (hereafter RG 457, NA).

30. Ribbentrop to Papen, February 14, 1943, T-120/3969/3865/E045365.

31. Papen to Ribbentrop, March 2, 1943, T-120/3969/3865/E045489–490.

32. See Carl Boyd, *The Extraordinary Envoy: General Hiroshi Oshima and Diplomacy in the Third Reich, 1934–1939* (Washington, DC: University Press of America, 1980).

33. Shigemitsu's instructions to Oshima are contained in an appendix to "Magic" Summary No. 400, April 30, 1943, SRS 951, RG 457, NA.

34. Foreign Ministry memorandum, April 18, 1943, Document 2929-PS, *TMWC,* XXXI, 305–15.

35. Oshima to Shigemitsu, "Magic" Summary No. 392, April 22, 1943, SRS 943, RG 457, NA.

36. Extracts of Shigemitsu to Oshima, "Magic" Summary No. 414, May 14, 1943, SRS 965, RG 457, NA. Stahmer's version is reproduced on T-120/1014/1707H/398588.

37. Stahmer to the Foreign Ministry, May 18, 1943, in *ADAP*, E: VI, 75–76.

38. Ott's comments quoted by the Japanese minister to French Indochina, "Magic" Summary No. 427, May 27, 1942, SRS 978, RG 457, NA.

39. Oshima to the Foreign Office, May 21, 1943, SRDJ 37450–452, RG 457, NA. Ribbentrop's version of the meeting is on T-120/11/27/17248–252.

40. Tokyo (Shigemitsu) to Kuibyshev legation, June 12, 1943, SRDJ 33427–428, RG 457, NA.

41. Oshima to Foreign Office, June 28, 1943, SRDJ 39683–685, RG 457, NA.

42. Goebbels, *Diaries,*, p. 348.

43. Oshima to Shigemitsu, in "Magic" Summary No. 469, July 8, 1943, SRS 1019, RG 457, NA.

44. Oshima's report to Shigemitsu on his conference with Hitler, August 4, 1943, appendix to "Magic" Summary No. 501, August 9, 1943, SRS 1054; extracts from his

conference with Himmler in "Magic" Summary No. 502, August 10, 1943, SRS 1052, RG 457, NA.

45. See Deakin, *Friendship*, pp. 244–75; and Robert Edwin Herzstein, *When Nazi Dreams Come True* (London: Abacus Books, 1982), pp. 200–12.

46. Memoranda of Foreign Ministry official Schmidt, April 10 and 11, 1943, in *ADAP*, E: V, 543–55 and 566–71.

47. See Deakin, *Friendship*, pp. 264–75.

4

FROM *OSTPOLITIK* TO *REALPOLITIK*: PROPOSALS FOR A GENERAL REFORM

As Germany's 1942 summer victories faded with the autumn, the failure to eliminate Russia prompted many Germans again to consider the advantages of a political solution to the eastern question. The reforms half-heartedly enacted the previous spring provided the foundation for a renewed effort. Germany's reverses in the winter of 1942–43 reinforced the reformers with a rush of converts and established a bureaucratic proselytism that characterized the entire period, while the lateness of the hour imparted a new urgency to the reform proposals. But could the führer be induced to join them on the road to Damascus?

The murmurings began among those least susceptible to victory bulletins, the soldiers at the front. At the end of August 1942 Dr. Giselher Wirsing, journalist and eventual editor of *Signal* magazine, reported to the Foreign Ministry the views expressed by officers of one of Army Group Center's panzer corps. Acknowledging the improbability of outright military victory, they urged instead the establishment of increased self-administration for the population and a premium system to reward pro-German services. Firm adherents to the "divide and rule" precept, they also proposed to "re-awaken the civil war between White and Red in the rear areas and later throughout the East."[1] The Foreign Ministry representative attached to the Ninth Army reported similar views there in early September, but added that the requisition of Russian nationalism for the German cause entailed at least a recognition of Russian membership in the "great European community of peoples."[2]

In September and November Dr. Theodor Oberländer, a Canaris associate and commander of the *Abwehr's* "Bergmann" unit of Caucasian troops, added to his earlier attacks on German occupation policy.[3] The abysmal living conditions in the Ukraine provided the focus of his September memorandum, emphasizing the need for "consideration of the most basic economic and national-cultural vital interests of the Ukrainian people," which Oberländer believed only possible through a "a fundamental change in current German policy."[4] He followed this in November with a memorandum to the headquarters of Army Group A, urging increased participation in self-government and the complete dissolution of the *kolkhozy*.[5]

Other individuals picked up on the same theme as the autumn wore on. Dr. Paul W. Thomson of the Geological-Paleontological Institute at the Reich University, Posen (Poznan), took time out from his scientific research to compose a blistering attack on the excessive brutality practiced by many civil officials in the East and pointed to the need for the collaboration of the indigenous workers in any serious economic development of occupied Russia.[6] Edwin E. Dwinger, a writer and SS war correspondent who had been a Russian captive during World War I, disapproved of the *Untermensch* stereotype and sought to replace it with a greater appreciation of Russian attitudes and values through newspaper articles and official memoranda.[7]

The most concise and devastating critique of *Ostpolitik*, however, came from *OMi*'s own Dr. Otto Bräutigam. On October 25, while serving in the Caucasus as political liaison officer, Bräutigam submitted his views to Rosenberg in a 13-page memorandum. With the premise that German colonial methods had wasted anti-Stalinist sentiment and aroused widespread resistance among the population, Bräutigam argued that a sincere redirection of policy might yet bring about the "decomposition" of the Red Army. Specifically, Bräutigam proposed: the establishment of a counter-regime in the manner of DeGaulle; immediate improvement in the treatment of Soviet prisoners-of-war and civilian *Ostarbeiter*; and above all, a positive reorientation of policy toward the Ukraine, starting with the replacement of *Reichskommissar* Koch.[8]

Bräutigam's indictment of German occupation policy and the reforms he proposed mapped the terrain which would become the battlefield of German policy for the next eight months. For the present, however, Bräutigam achieved nothing. When he met with Rosenberg and the latter's deputy, Alfred Meyer, in early November, Meyer mentioned Bräutigam's memorandum with the warning that such strong criticism of *Gauleiter* Koch "would not do." When Rosenberg, after confessing he had still not read the paper, expressed sympathy with Bräutigam's concerns, Meyer immediately retorted: "But to heap criticism upon a Gauleiter, that won't do." Rosenberg acquiesced, "At least not in writing."[9]

At this time many moderate officials in the Foreign Ministry favored a different political solution to Germany's military dilemma, the conclusion of a separate peace with Stalin.[10] Some thought was given to *Ostpolitik* reform, however, as when Dr. Karl Megerle, deputy for propaganda on Ribbentrop's staff, approached State Secretary Ernst von Weizsaecker on November fourteenth with the proposal of establishing an opposition regime in occupied Russia. Weizsaecker conditionally accepted the plan, pending the outcome of the exploratory negotiations with the USSR.[11]

More than any other agency, the Army High Command developed into a center of reform agitation. In October, Major Stauffenberg and Colonel Altenstadt closed a conference on agricultural policy in Russia by criticizing "the disastrous course of Germany's Eastern policy" and claiming that "victory in the East was possible only if Germany succeeded in winning over the local population."[12] The next month Altenstadt addressed a conference of senior Army medical officers on the need for a correct and sympathetic treatment of the Russians serving with German forces; conceding that no political promises could be made, Altenstadt contended that this very fact required every other possible consideration on behalf of the *Osttruppen*.[13] The day after this speech Colonel Reinhard Gehlen, head of the FHO intelligence section, submitted a lengthy memorandum on the need for agrarian reform, religious toleration, the restoration of private property, increased self-government, and a proclamation which guaranteed Russian independence.[14]

In the wake of the successful Soviet counterstroke at Stalingrad in late November came fresh calls for reform. Dr. Giselher Wirsing, this time writing on his own behalf, strongly criticized the disparaging attitudes toward the Russian population at the heart of *Ostpolitik*, in a report to the Foreign Ministry in early December. Yet, Wirsing concluded, the opportunity to win over the population "remains open to us, probably only for a short time . . . if this winter slips by us unused, this opportunity will be gone with it."[15] More importantly, civil officials within the *Ostministerium* began to speak out on the need for change. On December ninth, the head of the Legal Department, Dr. Friedrich Markull, wrote Rosenberg in support of "New Measures in the East," particularly economic concessions in the Baltic states and cultural reforms in the Ukraine (for example, the expansion of the Ukrainian school system).[16] That same month Rosenberg received a more detailed critique from his liaison officer to the headquarters of Army Group North, who had just completed an inspection tour of the southern areas. The report dealt largely with the practical problems of occupation and administration, but its message was unequivocal:

It is the opinion of all military commanders as well as of the leaders of the civil administration areas . . . that the present Eastern policy must undergo a fundamental change in its basic points.[17]

Beyond its contents, the report offered evidence of the cooperation between the army and the *Ostministerium* on behalf of *Ostpolitik* reform. The army had in November modified its liaison channels with the Eastern Ministry to ensure closer coordination on political and administrative matters.[18] Prospects for a reform alliance therefore seemed promising in December when Dr. Georg Leibbrandt, head of Rosenberg's political department, and General Eduard Wagner, quartermaster-general of OKH, took advantage of Christmas leave to convoke a grand conference of military and civil officials in Berlin concerning Germany's eastern policy.[19]

The Eastern Ministry hosted the conference in its spacious new Berlin headquarters, the former Soviet embassy, on December 18, 1942. The 15 military representatives included Stauffenberg and Altenstadt from OKH and military government officers from the field; they had the opportunity to express their views to the top echelons of the *Goldfasanen*, Rosenberg, Meyer, Leibbrandt, and most of the department and section chiefs of the ministry. After Rosenberg opened the meeting with a speech on the difficulties of German colonization and economic requirements in Russia, the military officers took control of the conference. One after another they described the poor living conditions of the occupied population, and pointed to the military implications of popular disaffection for a German Army which included half a million Russian volunteers and depended upon supply lines exposed to partisan attacks. To remedy this situation, they proposed: improvements in food supplies, restrictions upon slave labor conscription, a generous and prompt agrarian reform, the restoration of private property, the reopening of schools and churches, an expanded role in self-government, closer coordination between the civil and military administrations, and the pronouncement by Hitler himself of these reforms to emphasize the change in policy.[20]

These proposals, however, served merely to underscore the differences between the army and the Eastern Ministry regarding *Ostpolitik*. Lieutenant Hans Herwarth von Bittenfeld, representing army Group A, bluntly asserted what many army officials present believed: "Russia can be conquered only by Russians." Rosenberg reaffirmed his own commitment to the minority nationalities when he "once more emphasized the necessity to check the danger of centralized Russian Government by splitting the country into numerous regions."[21] Bräutigam's absence from Berlin (he was still in the Caucasus) denied both parties a valuable official who could bridge their differences in a common cause. Nevertheless, a start had been made; and Rosenberg, already embroiled in a major dispute with *Reichskommissar* Koch, certainly welcomed the army's support. Three days after the conference he submitted its conclusions to Hitler, requesting a decision.[22]

Hitler wasted no time in smashing the alliance before it could solidify. Some days after the receipt of Rosenberg's report he admonished both parties, in effect, to mind their own business.[23] For Rosenberg, this was enough. He concluded an agreement with the army in January 1943 that enhanced potential cooperation through the direct assignment of *OMi* liaison officers to army group headquarters staffs.[24] But locked as he was in a bitter struggle with Koch, Rosenberg knew he needed Hitler's goodwill and was moreover courting an alliance with Himmler. Henceforth he begrudged the army's reform advocates only limited support and bickered with them constantly. [25]

The Eastern minister's bickering, however, was not restricted to the army.

The attempt to obtain an official führer proclamation of German war aims in the East in early 1943 provides an excellent example of how a reform issue—even one that amounted only to a propaganda measure of words and not deeds—could be swallowed up in the personal and organizational rivalries of *Ostpolitik*. Picking up on the army's suggestion at the December conference, Leibbrandt's staff at *OMi* produced a draft führer proclamation before the end of January 1943, together with carefully reasoned justification for its issuance.[26] A copy was forwarded to the *Wehrmacht* Propaganda Office (OKW/WPr), which, after consultation with OKH, recommended strengthening its tone and accelerating its publication.[27] The proposed revisions were incorporated in a new version drafted for Rosenberg on February third.[28] Five days later the latter met with Hitler to present a general reform program for the areas under civil administration, including the issuance of the proclamation. Hitler, preoccupied with the military crisis confronting the southern wing of the Eastern Front after Stalingrad, put off Rosenberg with a request to see "more concrete proposals," and even the *Ostminister* concurred in delaying any proclamation until the military situation stabilized.[29]

Rosenberg, however, now found himself in stiff competition with Goebbels, whose ministry included an Eastern Department (*Abteilung Ost*) deeply involved in propaganda activities.[30] The department was directed by Dr. Eberhard Taubert, a tireless critic of German occupation policy and propaganda in Russia who was already engaged in a protracted covert struggle to force the withdrawal of the SS pamphlet *Der Untermensch*.[31] In the winter of 1942–43 Taubert pressed Goebbels to become directly involved in *Ostpolitik* generally and in the issuance of an *Ostproklamation* specifically.[32] Goebbels apparently took this to heart, for by the end of January 1943 he secured Hitler's permission to draft his own proclamation. [33] By the time of Rosenberg's meeting with Hitler on February eighth, Goebbels' draft was already being circulated for comment to the army and Foreign Ministry.[34]

A reviewing official at the latter derided Goebbels' proclamation as little more than a collection of vague promises, warning that its publication would "smash the last porcelain in the occupied East."[35] Yet this had not deterred another senior Foreign Ministry official, Cecil von Renthe-Fink, from composing his own eastern proclamation. With more boldness than either Rosenberg or Goebbels, Renthe-Fink went so far as to promise independence for the Baltic states and an enlarged "Greater Ukraine" after the war.[36]

The Goebbels-Rosenberg confrontation had meanwhile degenerated into a jurisdictional dispute. Both parties appealed to Chief of the Reich Chancellery Hans-Heinrich Lammers; when Lammers proposed a compromise of shared authority, Goebbels rejected it.[37] But the issue had become academic. Hitler's consideration of a proclamation evaporated with the restoration of the military situation on the southern wing in early March, an event Hitler rated "of the first magnitude, [that] simply cannot be overestimated."[38] Lammers informed Rosenberg on March eighth that "the Führer rejects any proclamation to the Eastern peoples . . . at this time.''[39] Goebbels had learned as much from OKH Chief of the General Staff General Kurt Zeitzler on March second, and confirmed it in direct approaches to Hitler on March ninth and seventeenth; next month Army Group Center's commander Field Marshal Günther von Kluge appealed to Goebbels to renew his efforts, but the frustrated propaganda minister dared not raise the issue again in view of "such a positive stand" by the führer.[40] The Rosenberg-Goebbels dispute dragged through the summer of 1943 until Hitler formally granted Goebbels broad propaganda powers in the East on August fifteenth.[41] Thus the reform issue which offered the least painful first step toward a general conversion of *Ostpolitik* dissolved into a bureaucratic power play, and Goebbels' hollow victory was celebrated by the Red Army's sweep through the eastern Ukraine.

While the "battle of the proclamations" ran its course, many reformers withdrew into their respective jurisdictions to concentrate their efforts on specific and limited concerns. While they regrouped, others fought a delaying action on behalf of a general reform of policy throughout the first half of 1943. This rearguard was composed of men on the fringes of *Ostpolitik* but with special qualifications that commanded some respect, and through individual lobbying they kept the issue alive.

One early effort featured a direct encounter with Hitler. On January 13, 1943 the führer conferred upon Colonel Helmuth von Pannwitz, combat commander of a group of Cossack cavalry units in German service, the oakleaf cluster to the Knight's Cross of the Iron Cross. During the brief conversation that followed Pannwitz offered his own views on the major German misconceptions and blunders in the treatment of the Russian population, to which Hitler replied that Germans lacked the imperial Austrian experience of managing a dozen nationalities; when Pannwitz later extended his analysis to Poland as well, Hitler said nothing and the interview ended.[42]

The most prominent figure involved in these efforts was Vidkun Quisling, minister president of the Norwegian "government" under German occupation. Quisling's name had already become synonymous with collaboration, but he also qualified as a Russian authority: He had served eight years in the USSR with the League of Nations' famine relief organization, married a Ukrainian, and authored a polemic on Soviet Communism.[43] Germany's mishandling of occupied Russia so distressed Quisling that on February 2, 1943 he set forth his thoughts on "the Russian question" in a 29-page memorandum that eventually wound its way to Hitler, Himmler, Goebbels and the OKW Operations Staff. Quisling argued that this issue was "decisive" for the outcome of the war, and outlined an elaborate scheme to square the circle of indigenous nationalism and Nazi colonialism: The Baltic states, "White Russia" and the Ukraine west of Dnieper River should be granted national autonomy and bound to Germany, while an anti-Soviet Russian regime should be built up for eventual installation in the Kremlin and alliance with the Axis against Britain and the United States. At the same time Germany could establish military colonies in both the autonomous states and Russia to secure her predominance and initiate a gradual "Germanization" of the East for future generations.[44]

Whereas Quisling tried to reconcile the divergent aims of all concerned, a former Austro-Hungarian official proposed applying the lessons of 1918 to the Soviet Union as a new basis of policy. Richard Riedl had served in the Dual Monarchy's Economic Ministry during the First World War, and as Austrian ambassador to Germany from 1921 to 1925; in March 1943 he was a senior executive with the I. G. Farben Combine in Vienna, when he composed a massive essay on "The Russian Question." Riedl accepted Rosenberg's premise of the importance of the non-Russian nationalities and proposed to dismember the European Soviet Union through an enlarged Finland, independence for Baltic states, White Russia, and the Ukraine, and a military colony along the southeastern frontier of occupied Russia. Riedl bluntly declared the victory could be gained only with the cooperation of all the occupied peoples, which required Germany "to content herself to be *a leading* power but not *the ruling* power in Europe" (emphasis in original). Riedl's report was warmly endorsed by Max Ilgner, a member of I. G. Farben's managing board of directors, who forwarded an abstract to Lammers for submission to Hitler; other copies were circulated to the Foreign Ministry, where Soviet specialist Gustav Hilger supported Riedl's views to Ribbentrop, and to Gehlen at OKH.[45]

Riedl's critique also drew a response from the SD's research organization specializing in Soviet studies, known as the "Wannsee Institute" (after the Berlin suburb in which it was located). Their reply assessed Riedl's views as outdated, with an exaggerated emphasis on Ukrainian nationalism ("looking at the Ukrainian problem through Galician glasses") and insufficient consideration for the role of the Communist Party. On the other hand, the Institute endorsed one of Riedl's lesser points—an accelerated agrarian reform—as an economic and social measure of significant value in winning over the occupied population.[46]

This commentary illustrated the Wannsee Institute's own unusual position in *Ostpolitik* reform. Under the direction of Dr. Mikhail Akhmeteli, a native of Soviet Georgia and pre-war faculty member of the University of Berlin, the institute collected and evaluated intelligence data on the Soviet Union for the SD's Foreign Intelligence Section.[47] Akhmeteli, however, also attempted to influence policy in the direction of moderation. At the beginning of BARBAROSSA he put forward a detailed program for agrarian reform.[48] In December 1942 Akhmeteli composed a scathing criticism of *Reichskommissar* Koch's Ukrainian policy in a tone deemed "more than dangerous for state security" by SS-*Gruppenführer* Gottlob Berger.[49] Following an extended inspection tour of the occupied areas Akhmeteli drew up a lengthy analysis of the mistakes of German policy and recommended cures, including the recall of the Reich commissioners and increased self-government; Schellenberg summarized and elaborated these proposals in a report to Himmler in April 1943. The result was very nearly the arrest of the author on a charge of "defeatism," averted only by Schellenberg's intercession with Himmler.[50]

Anatol von der Milwe-Schröden, deputy chief of the *Ostministerium*'s cultural department, employed quite another argument in a memorandum written in May 1943. Milwe-Schröden did not question the colonialist nature of Hitler's war aims, but simply considered that the best way to achieve them was to assimilate eligible Russians as partners. Citing the historical lessons taught by Bismarck and the Ottoman Empire's use of Janissaries, he proposed a gradual reconstruction of the Reich through the absorption of autonomous eastern states and assimilation of those Russians and Ukrainians sufficiently "Germanized" to identify the Reich's interests as their own. Milwe-Schröden practiced what he preached, for the previous November he had formally changed his name from Milewski-Schröden.[51]

The would-be beneficiaries of Milwe-Schröden's plan, however, shared only his general concerns and timing. Russian collaborationists who followed the example of their German sponsors and submitted their own memoranda shared two distinguishing qualities: first, they subordinated the issue of the minority nationalities to a broader anti-Stalinist movement; and second, they served as the only gauge of popular response to indicate that a change in policy might not yet be too late—but time was running out.

Sergei Pavlov, a member of the local administration for the Pochep district in central Russia, advised the Germans in February 1943 that an allied Russian government was necessary if Germany hoped to secure popular support.[52] In an undated letter to Adolf Hitler, Vladimir Aksenov from the city administration of Ostrov proposed the establishment of a Russian Nazi Party and of a counter-regime allied to the Axis powers, which would deliver up to 50 percent of its economic production and an army to Germany in return for the release of Russian prisoners-of-war.[53] And in early April one of the leaders of the Russian emigré community in Warsaw suggested the establishment of a "Russian Central Committee" whose 15 to 20 members would exercise immediate administrative and economic powers in the occupied areas; he added that the anti-Bolshevik struggle must include the minority nationalities before their political status was resolved.[54]

Perhaps the most representative and articulate among Russian civilian collaborationists was a Professor Dimitri Soschalski of Minsk, who wrote in the late spring of 1943 that it was still possible " . . . in spite of all events, all misunderstandings and all mistakes, willful or otherwise . . . to build the bridge between the Russian and German peoples." But this required Germany to openly endorse a true liberation movement that transcended Vlasov's "Russian Committee" and discarded the "political unreality" of Ukrainian and White Russian separatism.[55] Soschalski repeated his views in another memorandum on July second urging the establishment of sovereign Russian government and a formal treaty of alliance with Germany.[56]

The same point had just been raised again by Theodor Oberländer: on June 22, 1943, the second anniversary of the German invasion of Russia, he composed another critique of German policies entitled "Alliance or Exploitation." Oberländer advocated a clear and total change in *Ostpolitik* through an accelerated agrarian reform, greater self-rule, concessions in cultural and social policy, and the formal establishment of a Russian army from the 800,000 Soviet nationals in German service. Oberländer registered his bitterness at two years of wasted opportunity and stupidity by quoting a captured Communist Party member: "We have treated our people badly, so badly that it would be a true art to treat them worse. You Germans have managed it."[57]

While Oberländer's arguments sounded a familiar litany, his timing and indiscretion proved his undoing. Two weeks earlier Hitler had categorically rejected anything more than a propaganda use of Vlasov movement, effectively shelving the alternative of political reform in favor of another major military effort. Oberländer's distribution of 50 copies of his memorandum throughout governing circles embarassed even his sympathizers; though Zeitzler retrieved and destroyed about one-fourth of the copies, the OKW Operations Staff called for Oberländer's sacking while SS officers spoke of his arrest.[58] In the end Oberländer did lose his command and was banished to a training camp in Antwerp until his release from the *Wehrmacht* in October 1943. He would spend most of the rest of the war in Prague in academic work, until recalled to duty with Vlasov's Russian units in spring 1945.[59]

Oberländer's case typifies the paradoxical nature of the individual efforts that initiated and closed the movement for a general reform of *Ostpolitik* in 1942–43. Though consistent and strong in his criticisms, Oberländer nevertheless began with the unspoken, optimistic premise that rational arguments, if necessarily cloaked in Nazi rhetoric, openly submitted through official channels could alter the course of policy. That so many followed this course indicates serious misinterpretations among National Socialist officials of the essentially irrational nature of National Socialist policy. The candor of the arguments advanced illustrates a misplaced faith in the dictates of *Realpolitik* over ideology, a supremacy achieved only partially and very late in the Third Reich's history. In 1942–43 such frankness merely exposed the isolation of these individual efforts: without an institutional foothold, they could be ignored or intimidated.

The larger framework which might have unified these efforts disintegrated with the collapse of the army-*Ostministerium* alliance at the end of 1942. Several factors contributed to the premature death of this "reform coalition," including the natural antipathy of civilian and military agencies bumping shoulders over shared responsibilities, and the particular contempt in which many soldiers held the "Golden Pheasants" behind the lines. Key individuals who might have served as cohesive bonds in the alliance were unavailable: Bräutigam paid for his contributions in the Caucasus with his absence from Berlin, Stauffenberg ended a promising role in *Ostpolitik* with a field duty rotation to North Africa in January 1943.[60] Above all, Alfred Rosenberg cared little for the alliance. The December eighteenth conference confirmed a major difference between the *Ostminister*'s nationalities concept and the army's view of a more general reform. Rosenberg's quick acquiescence in Hitler's reproof may be attributed in part to his weakness of character, in part to his preoccupation with the Ukraine; perhaps most of all, it reflects Rosenberg's inability to compromise his principles in the interests of pragmatism.

But with allowances for the actions of individuals, the aborted alliance of army and Eastern Ministry resulted fundamentally from the fragmented structure of *Ostpolitik*. Lacking coordinating mechanisms, dependent on access to the führer rather than regular channels, and usually in constant competition with rival offices for the same functions, the Nazi political structure discouraged cooperation and rewarded individual initiative. For the reformers this offered the advantage of effecting immediate if limited changes within their own jurisdictions, and this shaped the course of the reform efforts from the end of 1942. Accepting that Hitler had not yet seen the light, the reformers withdrew and directed their efforts toward those areas where their authority and discretion permitted improvements. The fait accompli and direct confrontation replaced the lengthy memorandum as the chief instruments of change. The army reformers concentrated on military government and political warfare. Rosenberg meanwhile prepared himself for battle with the nemesis of his Ukrainian policy, *Reichskommissar* Erich Koch.

NOTES

1. Dr. Giselher Wirsing, "Die Zukunft der deutschen Herrschaft in Russland," end of August 1942, T-120/695/1083/316916–39.

2. Der Vertreter des Auswärtigen Amtes beim AOK 9 (Schmidt) an das A.A., "Der russische Nationalgedanke in der propagandistischen Auseinandersetzung," September 5, 1942, T-120/270/339/198617–620.

3. Compare Aleksander Drozdzynski and Jan Zaborowski, *Oberländer: A Study in German East Policies* (Poznan/Warsaw: Wydawnictwo Zachodnie, 1960) and Herman Raschhofer, *Political Assassination: The Legal Background of the Oberländer and Stashinsky Cases* (Tübingen: Fritz Schlichtenmayer, 1964). Oberländer's earlier memoranda are published in his *6 Denkschriften aus dem Zweiten Weltkrieg über die Behandlung der Sowjetvölker* (Ingolstadt: Zeitgeschichtliche Forschungsstelle Ingolstadt, 1984), Nos. 1 and 2.

4. Theodor Oberländer, "Die Ukraine und die militärischen (psychologischen) Notwendigkeiten der weiteren Kriegführung im Osten, besonders im Kaukasus," file EAP 99/1144 (not microfilmed), RG 242, NA, and *6 Denkschriften*, No. 3, pp. 1–17.

5. Oberländer, "Die besetzten Gebiete Osteuropas und der weitere Verlauf des Krieges," November 9, 1942, T-311/101/7134307–319, published in *6 Denkschriften*, No. 4, pp. 1–16.

6. Dr. Paul W. Thomson, "Politischer Bericht," October 19, 1942, Document 303-PS, *TMWC*, XXV, 342–46.

7. Edwin E. Dwinger, "Wesensfundamente einer Ostraumpolitik," autumn 1942, on T-120/363/876/288649–64.

8. Dr. Otto Bräutigam, "Aufzeichnung," October 25, 1942, Document 294-PS, *TMWC*, XXV, 331–42.

9. Bräutigam, *So hat es*, pp. 514–15.

10. See Ingeborg Fleischhauer, *Die Chance des Sonderfriedens: Deutsch-sowjetische Geheimgespräche 1941–1945* (Berlin: Siedler, 1986), pp. 101–13.

11. Dr. Karl Megerle to Ernst von Weizsaecker, November 14, 1942, T-120/393/982/303879; Weizsaecker to Megerle, November 16, 1942, *ADAP*, E: IV, 324–25.

12. Eberhard Zeller, *The Flame of Freedom: The German Struggle against Hitler*, trans. R. P. Heller and D. R. Masters (Coral Gables, FL: University of Miami Press, 1969), pp. 189–90.

13. "Vortrag: Oberstleutenant i.G. v. Altenstadt anlässlich der Heeresgruppen- und Armeearztbesprechung am 24.11.1942," on T-120/695/1083/316857–863.

14. Gehlen, "Dringende Fragen des Bandenkrieges und der 'Hilfswilligen'-Erfassung," November 25, 1942, T-78/556/536–52.

15. Wirsing, "Kernfragen zur Beherrschung des Ostraums, Anfang Dezember 1942," T-120/2553/5079/E292527–534.

16. Markull to Rosenberg, "Neue Massnahmen im Osten," December 9, 1942, T-454/18/617–21.

17. The Representative of the Reich Ministry for the Occupied Eastern Territories with the Headquarters of Army Group North, "Political and Economic Problems of the Military and Civil Administration of the Occupied Eastern Territories," December 1942, Document 1381-PS, published in *NCA*, III, pp. 932–58.

18. OKH GenStdH/GenQu, Abt. Kriegsverwaltung, "Vertreter des Reichsministeriums f.d.b. Ostgebiete bei den Heeresgruppen," November 12, 1942, file EAP 99/1143 (not microfilmed), RG 242, NA.

19. Dallin, *German Rule*, p. 152.

20. See SS-*Brigadeführer* Zimmermann, "Protokoll der Besprechung des Reichsministers für die besetzten Ostgebiete mit den Befehlshabern der Heeresgebiete und den Beauftragten der für die besetzten Ostgebiete zuständigen höheren Wehrmachtsdienststellen am 18. Dezember 1942," January 4, 1943, Document NO–1481, RG 238, NA; minutes of Befehlshaber Heeresgebiet Mitte, "Besprechung im Ostministerium am 18.12.1942," on T-501/27/278–83; and the minutes of Dr. Leibbrandt, folder 547, roll ML 465, RG 242, NA.

21. Zimmermann, "Protokoll," Document NO–1481, RG 238, NA.

22. Rosenberg to Hitler, "Conference with the commanders in chief of the army areas behind the front," December 21, 1942, published in translation in Brandt, *Management*,, pp. 671–74.

23. Dallin, (*German Rule*, p. 154n) citing interviews with three unidentified *Ostministerium* officials. Jürgen Thorwald, *Wenn sie verderben wollen. Bericht des grossen Verrats* (Stuttgart: Steingrüben-Verlag, 1952), pp. 189–90, asserts that Hitler's decision came on December 22 but cites no source.

24. Leibbrandt, "Stellung der Vertreter des Ostministeriums bei den Heeresgruppen," January 11, 1943, EAP 99/1143, RG 242, NA.

25. See below, Chapters 5 and 12.

26. Separately annotated drafts of the proclamation with accompanying correspondence dated January 14–26, 1943, appear on T-454/21/841–43, T-454/24/974–1002, and in Akten R6/35, Bundesarchiv, Koblenz (hereafter BA). See also Hans-Erich Volkmann, "Das Vlasov-Unternehmen zwischen Ideologie und Pragmatismus," *Militärgeschichtliche Mitteilungen*, Bd. XXI, 2/1972, pp. 139–42.

27. Ostministerium/Hauptabt. Politik (signature illegible), "Führerproklamation," February 3, 1943, T-454/21/430.

28. Ostministerium draft, "Völker der Sowjetunion! Aktennotiz für den Führer," February 3, 1943, T-454/45/00027–31.

29. Paul Körner's letter to Goering, February 20, 1943, and Dr. Wilhelm Kinkelin, "Aufzeichnung über die Besprechung beim Herrn Minister am 10. Februar 1943," T-454/89/446–52, 461–64. See also Chapters 5, 6 and 12, below.

30. See Buchbender, *Tönende Erz*, pp. 33–51.

31. See Jay W. Baird, *The Mythical World of Nazi War Propaganda, 1939–1945* (Minneapolis, MN: University of Minnesota Press, 1974), pp. 161–63.

32. See Taubert to Goebbels, "Deutsche Politik im Ostraum," December 28, 1942, on National Archives microcopy T-580, Captured German records filmed at Berlin (American Historical Association), roll 647, Ordner No. 406; and Taubert, "Die Politik in den besetzten Ostgebieten," February 24, 1943 (with accompanying cover letter, February 25, 1943), file R 55/567, Reichsministerium für Volksaufklärung und Propaganda, BA.

33. Boelcke, *Secret Conferences*, pp. 325–26.

34. "An alle Völker des Ostens!", n.d., and Rosenberg's letter to Goebbels, February 11, 1943, both in file Occ E 18–19, YIVO Institute for Jewish Research, New York, (hereafter YIVO).

35. See *Legationsrat* Dittmann, "Bemerkungen zu den Entwurf einer Proklamation an die Völker der Sowjetunion," February 5, 1943, T-120/1069/1898/427363–366.

36. See Herzstein, *Nazi Dreams*, pp. 233–35. Renth-Fink renewed his efforts in August 1943 (ibid., pp. 242–47).

37. See Rosenberg to Goebbels, February 11, 1943, and Goebbels to Lammers, February 13, 1943, both in Occ E 18–19, YIVO.

38. Goebbels, *Diaries*, p. 280 (entry for March 9, 1943).

39. Lammers to Rosenberg, March 8, 1943, file EAP 99/76, microfilm MR 260, RG 242, NA.

40. Goebbels, *Diaries*, pp. 261, 280, 284, 302, 330 (entries for March 2, 9, and 17 and April 16, 1943).

41. The Rosenberg-Goebbels correspondence of June 1943 can be found in file Occ E 18–19, YIVO, and Buchbender, *Tönende Erz*, pp. 202–03.

42. Erich Kern, *General von Pannwitz und seine Kosaken* (Oldendorf: Verlag K. W. Schütz KG, 1971), pp. 47–49.

43. See Paul M. Hayes, *Quisling: The Career and Political Ideas of Vidkun Quisling 1887–1945* (Bloomington, IN: Indiana University Press, 1972), pp. 22ff.

44. Vidkun Quisling, "Denkschrift über die russische Frage," February 2, 1943, T-175/60/2575933–961. On the memo's circulation: Berger to Himmler, March 1, 1943, T-175/60/2575932; Goebbels, *Diaries*, p. 328 (entry for April 14, 1943); and *KTB/OKW*, 1943 Teilband I, p. 228 (entry for March 19, 1943).

45. R. Riedl, "Die russische Frage. Gedanken zur Neugestaltung Osteuropas, März 1943," T-78/486/6471226–1419; Hilger, "Notiz für den Herrn Reichsaussenminister," August 17, 1943, T-120/395/997/305083–091. See also Dietrich Eichholtz, " 'Wege zur Entbolschewisierung und Entrussung des Ostraumes,' Empfehlungen des IG-Farben-Konzerns für Hitler in Frühjahr 1943," *Jahrbuch für Wirtschaftsgeschichte*, 1970, Teil II, pp. 13–44.

46. RSHA/Wannsee-Institut, "Stellungnahme zu der Denkschrift von Richard Riedl, im Juli 1943," file R 58/237, BA.

47. See U.S. State Department Propaganda Investigation Team: Interrogations of Dr. Franz Six and Dr. Horst Mahnke, April 30, 1946, RG 238, NA; and Walter Schellenberg, *The Labyrinth: The Memoirs of Walter Schellenberg* (New York: Harper and Bros., 1956), pp. 273–76.

48. See below, Chapter 7.

49. Gottlob Berger to Walter Schellenberg, January 6, 1943, Document NO–3022, RG 238, NA. See also Chapter 5, below.

50. Interrogation of Walter Schellenberg, April 30, 1947, RG 238, NA; see also Schellenberg, *Labyrinth*, pp. 274–76.

51. Anatol von der Milwe-Schröden, "Gedanken über den Reichsaufbau im Osten," May 1943, T454/33/632–45; Milwe-Schröden to Rosenberg, November 9, 1942, EAP 99/143, MR 278, RG 242, NA.

52. Memorandum of Sergei Pavlov, February 11, 1943, quoted in Sven Steenberg, *Vlasov*, trans. Abe Farbstein (New York: Alfred A. Knopf, 1970), pp. 81–82.

53. Aksenov, "An den Führer des deutschen Volkes und der deutschen Armee Herrn Adolf Hitler!" n.d., Document Occ E–8, YIVO.

54. Strecker (first name unknown), "Aufzeichnung über eine Unterhaltung mit dem Vorsitzender der russischen Vertrauensstelle in Warschau, Herrn Sergius Woizechowski," April 6, 1943, file EAP 99/498, microfilm MR 336, RG 242, NA.

55. "Ansichten des Professors D. Soschalski über die deutsche Politik in Zusammenhang mit Russland und der sogenannten russischen Befreiungsbewegung (Übersetzung)," ca. May–June 1943, Document Occ E–6, YIVO. "Soschalski's" biographic file is in Document Occ E–41, YIVO.

56. D. Soschalski, "Gedanken eines Russen über die Zusammenarbeit Deutschlands mit den Völkern im Osten," July 2, 1943, on microfilm ML 469, RG 242, NA.

57. Theodor Oberländer, "Bündnis oder Ausbeutung. Zum Jahrestag des deutscheuropäischen Kampfes gegen die Sowjets am 22.6.1943," in Oberländer, *6 Denkschriften*, No. 6, pp. 1–8.

58. Heinz Danko Herre, "Denkschrift von Professor Oberländer," ZS 406/II, p.9, IfZ.

59. Drozdzynski and Zaborowski, *Oberländer*, pp. 105–07, 310–21. See also Hoffmann, *Geschichte*, p. 123.

60. See Kramarz, *Stauffenberg*, p. 113.

5

REFORM IN
REICHSKOMMISSARIAT
UKRAINE: ROSENBERG VS.
KOCH

With no immediate prospect of a general reform of *Ostpolitik*, reformers turned their efforts to the more limited possibilities presented by specific subjects (for example, agrarian reform) and regions. In the *Reichskommissariat Ukraine* (RKU) such an approach offered cause for optimism, as the proposed agrarian reform perfectly complemented a redirection of Ukrainian policy from above. The fate of the former will be discussed in a later chapter; here we shall examine the attempt to remove Erich Koch as *Reichskommissar*. Above all this featured a confrontation between Rosenberg and Koch, a personal feud transformed by a year's occupation into a major debate on the future of Germany's course.

The *Wehrmacht*'s advance into the Ukraine in the summer of 1941 marked the beginning of the second German occupation of the region in 23 years. Germany's Ukrainian policy in 1918 had wavered between short-term and long-range objectives and vacillated in its attitude toward irredentist nationalism; the result was a short-lived "satellite" state, nominally sovereign but with a commanding German influence in her foreign and economic affairs.[1] Though bitterly disappointed, many Ukrainian nationalists still looked to Germany for refuge and support after Bolshevik forces regained the Ukraine in 1920.[2] By the late 1930s a special cooperation had developed between the Organization of Ukrainian Nationalists (*Organizatsiia Ukrains'kykh Natsionalistiv*, or OUN) and Admiral Canaris' *Abwehr*, a bond that survived further disappointments in the surrender of the Carpatho-Ukraine to Hungary and Galicia to Stalin—as well as a major split within the OUN—to bear fruit in the early days of BARBAROSSA.[3] On January 1, 1942 Colonel Tymosh Omel'chenko, head of an OUN-affiliated organization, combined a New Year's greeting to Foreign Minister Ribbentrop

Map 2
Reichskommissariat Ukraine, November 1942

with a plea for Ukrainian independence, and a warning that Germany could not afford to "repeat the mistakes of the year 1918, when she employed colonial methods in her treatment of the Ukraine."[4]

Hitler indeed intended to avoid "the mistakes of 1918" in the Ukraine, but his perception of those mistakes stood directly opposite to Omel'chenko's. This became evident in July 1941 after the activist OUN faction, with tacit German Army approval, established a provisional government in L'vov and proclaimed an independent Ukraine: SS and security police units moved quickly to crush the coup and arrest its leaders. Through the autumn of 1941 the SD extended its repression of both OUN factors with numerous arrests and executions.[5] And in setting up the civil administration, Hitler overrode the protests of the *Ostministerium* and amputated Galicia—the stronghold of Ukrainian nationalism— from the rest of the Ukraine and appended it to the Government-General of Poland.[6]

Paradoxically, the Galician Ukrainians enjoyed a relatively privileged status vis-à-vis the Polish population in the *Generalgouvernement*. German policy here followed the principle of "divide and rule," exploiting the animosity between the two occupied peoples to the benefit of the Ukrainians. Dr. Otto Wächter, governor of the district from January 1942, granted a number of concessions in the former Habsburg province: the number of Ukrainian language schools was greatly increased, Ukrainian cooperatives and small businesses multiplied, and Ukrainian officials predominated in the local administration. German authorities offered no political promises but these concessions secured a widespread cooperation and paid military manpower dividends in the spring of 1943.[7]

For their compatriots living in the RKU, however, the German occupation exhibited its worst features. The commandos of *Einsatzgruppe* C and related SS and police units massacred no less than 175,000 Ukrainian Jews by early December 1941.[8] Ukrainian cities starved in the late winter of 1942 as a result of wartime dislocations, priority requisitions by the *Wehrmacht*, and a lack of German planning: some 26,000 died in Kharkov alone.[9] In the countryside, Ukrainian peasants endured both the retention of collectivization and the introduction of German colonization.[10] The RKU also provided the majority of the *Ostarbeiter* shipped to Germany as slave labor.[11] The German criminal code became the law of the land, dispensing justice in direct relation to German interests: murders arising from domestic quarrels were punished less severely than the illegal slaughtering of livestock.[12]

The colonial mentality was personified by *Reichskommissar* Erich Koch, the lapsed Marxist whose pro-Soviet sympathies had earned Rosenberg's enmity in the 1920s.[13] Typical of Koch's proclamations was the following of January 5, 1943: "The Ukraine is Germany's most precious pawn of victory. . . . [O]ur soldiers did not bleed in this country to achieve some concept for mankind's happiness, but in order to make the natural resources of this country available for the Front and Germany."[14] To accomplish this mission, Koch willingly gave free rein to the economic agencies and police apparatus. For all his rhetoric,

Koch devoted little time to the actual administration of the Ukraine in preference for his alternate duties as *Gauleiter* of East Prussia; consequently the Reich Commissioner's headquarters in Rowné was virtually abandoned as Koch spent the bulk of his tenure in Königsberg.[15] Only in the field of cultural policy education did Koch regularly intervene,[16] and one such intervention would spark the Ukrainian policy debate of 1942–43.

To be sure, Koch's reign yielded impressive economic results.[17] What might have been accomplished through a policy based on cooperation can only be imagined, particularly in view of Germany's ultimate reliance upon the native population. In January 1943, roughly 25,000 Reich Germans governed 16,910,008 inhabitants scattered throughout the *Reichskommissariat*'s five cities and 443 *raions*, each of the latter averaging five villages; these dimensions alone ensured that the most basic levels of administration depended entirely on Ukrainians.[18] Recognizing this, several German agencies undertook studies of Ukrainian morale through the 1942–43 period as Soviet forces advanced from their victory at Stalingrad into the Ukraine. The results underscored the effects of German policy. Intercepts of nearly six hundred letters written by Ukrainian *Ostarbeiter* from September to November 1942 noted a steady deterioration of morale due to the slave labor recruitment measures.[19] Later surveys conducted independently by the OKW/WPr and the SD in the Ukraine confirmed the hostility of the majority of the population toward their occupiers.[20]

Particularly ominous for the Germans was the growth of armed resistance in previously quiet areas. The northern sectors of *Generalbezirke* Volhynia-Podolia and Zhitomir and the northwestern corner of *Generalbezirk* Kiev became in late 1942 a battleground among German security forces, Soviet partisans, and the OUN-sponsored Ukrainian Insurgent Army (*Ukrainska Povstanska Armia*, or UPA), the latter two alternately fighting, negotiating with, or implicating the other as dictated by their individual interests.[21] By August 1943 nearly two thousand Germans and twenty thousand Ukrainians had been killed or abducted, over a million tons of bread grain could not be harvested, and desertions among Ukrainian police and militia led one German official to estimate in March 1943 that no more than 10 percent of these units were reliable.[22] In the cities of Kiev, Dnepropetrovsk and Stalino to the east, a small but well-organized Soviet underground accelerated sabotage operations through the first half of 1943.[23]

These developments contributed to harsh attacks on Koch within the civil administration. Bräutigam, whose proposed recall of Koch has already been quoted, continued his attacks into the spring of 1943.[24] An *Ostministerium* official reported in August 1942 that 80 percent of Koch's own district commissioners (*Gebietskommissaren*) disagreed with his policy,[25] an observation strengthened by the scathing critique of Koch's "blindness and dilettantism" written by *Gauleiter* Alfred Frauenfeld, *Generalkommissar* of Taurida (the general commissariat for the hinterland of the Crimean peninsula), in February 1944.[26] Heinz von Homeyer, chief of the economics section under Frauenfeld, denounced Koch's policies in a memorandum to Rosenberg on December 30, 1942, urging

Koch's replacement, a shake-up of the structure of administration, and major economic concessions to the population.[27]

Criticism of Koch's policies was equally strong outside the *Ostministerium*. *Abwehr* officer Theodor Oberländer had already submitted four memoranda for improving policy in the Ukraine by the autumn of 1942.[28] In its assessment of Ukrainian morale in March 1943, the OKW/WPR's staff warned that the population's increasing hostility could materially affect German interests unless "a basic and decisive change" in policy and methods occurred.[29] Baldur von Schirach, leader of the *Hitler-Jugend*, independently approached Hitler in June 1943 with the suggestion that "an autonomous Ukraine served the Reich better than a Ukraine ruled by Koch."[30] Even Rosenberg's enemy Goebbels noted with regret in May 1943 the "very sad conditions" in the Ukraine.[31]

Most important for Rosenberg, Koch aroused opposition within the SS. Though he maintained excellent relations with SS-*Gruppenführer* Dr. Max Thomas, commander of Security Police and SD for the Ukraine,[32] the *Reichskommissar* treated his nominal superior, HSSPF *Obergruppenführer* Hans Prützmann, with abusive contempt.[33] The center of opposition, however, lay in the SD. As early as September 1941, when it struck against the OUN leadership, the *Sicherheitsdienst* had circulated its own argument that a successful occupation of the Ukraine required the cooperation of the Ukrainian peasants, attainable only through a major agrarian reform.[34] In July 1942, SS-*Brigadeführer* Otto Ohlendorf returned from command of an *Einsatzgruppe* in the Crimea to direct the *Inland* SD ("Spheres of German Life," Amt III of the RSHA) against corrupt Nazi party bosses, of whom Koch was a prime target.[35] As already noted, Dr. Akhmeteli of the SD's Wannsee Institute concluded an inspection tour of the occupied areas in late 1942 with a condemnation of Koch's policies.[36]

Rosenberg could therefore look for substantial support in the battle that Koch precipitated in the autumn of 1942. On October twenty-fourth the *Reichskommissar* ordered the closing of all schools and educational institutes beyond primary schools throughout the RKU, with the students over 15 years of age and their teachers slated for shipment to Germany as labor.[37] The decree disconcerted Rosenberg and his ministry's Cultural Department, who perceived the schools as a valuable tool to further collaboration and maximize the use of individual skills; the SD and German police moreover objected to the prospect of Ukrainian youths with time on their hands and nothing to do.[38] Rosenberg countered on November twenty-first with a carefully argued justification of the trade schools' value to the German war effort in increased productivity and a more efficient administration. He therefore "requested" that Koch withdraw the decree.[39]

Rosenberg's temperate reply may have been a ruse, for even as he dispatched it the *Ostminister* launched a grand campaign to eliminate Koch and resuscitate his own ministry. During the same week that Koch issued his decree Rosenberg sounded out SS-*Gruppenführer* Gottlob Berger, chief of the SS-*Hauptamt* (Central Office), on the need to reorganize the *Ostministerium*. Now, on November twentieth, he arranged a private meeting with Berger later that week to discuss the situation.[40] At this meeting Rosenberg emphasized his difficulties with Koch and his own ministry, which he largely attributed to Alfred Meyer and Policy Department chief Leibbrandt. Then he proposed a deal: In return for support against Koch, Rosenberg would bind his ministry to the SS by bringing in Berger as a "state secretary" in charge of policy and administration. Surprised, Berger promised to forward the proposal to Himmler but stressed that his own first loyalty would always remain to the *Reichsführer*.[41] The meeting ended, marking a critical moment for *Ostpolitik* reform.

Rosenberg's decision to seek an alliance with the SS is central to his role in the *Ostpolitik* debate throughout the period under study. Whatever his inadequacies as a Third Reich politician, Rosenberg here displayed a keen awareness of his own ministry's weakness and the *Schutzstaffel*'s growing strength. To overrule Hitler's own appointee Koch and exercise actual governing power, Rosenberg needed the most powerful allies possible; rather than attempt to piece together a coalition of diverse interests long enough for a tactical victory (such as toppling Koch), Rosenberg opted for a lasting cooperation with the strongest single force for long-term success. This would also account for Rosenberg's coolness toward the *Wehrmacht*'s reform proposals in November-December 1942: not only did the German Army lack political clout, but a flirtation with the army could jeopardize a courtship of Himmler. The danger, of course, lay in staking too much on single card. Time would prove whether Rosenberg's political skill in the execution of the solution matched his acute analysis of the problem.

In the aftermath of this conversation the debate over Ukrainian schools rapidly escalated into a conflict over the whole of Koch's policy. On November twenty-seventh the *Reichskommissar* contemptuously dismissed Rosenberg's requested repeal of the education decree.[42] On December fifteenth Koch and his deputy Paul Dargel dropped in unexpectedly at the *Ostministerium* in Berlin, where they harangued Rosenberg and von der Milwe-Schröden against interference with their plans.[43] The day before, however, Rosenberg had already broadened his attack to the general conduct of policy in a letter to Koch that criticized labor recruiting methods, overly harsh punishments for minor offenses, and particularly the overbearing conduct of German officials in their relations with the population.[44] From this point, the Ukrainian education issue became secondary to that of Koch himself. In a subsequent exchange of correspondence both men actually moderated their stances, Rosenberg pushing only for the restoration of trade schools directly contributing to the war effort, Koch actually reopening 20 agricultural schools in January 1943.[45] But by then the protagonists were documenting their cases and playing to their audiences.

Rosenberg's careful groundwork paid off when he met privately with *Reichsführer* Himmler in Posen (Poznan) on January 25, 1943. The meeting, arranged by *Gauleiter* Arthur Greiser, lasted two hours and included no aides or staff members. According to Berger, Himmler explained afterward that all their personal differences had been resolved and that a unified course of action vis-à-vis

Reichskommissare Koch and Lohse has been worked out, apparently providing for the establishment of autonomy for Estonia and Latvia to regularize *Waffen-*SS recruiting in those areas. Berger himself would be transferred to the *Ostministerium* by April 1, 1943, pending Hitler's approval.[46]

The secrecy and lack of documentation characteristic of the SS-*OMi* negotiations preclude a proper analysis of the nature and scope of the envisioned alliance. What Rosenberg hoped to accomplish, however, is evident in his discussion with Hitler only two weeks after his meeting with Himmler. On February eighth, Rosenberg personally presented his reform program to the führer. In addition to its provisions for the Baltic states and the areas inhabited by ethnic Russians, Rosenberg's plan called for the establishment of a "Ukrainian National Committee" for immediate propaganda value and as a step toward eventual autonomy, together with an accelerated agrarian reform to win the support of Ukrainian peasants. Perhaps on Himmler's advice Rosenberg avoided going into details, as Hitler deferred a decision pending Rosenberg's refinement of these proposals into concrete measures; and nowhere is there a direct reference to Koch.[47]

Rosenberg's concept of a Ukrainian state, however, had weakened considerably since June 1941. Draft proclamations for the Ukraine prepared by the *Ostministerium* in January 1943 diluted the appeal to Ukrainian nationalism by revising promises of "an independent state" to "equal partnership in the new Europe."[48] In a staff conference of February tenth, Rosenberg did push for such significant economic measures as the restoration of small businesses and an agrarian reform with a minimum of 30 percent of the collectives to be converted to farm cooperatives. But in the terms of political concessions, Rosenberg opted for shadow rather than substance, as one conference participant observed: "The Minister rejects the creation of a 'National Council' and of workers' councils at the levels of *Gebiets-* and *Generalkommissar* [which] would do nothing more than find fault with our actions."[49]

Rosenberg's subordinates took these words to heart in their draft plans of the "Ukrainian National Committee's" envisioned powers, prepared two weeks later. These granted the committee authority over various social and cultural functions, but provisions for the nomination of Ukrainians to posts in the village and *raion*-level administrations and to the local judiciary were stricken from the final versions approved by Leibbrandt.[50] The committee's members were to be selected jointly by the Eastern Ministry, the SD, and the OKW Operations Staff (the Army High Command distinguished by its exclusion); the members would be recruited, however, from the areas under military government rather than the *Reichskommissariat*.[51] Though this tactic eliminated Koch from the process, it restricted representation to the eastern Ukraine, the region least affected by Ukrainian nationalism. By early May, when the establishment of a Ukrainian committee had become linked to the Vlasov movement, plans called for further limiting of the committee's powers to purely advisory in character, comparable to that of the regional councils operating in Galicia.[52]

The gap between German plans and Ukrainian expectations is evident in the proposal by Ukrainian emigré Yuri Muzichenko to the *Ostministerium* on May 25, 1943. Muzichenko urged the establishment of a national committee empowered to regulate the distribution of land, internal trade, education, law, religion, the press, cultural affairs, and welfare for the entire Ukrainain population. Muzichenko conceded sovereignty to Germany, and even nominated seven individuals for committee membership. Muzichenko's proposals, however, were merely filed and ignored by the *Ostministerium*.[53]

While his staff gutted the future Ukrainian committee of substance, Rosenberg moved toward a showdown with Koch over the education issue. On February twenty-third, in a decree issued directly to the RKU's *Generalkommissare*, he countermanded Koch's earlier order and established a school system featuring four years' primary and three years' secondary education, as well as expanded trade and occupational schools.[54] But Koch, probably aware of Rosenberg's machinations, refused to be drawn on any terms but his own: rather than fighting the decree he merely supplemented it with the directive that it only be implemented after war's end.[55]

The *Reichskommissar* meanwhile continued his practices in the Ukraine. On February twentieth he issued a warning to the administration against lenient treatment of the population in fulfilling produce and labor quotas, "as this will only display weakness."[56] Six days later Heinz von Homeyer resigned his economic post in the Ukraine, probably as a result of Koch's pressure.[57] On March fifth Koch reiterated his views to the Nazi party members of the Kiev city administration: "We are a master race that must remember, the lowliest German worker is racially and biologically a thousand times more valuable than the population here."[58]

By now the debate had "assumed such grotesque forms," remarked one observer, "that one can no longer speak of an orderly administration." Rosenberg ordered Koch's subordinates on March thirteenth to withdraw and destroy the *Reichskommissar*'s February twentieth decree; Koch parried with the instruction that the paragraph that offended Rosenberg be stricken out but the rest remain in force; and on the same day Rosenberg reiterated his educational decree and directed its full implementation.[59] But the end was in sight: even as Rosenberg fired off his last directive (March 16), Koch prepared a brief that recapitulated the debate with his nominal superior. Distributed to Bormann, Berger and apparently to all *Gauleiters*, the paper summarized Koch's case: a severe treatment of the population was justified with chapter and verse citations from *Mein Kampf*, Rosenberg's views were attacked as influenced by Russian and Ukrainian emigres, and the *Ostminister*'s measures criticized as impractical. Koch concluded that Rosenberg's interference in administration had so impaired his position that only the führer could restore it.[60] Koch thus set the terms by which he would be judged, on the whole of his Ukrainian policy and the limits of his authority.

Rosenberg accepted the challenge and summoned Koch to Berlin for a personal confrontation some days later, a meeting that degenerated into a shouting match. Rosenberg thereupon (March 26) formally requested of the führer that, as "it has become completely impossible to converse at all with *Reichskommissar* Koch," the latter be relieved of his duties.[61] For good measure, Rosenberg submitted a detailed refutation of Koch's critique to both Chief of the Reich Chancellery Lammers and Himmler.[62]

The *Ostminister* now prepared to play his trump card, the SS alliance. A stumbling block, however, had already arisen on March eighth when Lammers notified Rosenberg that Hitler had rejected the creation of a second "state secretary" in the *Ostministerium* for Berger as unnecessary.[63] Rosenberg met with Berger on March twenty-seventh to apprise him of developments and ask his support; Berger obliged in his report to Himmler where he described Koch's "disgraceful" behavior toward Rosenberg and commented that "the whole of Germany rejects as one Koch's methods in the Ukraine." But to the *Ostminister*'s request that he divide his working day between the SS-*Hauptamt* and a makeshift position within the Eastern Ministry, Berger balked.[64] At the decisive moment of his conflict with Koch, Rosenberg's concession of an institutional role in the ministry had been reduced to an offer of part-time employment.

On the other hand, Rosenberg received strong support from the SD. On March seventeenth two *OMI* representatives met with Ohlendorf at RSHA headquarters to discuss the Ukrainian Committee. Ohlendorf noted that the proposed committee would be useless so long as Koch's colonial policy continued, and that without an authorized change in policy the SD could not formally participate in the committee's constitution, but he nevertheless offered to assist in the selection of committee members.[65] Very likely other matters of interest were discussed as well, for exactly one week later Ohlendorf submitted a report to Himmler charging *Reichskommissar* Koch with abuse of his authority, citing Koch's procurement of one hundred kg. of caviar by special plane over the 1942 Christmas holidays.[66] Rosenberg, probably feeling the time to be right, wrote Himmler directly on April second with a report of a senseless massacre of Ukrainians by Koch to create a hunting preserve in December 1942. In his cover letter Rosenberg formally requested Himmler's "official pronouncement in this case."[67]

But Himmler did nothing. Whatever the state of personal relations between Koch and Himmler, both shared the colonialist vision of the occupied East as the future *Lebensraum* for Germany. In October 1942 Himmler smoothed over the troubles between Koch and HSSPF Prützmann with a cordial and conciliatory letter to the *Reichskommissar*.[68] Of more material interest to Himmler was the possible control of a valuable quartz deposit near Zhitomir, for which Himmler had cultivated good relations with Koch since August 1942.[69] Himmler's January 1943 meeting with Rosenberg in Posen probably resulted from the opportunity to establish a dominant influence within the civil administration and concern over a rapidly deteriorating military situation; by April, Hitler's veto of Berger's promotion and the stabilization of the southern German flank had removed both considerations. On March eighteenth Himmler invited the *Reichskommissar* to a meeting at the beginning of April "so that we may be able to speak at length of all things."[70] In the Rosenberg-Koch duel, Himmler had made his choice.

With Himmler removed from the conflict, Koch enjoyed the upper hand. Sometime in early April 1943 he met with Party Secretary Bormann, who concluded the three-hour session with the promise that "he would cover Koch completely" in the approaching showdown.[71] Rosenberg tried to force the issue while unaware that his SS connection had been severed. On April ninth he again wrote to Lammers to request Koch's dismissal, accompanied by an endorsement by Paul Pleiger, director of the Reich mining corporation in the Ukraine. Six days later he appealed directly to Hitler to relieve the *Reichskommissar* of his post.[72] The very next day Rosenberg contacted Berger for support and again raised the possibility of sharing duties in the *Ostministerium*.[73] One month later, on May eighteenth, he approached Berger yet again, but all Berger could offer was a proposed subterfuge that all *Gauleiters* in the ministry be furloughed to deal with the problems in their home areas due to air raids.[74] But events had already overtaken Rosenberg, for the next day he confronted his nemesis before Hitler.

The meeting took place in Hitler's headquarters at Vinnitsa in the early evening of May 19, 1943, with Bormann also in attendance. After listening to the two protagonists present their cases, the führer rendered judgment in favor of his *Reichskommissar*. In a summary of the conference later prepared by Bormann, Hitler's comments refuted Rosenberg's every argument:

We can never expect the political approval of the Ukrainians for our actions . . . Ukrainians and the peoples of Great Russia are not opposed to each other . . . Too much education [for Ukrainians] must be prevented . . . It is after all pointless for the Ministry to issue decrees that cannot be carried out.[75]

Hitler's remarks during this conference also reveal his correct identification of Rosenberg's ideas with the *Ostpolitik* of 1914–18, rejected by Hitler. A few weeks later he drew an exact parallel: "We must not get into a state of mind in which one day the military will again come, as in 1916, and say, 'Now it's up to politics to do something, to create a Ukrainian state, just as a Polish state was established then.'"[76] During the conference Hitler reminded Rosenberg that "the greatest friend of the Ukrainian people during the last world war, Field Marshal Eichhorn, was himself murdered by the Ukrainians."[77]

Rosenberg thus emerged from the conference with his political program completely repudiated. One can therefore imagine his surprise when he received a letter from Hitler on June fifth that enjoined cooperation between the rivals and seemingly asserted Rosenberg's superior authority: Koch was not to employ "obstructive tactics" as in "ignoring and willfully failing to execute [Rosenberg's] orders." Hitler closed with the admonition that both men should meet "at least twice a month for an exchange of opinions," and that any differences over "fundamental" issues should be referred to the führer for his personal decision.[78]

By this action Hitler merely reaffirmed the contradictory relationship between the protagonists as it had existed all along. Rosenberg accomplished the reopening of Ukrainian schools, but this was a hollow victory against Koch's continued rule of the Ukraine.[79] For the *Ostminister*, Hitler's verdict of May nineteenth produced a lasting bitterness toward Himmler and a documented report to Hitler "proving" that Eichhorn's assassins were a Russian revolutionary and two Jews, not Ukrainians.[80]

Rosenberg himself furnished an appropriate epilogue to this episode when he departed Berlin on a three-week tour of the Ukraine on June third, the day the *Ostminister* also issued his declaration of property rights for Soviet farmers. As the tour hoped to capitalize on improvements in policy, one *OMi* official approached Rosenberg on May thirty-first with a proposed reorganization of the civil administration to allow an expanded role for Ukrainian leaders;[81] Rosenberg did nothing. Koch accompanied Rosenberg for most of the trip, and the two avoided any major clashes. Indeed, the greatest tension occurred in meetings with German military leaders: the *Ostminister* openly cautioned Field Marshal von Manstein against involvement in political matters, then Koch and Rosenberg united against Field Marshal von Kleist to criticize the liberal economic measures instituted in the Crimea. On his return to Berlin Rosenberg reportedly described the trip as "a complete failure."[82] The same could be said of Rosenberg's entire effort against Koch.

Koch's successful defense of his post in itself did not kill the reform issue in the Ukraine, which was kept alive by the agrarian reform and developments in the areas under military government. Ironically, Koch's very intransigence led to Berger's replacement of Leibbrandt in August 1943, when the latter embarrassed Rosenberg in a covert attempt to expose corruption in Koch's administration. Without any concessions to Rosenberg, a senior SS official thus assumed control of the *Ostministerium*'s Political Department, where he quickly proved a great disappointment to reformers like Bräutigam.[83] Even as these events transpired, however, their significance dimmed as the Red Army advanced into the Ukraine.

In perspective, the differences that so bitterly divided *Reichskommissar* and *Reichsminister* were far less than both perceived, a question of the manner of German domination rather than the fact. Beyond the conflicts of personality and ideology, Koch's victory represented the triumph of immediate gains through intensive exploitation over a long-term policy of indirect control and more popular cooperation. Germany's strategic situation in 1943 could not have dictated otherwise. As Koch epitomized the colonialist viewpoint, so his recall would have signalled a change in policy; yet without major revisions in the system of economic exploitation it could remain only a gesture. Rosenberg's ill-fated sortie into National Socialist power politics failed even to accomplish this prerequisite for change, and absorbed his energies to the exclusion of other and more promising opportunities for *Ostpolitik* reform.

NOTES

1. See Oleh S. Fedyshyn, *Germany's Drive to the East and the Ukrainian Revolution 1917–1918* (New Brunswick, NJ: Rutgers University Press, 1971), and Peter Borowsky, *Deutsche Ukrainepolitik 1918 unter besonderer Berücksichtigung der Wirtschaftsfragen* (Lübeck/Hamburg: Matthiesen Verlag, 1970).

2. Armstrong, *Nationalism*, (2d Ed.), pp. 26–45.

3. See Armstrong, *Nationalism*, pp. 19ff; Ilnytzkyj, *Deutschland*, Bd. I, pp. 73–78, 82, 164–207, 232–50, and II, pp. 78ff.; and Höhne, *Canaris*, pp. 315–27, 356–59, 451–52, 459–63.

4. Omel'chenko to Ribbentrop, January 1, 1942, T-120/289/444/221897. On Omel'chenko, see Armstrong, *Nationalism*, pp. 59–60.

5. Ilnytzkyj, *Deutschland*, Bd. II, pp. 173–94; Armstrong, *Nationalism*, pp. 74–111.

6. Dallin, *German Rule*, p. 121.

7. See Stefan Mekarski, "Die Südostgebiete Polens zur Zeit der deutschen Besatzung (Juni 1941 bis Juni 1943), Verwaltung und Nationalitätenprobleme," *Jahrbücher für Geschichte Osteuropas*, Bd. XVI, 3 (September 1968): 381–428.

8. Krausnick and Wilhelm, *Weltanschauungskriege*, pp. 618–19.

9. Brandt, *Management*, pp. 124–25.

10. Fleischhauer, *Dritte Reich*, pp. 174–84.

11. See Armstrong, *Nationalism*, p. 179n., and Chapter 8, below.

12. Nikolas Laskovsky, "Practicing Law in the Occupied Ukraine," *American Slavic and East European Review*, Vol. IX, no. 2 (April 1952): 123–37.

13. See Reitlinger, "Last," pp. 31–33, and Slawomir Orlowski, *Erich Koch pered polskim sudom* (Moscow: Institut Myezhdoonarodnikh Otnoshenii, 1961), pp. 24, 42, 56–58.

14. Quoted in U.S. State Department's "General Conditions in the Ukraine in December 1942 and January 1943 as Reflected in the German-Controlled Press," April 9, 1943, file 86OE.00/171, Records of the Department of State, RG 59, NA.

15. Reitlinger, "Last," p. 35.

16. In religious policy, Koch encouraged the factionalism dividing the Ukrainian Autocephalous and Autonomous Churches: See Fireside, *Icon and Swastika*, pp. 91–100, 151–60.

17. See Ihor Kamenetsky, *Secret Nazi Plans for Eastern Europe: A Study of Lebensraum Policies* (New Haven, CT: College and University Press, 1961), p. 148.

18. Fleischhauer, *Dritte Reich*, p. 166 (figure of 20,000 Germans adjusted to include other areas of RKU); "Übersicht über die Verwaltungseinteilung des Reichskommissariats Ukraine nach dem Stand vom 1. January 1943," T-454/92/933; OSS R & A No. 2500.8, "German Military Government," pp. 54–59, RG 226, NA.

19. Auslandbriefprüfstelle Berlin, "Stimmungsbericht aus Briefen," November 11, 1942, T-120/2533/5079/E29254912–914.

20. Compare Propaganda-Abt. Ukraine, "Stimmungsbericht," April 1, 1943, *KTB/OKW*, III (2), pp. 1424–25; SD *Meldungen* Nr. 43, T-175/236/2725591–595.

21. A full account of the complex guerrilla war in the Ukraine remains to be written.

For general information see Armstrong, *Nationalism*, pp. 131ff.; Yuriy Tys-Krokhmaliuk, *UPA Warfare in Ukraine*, trans. by Walter Dushnyck (New York: Vantage Press, 1972), esp. pp. 49ff., 225–60, 275–94; and Cherednichenko, *Collaborationists*, passim.

22. See "Zusammenstellung über die von Banden verursachten Schäden im Monat August 1943," T-77/1172/120; Koch to Rosenberg, "Derzeitiger Stand der Bandenlage," June 25, 1943, T-175/81/2601565–574; SD *Meldungen* Nr. 46, T-175/236/2725679–688; and Kommandeur der SD in Kiew, "Allgemeine Verwaltungsfragen," March 4, 1943, T-84/120/1419257–266.

23. *Istoriia Velikoi Otechestvennoi voiny Sovetskogo Soiuza, 1941–1945*, comp. Institut Marksizma-Leninizma Pri Tsk KPSS (6 vols.; Moscow: Voenizdat, 1960–64), Vol. III, pp. 482–87 (hereafter cited as IVOVSS).

24. See above, Chapter 4, and Bräutigam's memorandum, "Zwei Jahre deutsche Ukraine-Politik," May 14, 1943, T-454/92/957–63.

25. Markull to Leibbrandt, August 19, 1942, Document R–36, *NCA*, VIII, 54–55.

26. Frauenfeld's critique appears in H. D. Krannhals, "Politik der Vernichtung. Eine Denkschrift zur Besatzungspolitik in Osteuropa," in *Deutsche Studien*, Bd. IV, 16 (December 1966): 493–517.

27. Heinz von Homeyer to Rosenberg, December 30, 1942, T-454/18/112–20.

28. See Oberländer, *6 Denkschriften*, Nos. 1–4, pp. 1ff.

29. Propaganda-Abt. Ukraine, "Stimmungsbericht," *KTB/OKW*, III (2), p. 1424.

30. Schirach testimony, *TMWC*, XIV, 427–28.

31. Goebbels, *Diaries*, pp. 378–79 (entry for May 14, 1943).

32. Affidavit of Dr. Hans Ehlich, Ohlendorf Defense Document 10, RG 238, NA; and interrogation of SS-*Standartenführer* Constantin Canaris (CSDIC/CMF/SD 53), August 8, 1945, RG 165, NA.

33. See SS-*Obergruppenführer* Prützmann, "Aktenvermerk über Besprechung mit Gauleiter Koch am Sonntag, den 27.9.42 in Königsberg," T-175/56/2571350–355.

34. See SD *Ereignismeldung UdSSR* Nr. 86 (hereafter sited as *EgM* Nr. 86), September 17, 1941, T-175/233/2722381–391.

35. Ohlendorf testimony, *NMT*, IV, 238; Ehlich affidavit and Canaris interrogation, op cit.

36. See above, Chapter 4.

37. Reichskommissar Koch, "Schulen und Institute," October 24, 1942, T-454/84/949–50.

38. See OMi/Abt. I 6b to Rosenberg, "Die Schulen der besetzten Ostgebiete als Mittel zur Menschenführung," May 7, 1943, in file R–628, ML 465, RG 242, NA; and SS-*Hauptsturmführer* Brandenburg, "Vermerk," November 21, 1942, T-454/84/848. Position papers of the *Ostministerium* on this issue are reproduced in file EAP 99/384, T-454/84/828–886.

39. Der Ständige Vertreter (Alfred Meyer) to Koch, "Fortführung der Berufsausbildung einheimischer Jugendlicher im R.K. Ukraine," November 21, 1942, T-454/13/4921074–075.

40. Berger to Himmler, "Ostministerium," November 21, 1942, Document SS–870, RG 238, NA.

41. Berger to Himmler, November 26, 1942, T-175/139/2667357–359. Berger may well have encouraged Rosenberg's proposal out of personal ambition (interview with Gunter d'Alquen, May 26, 1984).

42. Koch to Rosenberg, "Schulen und Institute," November 27, 1942, T-454/84/849–53.

43. Thorwald, *The Illusion*, pp. 106–07, citing von der Milwe-Schröden's diary.

44. Rosenberg to Koch, December 14, 1942, Document 194-PS, RG 238, NA.

45. Compare Rosenberg to Koch, "Fortführung der Berufsausbildung," December 23, 1942, and Koch to Rosenberg, January 28, 1943, T-454/13/4921076–084.

46. See the interrogation of Gottlob Berger, December 12, 1946, and Berger's affidavit of June 14, 1947 (Document NO–3971), both in RG 238, NA. Rosenberg refers to the conference in his letter to Lammers, January 29, 1943, requesting Berger's transfer to *OMi* (T-454/100/656–57); Berger also mentions it in a letter to Himmler, April 16, 1943 (T-175/68/2584142–143).

47. See Paul Körner's report to *Reichsmarschall* Hermann Goering, February 20, 1943, T-454/89/446–52; SS-*Brigadeführer* Paul Zimmermann to Himmler, "Ergänzung zu dem Protokoll vom 4.1.1943," n.d. (ca. late February 1943), T-175/68/2584155–156, and Abwehrabt. II, "Vortragsvermerk für Amtschef," February 15, 1943, T-77/1505/861.

48. Compare the draft proclamations "An das ukrainische Volk!" of January 14, and January 25, 1943, T-454/21/826–29, 848–50.

49. (Dr. Kinkelin), "Aufzeichnung über die Besprechung beim Herrn Minister am 10. February 1943," n.d., T-454/89/461–64.

50. *OMi* Abt. I3 (Middelhauve), "Satzungen des ukrainischen nationalen Zentralkomitees im Bereich des Wehrmachtsbefehlshabers des rückw. Heeresgebietes," February 24, 1943, T-454/29/268–70.

51. *Omi*/Abt. I3 (Dr. Kinkelin), "Bildung eines ukrainischen Nationalkomitees," February 1943, T-454/91/681.

52. (Markull), "Ukrainisches Nationalkomitee," May 6, 1943, ML 474, RG 242, NA.

53. Juri A. Musytschenko [Muzichenko], "Organisation des Ukrainischen Komites," May 25, 1943, T-454/91/714–27.

54. Quoted in Koch's memorandum to Rosenberg, March 16, 1943, Document 192-PS, *TMWC*, XXV, 276–77.

55. Hans Riecke to Rosenberg, March 30, 1943, Document Rosenberg–19, *TMWC*, XLI, 196.

56. See Dr. Taubert to Goebbels, "Wirrwar in der Verwaltung des Ostraums," March 23, 1943, Document Occ E 18–19, YIVO.

57. Homeyer, "Aktennotiz," February 27, 1943, Document NG–1294, RG 238, NA; Dallin, *German Rule*, pp. 155–56.

58. Lieutenant Fähndrich an OKH/Gen StdH/GenQu, Abt. Kr. Verw., "Behandlung der Zivilbevölkerung in der Ukraine," April 1, 1943, Document 1130-PS, *TMWC*, XXVII, 9–11.

59. Taubert, "Wirrwar in der Verwaltung des Ostraums," March 23, 1943, Document Occ E 18–19, TIVO.

60. Koch memorandum to Rosenberg, March 16, 1943, Document 192-PS, *TMWC*, XXV, 255–88.

61. Rosenberg, "Meldung an den Führer," March 26, 1943, T-175/124/2599383–84.

62. See Rosenberg to Lammers, "Antwort auf die Denkschrift des RKU vom 16.3.1943," March 31, 1943, T-175/124/2599360–376.

63. Lammers to Rosenberg, "Staatssekretär im RmfdbO," 8 March 1943, T-120/2734/5830/E425116–119.

64. Berger to Himmler, "Besprechung bei Reichsminister Rosenberg," March 27, 1943, T-175/124/2599380–82.

65. Dr. Kinkelin, "Aufzeichnung über eine Besprechung beim Brigadeführer Ohlendorf," March 17, 1943, folder R–361, ML 473, RG 242, NA.

66. SD Amt III D Ost to Himmler, "Reichskommissar Gauleiter Koch, Rowno/Ukraine," March 24, 1943, T-175/275/2772032–033.

67. Rosenberg to Himmler, April 2, 1943, Document 032-PS, *TMWC*, XXV, 92–96.

68. Himmler to Koch, October 9, 1943, T-175/56/2571331–332.

69. See Speer, *Infiltration*, pp. 185–90.

70. Teletype message, Himmler to Koch, March 18, 1943, T-175/56/2571328.

71. Berger to Himmler, April 16, 1943, T-175/68/2584142–143.

72. Rosenberg to Lammers, "Aktenvermerk," April 9, 1943, and Rosenberg to Hitler, April 15, 1943, T-175/68/2584104–113.

73. Berger to Himmler, April 16, 1943, T-175/68/2584142–143.

74. Berger to Himmler, "Reichsleiter Rosenberg," May 18, 1943, T-175/128/2653901–903.

75. SD Amt III B to SD Amt III D Ost, "Bormann-Besprechungsprotokoll," June 10, 1943, T-175/275/2772034–043; see also Otto Hewel, "Auszug aus Notiz für RAM v. 24.5, " Document NG–3288, RG 238, NA.

76. "Besprechung des Führers, 8. Juni 1943," Document 1384-PS, RG 238, NA.

77. "Bormann-Besprechungsprotokoll," T-175/275/2772040.

78. Hitler to Rosenberg, June 1, 1943, Document NG–947, RG 238, NA; the *OMi* receipt stamp is dated June fifth.

79. See OMi/Abt. II7 (Dr. Kienzlen), "Vermerk: Erfahrungsbericht über die Verwaltung des RKU und Verbesserungsvorschläge für eine künftige Verwaltung," May 22, 1944, T-454/84/796–801.

80. Rosenberg, *Letzte Aufzeichnungen*, pp. 202–05, 214.

81. See OMi/Abt. IIIc (Dr. Guilleaume), "Vermerk für die nächste Dienstreise," May 31, 1943, T-454/24/53–56.

82. See Rosenberg's own "Besichtigungsreise durch die Ukraine vom 3.–23. Juni 1943," T-454/92/193–207; see also "The trip of newspaper representatives in the Ukraine, June 3 to 23, 1943," OSS Report 91978, RG 226, NA, and Bräutigam, *So hat es*, pp. 611–13.

83. On Leibbrandt's ouster and Berger's performance, see the interrogations of Otto Bräutigam, January 14–15, 1948, RG 238, NA.

6

REFORM IN
REICHSKOMMISSARIAT
OSTLAND

Under Reich Commissioner Hinrich Lohse, the *Reichskommissariat Ostland* covered an area of 90,425 square miles with over 8 million inhabitants partitioned into four *Generalkommissariate*; Estonia (roughly 1 million population), Latvia (1.8 million), Lithuania (2.8 million), and "White Russia" (2.4 million).[1] National identity, geography, and German war aims alike more naturally divided the region between the Baltic states and western Belorussia. By far the more important of these was the Baltic area, where the realities of nationalism and previous political sovereignty furnished an obstacle to German rule and an opportunity for *Ostpolitik* reform.[2]

When German forces swept through the Baltic states in the summer of 1941 they inherited both the debts left by their predecessors and the opportunities created by their enemies. A year of Soviet occupation characterized by political repression, forced collectivization, and especially the wave of executions and deportations after war's outbreak produced armed resistance against the Red Army throughout the Baltic states.[3] But to fully utilize this advantage Germany had to improve upon its own legacy in the Baltic area from 1915–19: a war aims policy that wavered between liberal imperialism and outright annexation, the requisition of the entire economy for the German war effort, and the bloody attempt by the Baltic German nobility and *Freikorps* adventurers to carve their own state out of Estonia and Latvia.[4] The Baltic peoples quickly discovered how National Socialism intended to build on this heritage.

In contrast to the Ukraine, plans for the Baltic states offered common ground for Hitler's visionary future and Rosenberg's Baltic German past: full incorporation with the Reich.[5] This was to be accomplished, Rosenberg wrote in May

Map 3
Reichskommissariat Ostland, November 1942

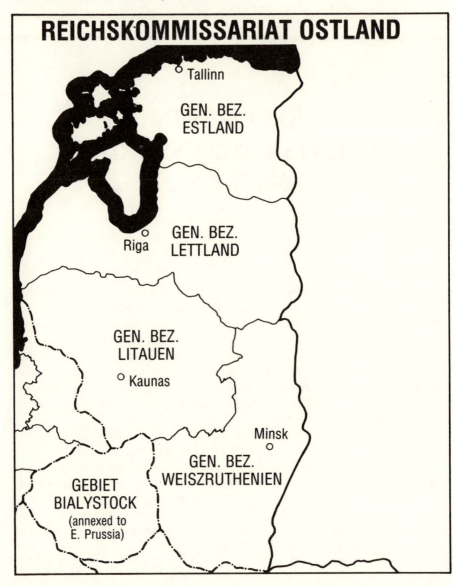

1941, "through Germanization of racially-suitable elements, colonization by Germanic peoples and resettlement of undesirable elements."[6] Before the end of 1942 every one of these programs had been initiated. SS and police units massacred over two hundred thousand Jews and concentrated the remainder in ghettos,[7] while in the Suwalki district of Lithuania thousands of Baltic Germans returned to farmsteads enlarged at the expense of their former inhabitants, who were resettled in neighboring *Weissruthenien*.[8] In November 1942 the *Ostministerium* completed an anthropological survey of the racial "value" of the Estonian and Latvian populations, with recommendations for a long-term cultural assimilation.[9]

The implementation of these long-range programs further padded the top-heavy superstructure of occupation administration. As noted earlier, *Reichskommissar* Lohse employed over 2200 officials throughout the Baltic states in his passion for regulation. An elaborate apparatus of economic controls geared the Baltic economy to the Reich's needs and inserted private German industry and finance into key positions of power.[10] The lowest level of this framework consisted of the "self-administrations," established in each state since the autumn of 1941 but legalized by the *Ostministerium* only in March 1942, and the limited administrative powers they exercised were often duplicated or undercut by German authorities.[11] In early 1943, however, these indigenous bodies assumed centerstage in the attempted restoration of self-government as the price for cooperation of the Baltic peoples.

Popular reaction to the occupation was probably best summarized by the anonymous Estonian who, when asked his opinion of the Germans, replied that he thought "they were not Germans at all but merely Russians who had donned other uniforms."[12] The occupied inhabitants endured wages and food rations that represented only a fraction of those for German civilian employees working in the *Reichskommissariat*.[13] Though starvation did not affect Baltic cities as it did Ukrainian, the reduced diet contributed to a significant increase in infant mortality.[14] Yet by their relatively privileged status in the occupied East the Baltic nationalities preserved their cultural identities through youth organizations and especially through the educational system (in German-occupied Europe, Baltic students alone attended their own universities).[15] And though Estonians and Latvians might offer passive resistance,[16] the SD found that the majority of the population considered the Germans "the lesser evil" to the Soviets, at least until the Western Allies could intervene in the region.[17]

This was evident in the participation of Baltic units in combat, beginning in the autumn of 1941 when Estonian and Latvian police and security battalions were pressed into front line duties.[18] Their performance encouraged Germany to consider the advantage of a new source of manpower. All parties, however, quickly recognized the inseparable link between the military use of Baltic nationals and the political issue of Baltic self-determination. Propaganda exhortations of the "common struggle" against Bolshevism could only be effective if accompanied by political and economic concessions. Himmler had recognized this in October 1941, when he first rejected the idea of Baltic legions.[19] Renewed overtures to Himmler the following spring by both Estonian and SS officers began to weaken his resolve.[20] When SS-*Obergruppenführer* Friedrich Jeckeln, senior SS commander for the entire Baltic region, hinted to Latvian officers in June 1942 that independence might be their reward for cooperation, he earned a sharp rebuke from the *Reichsführer* for such "explicit political statements."[21] Yet, on virtually the same day, Himmler authorized the formation of an Estonian SS legion.[22]

Aware of this development, the Latvian "General Directorate" sought to bargain its cooperation for political concessions. When SS officers suggested in November that Latvia "offer" to form an SS legion, Director-General for Justice Alfreds Valdmanis bluntly stated the price for cooperation: a guaranteed restoration of independence at war's end and increased autonomy during the interim. The Latvian "Directorate" delivered this response to the Germans on December second, sweetened with the offer of a hundred thousand troops ready to take the field in three months if these conditions were met. Before the end of the month, however, Latvian Director-General of the Interior General Oskar Dankers was informed by Lohse and Dr. Otto Drechsler (*Generalkommissar* for Latvia) that these terms were unacceptable, and that the Latvians' antipathy "would no longer be tolerated."[23]

In fact, the Latvian petition had been initially referred to SS-*Gruppenführer* Berger for a decision. Berger rejected it as a "political trick" inimical to German interests, but urged Himmler to proceed with the establishment of a Latvian SS legion. The *Reichsführer* had by early 1943 overcome his reservations regarding Baltic SS units: the untapped source of manpower was too tempting to resist, and the legions could be seen as an instrument for Germanization. On January twenty-fourth Himmler secured Hitler's permission for the Latvian Legion, formally promulgated on February tenth. The Latvians continued to press for concessions, but were gradually reduced to lesser issues involving the legion's command, training, and status, on which the Germans were more willing to compromise.[24]

Throughout all this, the German civil administration for Latvia acted only as bystanders and middlemen. *Generalkommissar* Drechsler accepted the eventual incorporation of Latvia into a Greater German Reich, but felt this should have been intimated to the population from the start, rather than the combination of secrecy and inconsistency he characterized as an "unworthy game of hide-and-seek."[25] In December 1942 Drechsler unsuccessfully proposed a unified administration which would include Latvians in responsible posts.[26] When Drechsler received the Latvian "General-Directorate" on January 29, 1943, he offered his assistance in arranging the release of arrested nationalists, increased food rations and reprivatization in exchange for cooperation with the Legion; Latvian independence, however, was a matter he could not discuss.[27] Within these limitations, Drechsler did what he could, and by May 1943 the *Generalkommissar* could claim a new pension law, fewer restrictions on wage ceilings, and the restoration of the savings accounts of 32 thousand Latvians to the amount of 2.5 million *Reichsmarks.*[28]

An inhibiting factor for Drechsler was the proximity of *Reichskommissar* Lohse, who shared the Latvian capital of Riga. Lohse apparently intended to make his office hereditary.[29] His own views toward policy reform are revealed in a 51-page memorandum submitted to Rosenberg in December 1942. Lohse detested the "self-administrations" as incompatible with German interests and subversive influences on his *Generalkommissare* as well; he therefore recommended their dismantling through a reorganization of the *Reichskommissariat* that would concentrate power in his office. To secure popular support, Lohse advocated increased food rations, clothing drives and a "binding declaration" to reprivatize the economy after war's end.[30] But in the mobilization question, Lohse received the same treatment from the SS as had the Latvian leaders. When Lohse refused to approve a proclamation of mobilization for Latvia in February 1943, mobilization proceeded regardless under the guise of labor service registration.[31]

Within his own realm, however, Lohse encountered an even stronger challenge to his authority. The *Generalkommissar* for Estonia, SA-*Obergruppenführer* Karl-Sigismund Litzmann, enjoyed a relative independence from Lohse that reflected more than the distance separating Tallin from Riga. With the front stalemated before Leningrad, the northernmost Baltic state lay within Army Group North's Rear Area, creating a German civil-military condominium unique within the Reich Commissariat.[32] Litzmann also benefited from the displaced animosity of many Estonians, who considered Dr. Hjalmar Mäe, chief of Estonia's "National Directors," a Quisling worse than the Germans.[33] Above all, Litzmann maintained good relations with *Reichsführer* Himmler. From March through August 1943 the two corresponded regularly over recruitment for the Estonian SS Legion and the general topic of occupation policy in Estonia.[34]

These conditions allowed Litzmann to pursue his own course in Estonia. Litzmann sabotaged or defied dozens of Lohse's edicts, ignoring fish and grain quotas and publicly commemorating Estonian independence day. Replying to Lohse's attacks on his conduct, the *Generalkommissar* pointed out: "We cannot incur the enmity of a people and at the same time demand that they fight alongside us."[35]

To his surprise, Lohse discovered he could not simply overrule him. The *Reichskommissar*'s appeal to Rosenberg for support on March third was brushed off with the comment, "A very difficult jurisdictional and personal conflict has broken out here with *Reichskommissar* Koch . . . I beg you not to harass me to resolve the questions of other offices."[36] The parallel drawn by Rosenberg was more appropriate than he realized. In both the Rosenberg-Koch and Lohse-Litzmann confrontations, a subordinate successfully defied his nominal superior and implemented his own concept of occupation policy; and in both cases higher authority condoned the insubordination but left the chain-of-command intact. Lohse and Litzmann exchanged paper salvoes into June 1943, but without effect.[37]

Yet Litzmann's successful defense against Lohse could not halt the steady decline of Estonian morale under occupation, reaching its nadir in early 1943.[38] With the proclamation of compulsory labor service in March, Estonian leaders followed the example of their Latvian counterparts and linked mobilization to political concessions.[39] Oskar Angelus, one of Estonia's "National Directors," submitted a memorandum to Litzmann on March fifteenth that promised a national army 60 to 70 thousand strong in return for the restoration of independence.[40] One month later Estonian officers serving with the units attached to Army Group North made a more modest petition to replace the Estonian Legion with a regular field force of one or two divisions, under their own officers and *Wehrmacht* authority.[41] For his part, Litzmann wrote Himmler at the end of March with a proposed guarantee of autonomy for Estonia to be put before Hitler.[42] Himmler passed along Litzmann's memorandum to Bormann, but in his own reply he played down the importance of popular discontent and warned: "The Estonians should not make the mistake of presenting us with a bill today [for the Legion]."[43]

Like others involved in *Ostpolitik* reform, Litzmann cast about for more allies, and like others he found the Army willing. At the same time the *Generalkommissar* submitted his proposal to the führer he appealed for support to Field Marshal Georg von Küchler, commander of Army Group North. Von Küchler agreed immediately, though with what result is unclear.[44] Litzmann also found the Foreign Ministry cooperative in its attitude toward the Baltic population. Against the stated views of their own chief Ribbentrop, Foreign Ministry officials like Gustav Hilger continued to argue in February 1943 on behalf of post-war independence for the Baltic states.[45] On April sixteenth Litzmann discussed his views with Adolf von Windecker, the Foreign Ministry representative attached to the RKO, who passed them along to Berlin with his endorsement. Later Windecker pressed for an immediate granting of autonomy to the Baltic states on his own behalf.[46]

Litzmann's views were shared by many *Ostministerium* officials in Berlin by the end of 1942. *OMi* representatives had argued with Lohse for an expanded reprivatization of property at a conference on December eighth.[47] Upon reading Lohse's proposed "reforms" for the RKO, one member of the Political Department drafted a scathing reply on January 5, 1943 that criticized Lohse's entire approach to his task as *Reichskommissar*: the fact that his was a political rather than an administrative responsibility appeared "completely lost" upon him. To counteract the policy of exploitation and defamation of the population, the writer proposed that Lohse's reforms be supplemented by the reduction of the *Reichskommissariat* bureaucracy to small executive staffs, the expansion of the "self-administrations" with a view toward eventual self-government, and the restoration of the private economy.[48] The very next day other *OMi* officials composed a similar memorandum that recommended that the Baltic states be accorded the status of "protectorates" (as with Bohemia-Moravia), with the indigenous governments left in charge of administration, laws and cultural affairs while the Reich assumed responsiblity for foreign policy and defense. The paradox of the avowed purpose of the proposal, to facilitate the military mobilization of Baltic nationals, with the reservation of military defense to Germany, was not examined.[49]

These proposals formed the Baltic segment of the reform "package" Rosenberg would present to Hitler in early February. The minister presumably briefed Himmler on these two weeks earlier at Poznan as the concessions necessary to mobilize manpower for the Baltic legions.[50] When Rosenberg met with Hitler on February eighth, the former's primary concern remained the Ukraine, but the recommendations for the Baltic were less controversial and more clearly formulated: all three states were to be granted autonomy, with Germany retaining control of the military, railways, transportation, commerce, currency, customs and postal services; a "far-reaching" reprivatization of property should be implemented; and in return, each state would contribute a national legion, to be maintained by annual drafts of the male population. As already noted, Hitler deferred a decision until he saw more "concrete" proposals, yet Rosenberg departed in the belief that he had won approval for his program.[51]

Rosenberg and his staff returned to Berlin to prepare more specific provisions, only to discover that major disagreements divided the minister from his advisors. By February seventeenth the fifth draft of the proposed autonomy statute, though it embodied all the safeguards for Germany noted earlier, was nevertheless rejected by Rosenberg for allowing each state to retain its national flag and coat-of-arms.[52] But before these differences could assume significance, Reich Chancellery Chief Lammers informed a stunned Rosenberg on February eighteenth that Hitler had not endorsed an autonomy measure at the February eighth conference, but had merely postponed a decision until after the war.[53]

In its immediate impact, Hitler's verdict hardly affected the continuing discussion of reforms in Baltic administration. On March twelfth Lohse's chief political aide presented to the *Ostministerium* a restatement of Lohse's earlier proposals, updated by provisions for equalizing the wage and price structure in Estonia and Latvia with the Reich's and firing the incumbent members of the Latvian "General Directorate." Peter Kleist, a reform advocate and co-author of the autonomy statute that so offended Rosenberg, attacked these ideas and pointed instead to the example of Denmark, where a minimal German occupation executive had achieved impressive results.[54] But the continuing debate could not reverse policy, and when Himmler reopened the autonomy issue with SS support for the measure in autumn 1943, the political future of the Baltic states was no longer Germany's to determine.[55]

The economic aspects of reform fared little better. Control of the valuable phosphorite and shale-oil industries in Estonia would remain entirely in German hands under any circumstances.[56] The only positive measure—and the sole accomplishment of Rosenberg's presentation to Hitler—was the reprivatization decree, issued February 18, 1943 and applicable to all properties nationalized under the Soviet regime except where such actions "oppose public interests, particularly the war effort."[57]

Yet even this measure miscarried in its planning and execution. Reprivatization of small businesses had actually begun in October 1941, and the long delay in completing the process, while German officials argued over its timing and nature, stripped the decree of much of its effectiveness.[58] Popular suspicions of German motives were well-founded: "public interests" alone did not account for the exemption of large business and industrial enterprises, which Rosenberg intended to reserve as post-war rewards for German soldiers.[59] The decree and its accompanying directives for implementation made very clear that reprivatization came with strings attached. Restitution required formal application through the German administration, whose approval obligated the recipient to greater cooperation and higher production for the New Order; preferential treatment would be accorded families with members serving in the Legions or who had proven their reliability; reprivatized businesses had to pay a cash settlement on their goods; and each *Generalkommissar* was free to grant or deny restitution on his own judgment in any case.[60]

With such discretionary powers vested in the *Generalkommissar*, the implementation of the decree varied considerably. In Estonia and Latvia, a planned reprivatization rate of 20 to 30 percent for farms and agricultural businesses contrasted sharply with the views of Lithuania's *Generalkommissar* Adrian von Renteln, who declared his intention to restore no more than 5 percent of collectivized property annually.[61] Available statistics indicate that even these modest estimates proved optimistic. By the beginning of October 1943, the numbers and percentages of reprivatized farms stood as follows: Latvia, 35,635 (about 15 percent); Estonia, 10,723 (about 10 percent); and Lithuania, less than 9000 (about 2 percent). In the area of small businesses and industries, reprivatization became a limbo of delays and indecision: as of the end of 1943, the bulk of the applications (418 of 800 in Latvia, 296 of 418 in Estonia, 504 of 558 in Lithuania) had not been decided, and one-fourth of those that had been approved had not yet been carried out.[62]

If Rosenberg and Lohse expected the decree to promote collaboration among Baltic nationals, the *Sicherheitsdienst*'s surveys of public opinion quickly disabused them. Faith in a German victory after Stalingrad hardly existed; in Estonia and Latvia rumors circulated of reforms in the German administration, of the recall of Lohse and Drechsler, even of a restoration of independence to be proclaimed by Hitler himself in the Reichstag on January 30, 1943. Instead of these, the occupied inhabitants received only that which already rightfully belonged to them, but dispensed by the Germans as "a damned obligation." Lithuanians suspected that reprivatization represented merely a down payment on the compulsory mobilization of their society for the German war effort.[63]

These suspicions proved correct. *Ostministerium* edicts of August and December 1941 had already established the inhabitants' liability for labor service as needed. On March 29, 1943 a third decree ordered all adults between the ages of 15 and 65 to report to the nearest labor office for work assignment. The key aim of the measure, however, was the conscription of young men born between 1919 and 1924 into the SS legions.[64]

In Estonia and Latvia the SS judged the action a success. From March to August 1943 nearly 100,000 young men (over 87 percent of those summoned) duly registered for labor or military service, of whom over 23,000 (5000 Estonians, almost 18,000 Latvians) qualified for active duty in the SS or police.[65] These figures reflected not only a revision of the racial standards for the SS (the Reich Labor Service, for example, appears to have been more selective in accepting Baltic recruits), but the use of intimidation and occasional coercion by SS recruiters at the registration stations.[66] Dankers and Mäe actively participated in the recruitment drives as did such former senior officers of the national armies as Latvian Rudolfs Bangerskis and Estonian Johannes Soodla, each of whom assumed the post of inspector-general for their respective legions.[67] As Himmler had already pressed 4000 auxiliary policemen from all the Baltic states into front line service with the 2nd SS-Brigade near Leningrad in late January 1943, the net gain of valuable manpower for the Reich in this period was considerable.[68] These numbers, of course, represented only a fraction of what had been offered Germany, but from Himmler's perspective they came without strings attached.

The SS recruiting statistics, moreover, disguised both the widespread disaffection among the population and the growth of resistance among the young. An examination of the mobilization statistics for one Estonian district from March 9 to April 28, 1943 confirms the high compliance with registration (92.6 percent), nearly half of whom were released or exempted from service; 17.5 percent were assigned labor duties in war-related industries, and 27 percent were ordered to report for auxiliary service with the *Wehrmacht* or police, including most of the students. Only 2.6 percent of the total summoned actually volunteered for the Estonian Legion.[69] In Riga university students actively campaigned against recruitment, resulting in the arrest of more than 20 of their number in April 1943.[70]

These developments mirrored on a much smaller scale the situation in Lithuania, where the total failure of mobilization reflected that country's distinct experience under German occupation. Ironically, initial German prospects for a fruitful collaboration appeared better here than for Lithuania's northern neighbors. With German assistance, former Lithuanian Army Colonel Kazys Kirpa organized the Lithuania Activist Front in Berlin in November 1940 as the future pro-German government, which prepared and coordinated the activities of a widespread Lithuanian partisan movement behind Soviet lines in 1941. But as a reward for its services, the organization was first prevented from assuming power in Lithuania and then disbanded, with several of its leaders arrested. In its place the German civil administration established a "General Council" under former General Petras Kubiliunas, one of the organizers of a 1934 *putsch* against the Lithuanian government.[71]

Except for this concession, German policy subjected Lithuania to a much harsher treatment than Estonia or Latvia. The *Ostministerium* racial specialists rated the "Germanizable" element of the most populous Baltic state at no more than 25 to 30 percent and recommended that this could best be done only by resettling them in German-inhabited areas.[72] Though this project remained on paper, German colonization proceeded unabated throughout 1943 in the Suwalki district: By November about 28,000 Baltic Germans had returned to much larger farmsteads in Lithuania than they had left in 1940. German authorities cleverly imposed the bulk of property confiscation upon the ethnic Russian and Polish elements of the population, but could not afford to be so discriminating in meeting the labor needs of German industry.[73] Throughout 1942 thousands of Lithuanians were dispatched to the armaments factories of Gau Hessen, and when the labor quotas for the Baltic states were established in May 1943, the requirements for Estonia (3000) and Latvia (10,000) stood in sharp contrast to that for Lithuania (40,000).[74]

Above all, the distinguishing characteristic of German policy in Lithuania remained brute force. With its large Jewish population, Lithuania provided the firing squads of *Einsatzgruppe* A with over 76 percent of its victims in the Baltic states through January 1942.[75] In retaliation for two German agricultural specialists killed by partisans near Vilnius in May 1942, German authorities shot four hundred "saboteurs and terrorists."[76] Yet the death penalty was by no means restricted to acts of armed resistance. In February 1943 the *Gebietskommissar* for the Vilnius district, obsessed by the failure of native peasants to meet their agricultural quotas, executed 40 peasants who were in chronic arrears. The massacre aroused strong protests among reform advocates within the Eastern Ministry, but Lohse and von Renteln backed their subordinate. The *Gebietskommissar* received only an admonition not to exceed his authority, while Peter Kleist's continued protests ultimately led to his dismissal.[77]

Ironically, this incident coincided with Germany's effort to enlist Lithuania's aid against Stalin. The initial developments followed the pattern set in Latvia: German authorities approached prominent Lithuanians in early February with the suggestion that an offer to raise a Lithuanian Legion would be favorably received by the führer. The General Council vetoed such a measure without political concessions, and so advised *Generalkommissar* von Renteln on February thirteenth; they were nevertheless commanded to report to Riga to discuss mobilization. Before departing on February twenty-second the councillors drafted a petition for Lithuanian independence as the price for military conscription, but the next day *Obergruppenführer* Jeckeln declined to accept it on the grounds that the purpose of the conference concerned only military affairs, not political. The Lithuanian delegates returned to Kaunas on February twenty-fourth to discover that the Germans had already proclaimed mobilization. A tension-filled conference convened by von Renteln on March second produced the endorsement of only Kubiliunas and two other general councillors to a popular appeal supporting mobilization.[78]

If the majority of the Lithuanian "Self-Administration" refused to uphold the German measure, the public response was overwhelmingly negative. The average Lithuanian could see that the Germans allowed the traditional Lithuanian independence day (February 16) to pass without the slightest recognition, in contrast to the well-publicized celebration in Estonia the very next week. The Lithuanian nationalist underground encouraged and assisted eligible youths to escape into the countryside before they could be registered. Out of 3230 candidates summoned to register in six Lithuanian cities, only 177 complied.[79] Through the summer of 1943 the mobilization produced a grand total of only 1464 recruits for military and police service.[80]

German rage at this response transformed what had been merely a failure into a disaster. In order to prevent "further damage to the healthy segment of the Lithuanian people," *Reichskommissar* Lohse directed von Renteln on March twelfth to suspend further reprivatization actions, restrict the activities of the General Council, and "eliminate these negative influences at their source."[81] Before the end of the month SS and police units closed down the Lithuanian universities at Kaunas and Vilnius and arrested some 89 academics and three members of the General Council.[82] The warnings of *Ostministerium* critics against such policies were ignored.[83] Himmler instead drew the lesson that Lithuanian resistance resulted from German lenience and softness, and relieved his commander for the district.[84] Increased repression only strengthened the ranks of the nationalist resistance, whose separate leaders came together in June–July 1943 to coordinate a unified movement.[85]

Yet at least one German official was probably relieved at the miscarriage of the mobilization and reprivatization decrees. Dr. Duckart, chief of the resettlement staff in Lithuania, complained to Himmler on March eighth that restoring property rights and weapons to Lithuanians marked a "decisive change" in policy and was incompatible with the colonization well under way in the Suwalki region.[86] Duckart's commentary, essentially applicable to all the Baltic states, emphasized what Himmler and Berger chose to overlook—that the mobilization of Baltic nationals irrevocably altered German war aims in the region.

Lithuania's experiences forecast future developments throughout the Baltic states. In Latvia, Director-General Valdmanis resigned his post in April 1943 and disseminated his memoranda among Latvian leaders to alert them to the reality behind German propaganda.[87] Recruiting drives for both SS legions through the remainder of 1943 proved far less effective, though the Soviet threat grew even greater.[88] A brief agreement in February 1944 to establish a "Lithuanian Territorial Defense Force" collapsed when the SS turned on their supposed allies.[89]

So ended the reform efforts of 1942–43 in *Reichskommissariat Ostland*, and with them a unique opportunity for Germany. Together with the Vlasov movement, the Baltic "Self-Administrations" offered the only initiatives for reform originated by the occupied population, but unlike Vlasov they could be trusted as both anti-Soviet and anti-Russian. For the price of increased autonomy, eco-

nomic reprivatization and guaranteed independence, Germany might have gained
as many as two hundred thousand fighting men for the front, buttressed the
domestic positions of her collaborationist regimes and strengthened her alliance
with Finland, all without surrendering predominance in the Baltic region in the
event of victory. The operational problems involved in such a mobilization were
not insignificant, but were not even considered. The initiatives failed because
Hitler, Himmler, and Rosenberg recognized them as incompatible with their war
aims: What Rosenberg established as his objective for the Ukraine, he rejected
for the Baltic states. The degree of popular support that produced twenty thousand
recruits for the legions can be seen as an act of good faith by those who yet
hoped for a change in German policy; when the Germans did not reciprocate
with the reforms known to be under consideration, that hope was crushed.
Insensitive to this result, the Nazi leadership continued on their course through
areas where reform opportunities were not so easily available.

NOTES

1. See the statistical data in Hans-Dieter Handrack, *Das Reichskommissariat Ostland:
Die Kulturpolitik der deutschen Verwaltung zwischen Autonomie und Gleichschaltung
1941–1944* (Hannover-Münden: Gauke Varlag, 1981), p. 220.

2. In addition to Myllyniemi's *Neuordnung*, a good monograph on German policies
in the Baltic states is that by East German scholar Roswitha Czollek, *Faschismus und
Okkupation: Wirtschaftspolitische Zielsetzung und Praxis des faschistischen deutschen
Besatzungsregimes in den baltischen Sowjetrepubliken während des Zweiten Weltkrieges*
(Berlin: Akademie-Verlag, 1974).

3. See August Rei, *The Drama of the Baltic Peoples* (Stockholm: Kirjastus Vaba
Eesti, 1970), pp. 286ff.

4. On Imperial Germany's policies in the Baltic, see Fischer, *Germany's Aims*, pp.
273–79, 313–14, 348, 353–54, 376–87, 456–72, 479–82, 598–607; on the *Freikorps*,
see Robert G. L. Waite, *Vanguard of Nazism: The Free Corps Movement in Postwar
Germany 1918–1923* (New York: W.W. Norton, 1969), pp. 94–139.

5. See Rosenberg's memorandum, April 2, 1941, Document 1017-PS, *TMWC*,
XXVI, 547–54; "Aktenvermerk," July 16, 1941, Document L–221, *TMWC*, XXXVIII,
86–94.

6. Rosenberg, "Instruktion für einen Reichskommissar im Ostland," May 8, 1941,
Document 1029-PS, *TMWC*, XXVI, 574.

7. See Krausnick and Wilhelm, *Weltanschauungskrieges*, pp. 294ff., 606–07.

8. Detailed documentation is located in the files of the Deutsches Ausland-Institut
on T-81/291–92/2415872–6323; see also Himmler's memoranda of January 31, and April
7, 1942, T-175/66/2582197–2200.

9. Dr. Wetzel, "Gedanken zur Frage der Eindeutschbarkeit der Völker des Ostlandes," November 16, 1942, Document OCC–49, RG 238, NA.

10. See OSS R & A Report No. 2500.8, "German Military Government over Europe:
Ostland and Ukraine," pp. 82ff., RG 59, NA; and Czollek, *Faschismus*, pp. 85ff.

11. See Myllyniemi, *Neuordnung*, pp. 103–120, and Oskar Angelus, "Die Einsetzung

der deutschen Zivilverwaltung im Estland,'' *Baltische Hefte*, Bd. XIX (1973), pp. 50–60.

12. Quoted in Hans Ronimois, "Estonians and World Affairs," (ca. January 1943), OSS R & A No. 40247, RG 226, NA.

13. See Angelus, "Wirtschaftsfragen im deutschbesetzten Estland 1941–1944," *Acta Baltica*, XVI (1976), pp. 158, 167; Alfred Bilmanis, *Latvia under German Occupation* (Washington, DC: Latvian Legation, 1943), pp. 79–80.

14. See SD *Meldungen* Nr. 42, T-175/236/2725564–565; Czollek, *Faschismus*, p. 126.

15. Handrack, *Reichskommissariat*, pp. 94–95, 126–49. Handrack's is an overstated defense of the policies of the RKO's *Kultur-Abteilung*.

16. For example, Latvian workers in a Riga armaments plant took an abnormally large amount of sick leave: see "Kriegstagebuch des We.Wi.Kdo. Riga, 1.1.–31.3.1943," T-77/691/1901134.

17. See SD *Meldungen* Nr. 42 and 44, T-175/236/2725560–63, 2725627–28.

18. Hugh Page Taylor and Roger James Bender, *Uniforms, Organization and History of the Waffen-SS*, Vol. 5 (5 vols.) (San Jose, CA: R. James Bender Publishing, 1982), pp. 57–58, 135–38. Over 7300 Estonians were serving with the *Wehrmacht* in January 1942 (*EgM* Nr. 154, T-175/234/2723579–580).

19. SS-*Obersturmbannführer* Brandt to SS-*Gruppenführer* Berger, October 17, 1941, T-175/22/2527941.

20. Taylor and Bender, *Waffen-SS* (Vol. 5), pp. 140–41; Himmler exchange of correspondence with SS-*Sturmbanführer* Witt, May 1942, T-175/66/2582806–816.

21. See the exchange of correpondence among Jeckeln, Lohse and Berger, July 30–August 17, 1942, T-175/122/2647579–585.

22. Brandt to Berger, August 14, 1942, T-175/22/2527939–940.

23. Oskar Dankers' affidavit of August 4, 1947, Document NO–4825, RG 238, NA; Valdmanis' reply and the accompanying supplement are reproduced on T-454/92/000053–65.

24. Dankers affidavit, Document No–4825; exchange of correspondence among Himmler, Berger and Jeckeln, December 11, 1942–January 12, 1943, T-175/22/2527892–7913; Stein, *Waffen-SS*, pp. 175–76; and Arthur Silgailis, *Latvian Legion* (San Jose, CA: R. James Bender Publishing, 1986), pp. 19–27.

25. Drechsler to Lohse, June 19, 1943, ML 473, RG 242, NA.

26. Drechsler to Lohse, December 7, 1942, T-454/102/000072–76, and Drechsler to Lohse, June 19, 1943, ML 473, RG 242, NA.

27. "Protokoll der Sitzung der Lettischen Selbstverwaltung und der Führung des Generalkommissariats," T-454/92/000035–42. A copy of this document was forwarded to Allied intelligence: See U.S. Legation, Stockholm, to the secretary of state, OSS R & A report No. 46,885, RG 226, NA.

28. U.S. Legation, Stockholm, to the secretary of state, "Review of Latvian Radio Broadcasts May 1943," June 7, 1943, decimal file 860N.00/225, RG 59, NA.

29. Kleist, *Zwischen*, p. 164 and *Documents Accuse*, pp. 43–46.

30. Lohse, "Denkschrift zur gegenwärtigen Lage der Verwaltung und Wirtschaft des Ostlandes," December 1942, T-454/14/000077–129.

31. RKO/Hauptabteilungsleiter I (Pröhl), "Vermerk," April 14, 1943, T-454/14/1332–333; Myllyniemi, *Neuordnung*, pp. 231–32.

32. Bräutigam, *Überblick*, p. 16.

33. See Political Memoranda Estonia nos. 4 and 5 from the Press Reading Bureau, Stockholm, to the British Foreign Office's Political Intelligence Department, August 10, and August 24, 1943, file FO 371/36770, Public Record Office, London.

34. Litzmann's correspondence with Himmler is scattered on T-175/22/2527816–854.

35. Lohse to Rosenberg, March 3, 1943, T-454/30/408–13; Litzmann to Rosenberg, April 5, 1943, T-454/14/143–78.

36. Rosenberg to Lohse, March 29, 1943, T-454/30/391.

37. See Lohse to Litzmann, May 1, 1943, and Litzmann's reply of June 3, 1943, T-454/14/179–208, 273–81.

38. Buchbender, *Tönende Erz*, p. 269.

39. Myllyniemi, *Neuordnung*, pp. 231–32.

40. Oskar Angelus, memorandum of March 1943, Akten R 6/76, BA.

41. The petition, forwarded by a Captain Cellarius to OKW, appears in Bender and Taylor, *Uniforms*, Vol. 5, pp. 154–54.

42. Litzmann to Himmler, March 31, 1943, T-175/22/2527853–854.

43. Himmler to Litzmann, April 24, 1943, T-175/22/2527846.

44. See "Anruf Chef an O.B. im Sonderzug, 2.3.43, 18,45 Uhr," T-78/352/6312160.

45. Gustav Hilger, "Notiz für den Herrn Reichsaussenminister," February 13, 1943, T-120/695/1083/316815–820.

46. Windecker to the Foreign Ministry, April 19, 1943, Document NG–2721, RG 238, NA; Windecker to Steengracht, "Aufzeichnung," May 8, 1943, T-120/1005/1659H/393345–347.

47. Myllyniemi, *Neuordnung*, pp. 222–23.

48. "Stellungnahme der HA I zur Denkschrift des RKO," January 5, 1943, ML 473, RG 242, NA.

49. Annotated but unsigned draft memorandum, "Der Einbau der ehemaligen baltischen Staaten in das neue Europa," January 6, 1943, T-454/15/127–34.

50. Interrogation of Gottlob Berger, December 12, 1946, and Berger affidavit of June 14, 1947, Document NO–3971, RG 238, NA.

51. Körner to Goering, February 20, 1943, T-454/89/446–452. See also above, Chapter 5.

52. "Erlass des Führers zur Ergänzung und Abänderung des Erlasses über die Verwaltung der neu besetzten Ostgebiete vom _____ 1943" (Fünfter Entwurf), February 17, 1943, T-454/15/267–69, and Kleist, *Zwischen*, p. 167. See also Myllyniemi, *Neuordnung*, pp. 217–18.

53. Lammers to Rosenberg, March 8, 1943, file EAP 99/76, MR 260, RG 242, NA.

54. Trampedach to Rosenberg, March 15, 1943; Peter Kleist to Leibbrandt, May 4, 1943, and Kleist, "Überflüssige Regierungsmassnahmen im Reichskommissariat Ostland," May 17, 1943, all in file EAP 99/158, MR 281, RG 242, NA.

55. See Myllyniemi, *Neuordnung*, pp. 246–51.

56. Körner to Goering, February 20, 1943, T-454/89/448–49.

57. *Verordnungsblatt des Reichsministers für die besetzten Ostgebiete*, 1943 Nr. 5, February 22, 1943, file EAP 99/1207 (not microfilmed), RG 242, NA.

58. See Myllyniemi, *Neuordnung*, pp. 219–23.

59. See Rosenberg's letters to Goering of December 1942 (specific dates not given), T-454/91/432–35, and April 1, 1943, T-311/166/7217578–581. Goering concurred in his reply of April 15, (T-311/166/7217582).

60. See Gerber, *Staatliche Wirtschaftslenkung*, pp. 168–80 and Dokumententeil Dok-

umenten Nr. 17, 19; also, *Landwirtschaftsrat* Dr. Westenhoff, "Die landwirtschaftliche Reprivatisierung," *Revaler Zeitung* of March 13, 1943 (file EAP 99/1207, RG 242, NA), and Oberkriegsverwaltungsrat Dr. Hans-Georg Szogs, "Restoration of Private Property in the Ostland," *Die Ostwirtschaft* Nr. 4/5 (1943), translation in U.S. Legation Stockholm dispatch no. 1890, June 26, 1943, decimal file 860N.00/233, RG 59, NA.

61. Compare Chefgruppe Ernährung und Landwirtschaft, "Stand der land- and ernähr-ungswirtschaftlichen Reprivatisierung im Ostland," October 19, 1943, file EAP 99/1207, RG 242, NA, and Bräutigam, *Überblick*, p. 51.

62. Chefgruppe Ernährung und Landwirtschaft, "Stand," EAP 99/1207, RG 242, NA; Myllyniemi, *Neuordnung*, p. 225.

63. See SD *Meldungen* Nr. 41, Nr. 44, Nr. 46, Nr. 48, and Nr. 49, T-175/236/2725547–548, 2725631, 2725691–692, 2725765–772, 2725796–798.

64. Myllyniemi, *Neuordnung*, pp. 231–33.

65. Ostministerium Hauptabteilung III-Arbeitspolitik und Sozialversicherung, "Vermerk über Ablauf und Ergebnisse sämtlicher seit dem Frühjahr 1943 durchgeführte Musterungen," February 1, 1944, T-454/15/339–41.

66. OMi/Hauptabteilung Ic, "Musterung der Arbeitsdienstfreiwilligen," September 15, 1943, file EAP 99/1218 (not microfilmed), RG 242, NA; Bilmanis, *Latvia* p. 91.

67. Dispatches of the U.S. Legation, Stockholm, "Review of Latvian Radio Broadcasts during March 1943," April 8, 1943, and "Political Events in Estonia during March 1943 as Revealed by the German-controlled Estonian Language Press," May 10, 1943, OSS R & A Nos. 34,831 and 37,264, RG 226, NA; and Taylor and Bender, *Uniforms*, Vol. 5, pp. 12–16, 155–56.

68. Himmler to Grothmann, February 2, 1943, T-175/66/2582771.

69. U.S. Legation, Stockholm, "Mobilization in Estonia," June 4, 1943, OSS R & A No. 39,550, RG 226, NA.

70. SD *Meldungen* Nr. 51, T-175/236/2725841.

71. See *Documents Accuse*, pp. 65–79, 93–101; and Krausnick and Wilhelm, *Weltanschauungskrieges*, pp. 349–51.

72. Wetzel, "Gedanken," Document OCC–49, RG 238, NA.

73. Der Generalkommissar in Kauen, Abteilung Politik, "Bericht über den Stand der Rücksiedlung der Litauen-Deutschen zum 10.11.1943," November 24, 1943, Document OCC–30, RG 238, NA.

74. Czollek, *Faschismus*, pp. 162–63, 168.

75. Krausnick and Wilhelm, *Weltanschauungskrieges*, p. 607.

76. A copy of the proclamation appears in *Documents Accuse*, pp. 250–51.

77. *Gebietskommissar* Wulff to *Generalkommissar* von Renteln, March 2, 1943, in *Documents Accuse*, pp. 268–70; on the background and aftermath see Czollek, *Faschismus*, pp. 123–24, and Kleist, *Zwischen*, pp. 226–27.

78. The fullest account of these developments appears in a German language report apparently prepared jointly by the Lithuanian underground and emigrés in Stockholm, "Zur Lage in Litauen, Februar–März 1943," OSS R & A No. 44,414; see also the dispatches of the U.S. Legation, Stockholm, May 11, and May 18, 1943, respectively, OSS R & A Nos. 38,226 and 38,178, all in RG 226, NA.

79. "Attempted German Military Mobilization in Lithuania," OSS R & A No. 38,226, RG 226, NA.

80. Hauptabteilung Politik III, "Vermerk," T-454/15/339. See also the report by the

same office, "Lagebericht für die Monate Juni and Juli 1943," August 31, 1943, Document OCC E 3b 7–8, YIVO.

81. Lohse to von Renteln, March 12, 1943, T-454/15/354–55.

82. SS-*Obergruppenführer* Jeckeln to Himmler, April 2, 1943, T- 175/73/2590225–226.

83. See Kleist, "Generalbezirk Litauen," May 14, 1943, file EAP 99/158, MR 281, RG 242, NA.

84. Himmler to Bormann, July 18, 1943, T-175/73/2590201.

85. See Algimantas P. Gureckas, "The National Resistance During the German Occupation of Lithuania," *Lituanus*, VIII, 1–2 (1962): 23–28, and Stasys Lusys, "The Emergence of Unified Lithuanian Resistance Movement Against Occupants 1940–1943," *Lituanus*, Vol. IX, no. 4 (December 1963): 123–27.

86. Duckart to Himmler, March 8, 1943, T-81/291/2416022–029.

87. SD *Meldungen* Nr. 51, T-175/236/2725843–845.

88. See Ostministerium Abt. III, "Erscheinen der Musterungspflichtigen," February 2, 1944, T-454/15/337–343.

89. Gureckas, "National Resistance," pp. 27–28.

7

AGRARIAN REFORM

Of all the aspects of *Ostpolitik*, none possessed more significance than the exploitation of the Russian soil itself. Not only would the land in the East provide the needed *Lebensraum* for Germany's future, but the expected agricultural production there would neutralize the effect of an Allied blockade insofar as foodstuffs were concerned. In planning for the occupation Undersecretary of Agriculture Herbert Backe, a Russian German like Rosenberg, sought to reverse the Soviet emphasis on food production for domestic consumption and restore Russia's former position as a major exporter of foodstuffs to Europe. This policy coincided with Hitler's colonialist view of starving Russian cities, deindustrializing the Soviet economy, and driving urban populations into the countryside; ironically, the planned increases in agriculture required the wholesale retention of the Soviet institution of the *kolkhoz*, the collective farm.[1]

At the same time, however, others valued the potential popular support for agrarian reform. A few days before BARBAROSSA began, Dr. Mikhail Akhmeteli, a Georgian-born economics expert, submitted a proposal that conceded the retention of the *kolkhozy* but guaranteed the peasants eventual ownership of farm plots between two and five hectares (five to twelve acres).[2] German Foreign Ministry representatives also urged immediate concessions of land and property rights to Ukrainian farmers.[3]

In practice German agrarian policy combined Backe's objectives with a diluted version of Akhmeteli's reform, while reserving the option of future German colonization. The New Agrarian Order of February 15, 1942 merely redesignated collective farms as ''joint-farming establishments'' (*Gemeinwirtschaften*), which granted Russian farmers property rights to the small plots of land adjacent to their homes and permitted individual cattle breeding. These would eventually become ''farm cooperatives'' (*Landbaugenossenschaften*), the key element in the reform that linked collectivism with capitalism: The land was distributed in the form of usufruct among the farmers in disconnected, scattered strips, with

Table 1
Soviet Foodstuffs Imported by Germany, 1939–June 1941

	1939		1940		Jan.–June 1941	
	Total Imports (Mill. RM)	Pct. From USSR	Total Imports (Mill. RM)	Pct. From USSR	Total Imports (Mill. RM)	Pct. From USSR
Wheat	123.7	0.0%	101.1	0.6%	50.9	55.6%
Rye	13.1	4.6%	19.7	69.5%	11.1	100.5%
Barley	37.8	0.0%	87.7	95.8%	17.2	70.3%
Oats	5.1	0.0%	13.8	99.3%	23.3	96.1%

Source: Taken from "Die kriegswirtschaftliche Beitrag Osteuropas für das deutsche Reich 1936–1944," prepared by the Institut für Weltwirschaft an der Universität Kiel, n.d. (ca. mid-1944), pp. 18-19, on T-84/72/1358680-681.

the plowing and cultivation shared by all; harvesting theoretically rewarded the individual for the higher yield of his areas, though delivery quotas were set collectively. Each peasant family in a cooperative would be responsible for a total area of four to eight hectares (about 10 to 20 acres). The final stage in the agrarian reform permitted the establishment of consolidated and independent family farms, but only to those who had proved their reliability and only as farm machinery and livestock became available.

The reform excluded, however, the Soviet system's state farms (*sovkhozy*) and machine tractor stations (respectively numbering 1875 and 900 in the Ukraine alone), which were taken over unchanged by German monopoly corporations. Neither did the decree divulge the planned conversion rate for individual farms: Dr. Otto Schiller, the reform's principal architect, concluded that nothing could be done during the first year but in the course of 1943 perhaps five to fifteen independent farms might be set up in each *raion* of the Ukraine. Small wonder that the OKW propaganda staffs were directed to speak of "land in usufruct" and avoid the term *land ownership*.[4]

But above all, the priorities and peculiarities of *Ostpolitik* reshaped agrarian reform in a manner not foreseen by its designers. The first economic commandment of BARBAROSSA required that the occupied area feed the invading army, an ironic reflection of Germany's increased reliance upon imported Soviet foodstuffs following the Nazi-Soviet Pact in August 1939 (see Table 1).

To minimize food disruption, German economic authorities hoped to maintain maximum agricultural production. The ravages of combat and the effectiveness of the Soviet "scorched-earth" policy crippled this goal from the start as only 40 percent of the farming tractors and very limited fuel supplies remained available for use. These conditions actually facilitated Berlin's approval of the agrarian reform, as private initiative was considered the best compensation for the loss in mechanization.[5] In the field, however, many German agricultural leaders distrusted the notion of peasant initiative and maintained the communes in the same or even more brutal manner than under Stalin.[6]

The application of the New Agrarian Order varied widely according to region. In the Baltic states, as already noted, German policy permitted a staged but inconsistent and incomplete restoration of agricultural enterprise through 1943. In the area of Army Group Center, Russian peasants had begun breaking up the collectives and redistributing the land among themselves at the beginning of German occupation: the agrarian reform here merely legalized existing conditions.[7] Army Group North, with the poorest farmland of all, carried out the conversion of *kolkhozy* to farm cooperatives and some individual farming by the beginning of 1943.[8] But in the key area of the Ukraine, from which Germany would draw nearly 78 percent of the total grain production in the occupied USSR, the meager progress of the agrarian reform provided the focus for the 1942–43 efforts.[9]

At the same time the Nazi commitment to colonization subverted the reform to suit its own purpose. In the Ukraine the ethnic German population was rewarded without regard to productivity by a rapid conversion to farm cooperatives.[10] Only four days after Hitler signed the New Agrarian Order *Ministerialdirektor* Hans-Joachim Riecke, chief of *Wi-Stab-Ost*'s agricultural section, developed a plan for grouping six to ten farm cooperatives along major transportation routes as agricultural strong points, which might later serve as colonization centers for German settlers.[11] In the summer of 1943, with Germany's fortunes markedly worse, Riecke still planned to use the state farms and 30 percent of the acreage set aside on each farm cooperative for settlement by German combat veterans.[12]

German policy further weakened the reform through the complexities of the tax structure imposed on agricultural production. Russian and Ukrainian farmers often paid multiple duties on the same yield from their fields, while taxes on the produce from individually cultivated lands amounted to several times that for lands under collective cultivation. As Riecke conceded, "We therefore strive through our agrarian policy to transfer the soil to individual peasant use on the one hand, and on the other establish taxes that benefit collectivization!"[13]

The most serious disruption of agricultural production, however, resulted from the activities of the partisans. The area most affected embraced *Generalkommissariat* White Russia and Army Group Center's sector, where Soviet partisans caused the loss of well over half the grain and meats produced during the economic year (June to May) 1942–43. The economic significance of this region was far less than that of the Ukraine, so it was with some alarm the *Wi-Stab-Ost* noted a significant increase in agricultural losses in the northern Ukraine through the depredations of Soviet and Ukrainian nationalist guerrillas in the spring of 1943. In all, partisans inflicted a loss of 10 percent of the total production of grain and 20 percent of the total in meats for the occupied USSR during 1942–43.[14] Perhaps more significant was the psychological impact on the farmers, who were virtually defenseless against the partisans: One German agricultural official reported from Kharkov that local peasants rejected offers of individual farms for fear of partisan reprisals.[15]

By the end of 1942 these factors left the agrarian reform in a moribund state. The supposed beneficiaries of the reform saw little if any change in their status, except that the available produce permitted for retention as domestic consumption had decreased sharply from that under the Soviet regime.[16] With the high expectations for the first year unfulfilled,[17] most German agricultural specialists determined to maintain the highest production possible by relying on the "joint-farming establishments": in the key area of the Ukraine (including both the *Reichskommissariat* and the area under military government), only 2195 out of 27,656 former collectives—less than 8 percent—had been converted to farm cooperatives by December 1, 1942.[18] When Riecke later polled his subordinates as to whether the reform should be expanded, the officers responsible for the Ukraine argued that conversion to cooperatives should remain solely a reward for proven performance instead of an incentive to boost production.[19]

Outside the *Wi-Stab-Ost*, however, pressure mounted to accelerate the agrarian reform as a primarily political measure. The petitions for an expanded land reform as part of a general revision of *Ostpolitik*'s course have already been described. Reich Coal Commissioner Paul Walter, an adviser to Goering on mining production, had already proposed the dissolution of the *kolkhozy* at the time the New Agrarian Order was proclaimed. On December 2, 1942 Walter reiterated his views in a memorandum to Riecke's section, condemning the existing policies as a doomed continuation of Soviet practices. Walter urged a return to the principles of Lenin's New Economic Policy of 1921: increasing production by guaranteeing the peasant's right to his land and the freedom to dispose of his surplus crops. Once an area was pacified, each collective should be divided among its members; permanent title to the land would be awarded after five years' performance with delivery quotas to German authorities of one-third the natural yield of the area.[20]

The strongest pressures were applied by the *Ostministerium*'s policy department and the army. On December 17, 1942—the day before Rosenberg hosted the great reform conference with army representatives in Berlin—Leibbrandt condemned the reform's dilatory execution in a memorandum to Alfred Meyer, recommending the immediate conversion of at least 30 percent of the remaining *Gemeinwirtschaften* into *Landbaugenossenschaften* by spring 1943 and another 20 percent after the autumn harvest.[21] What Liebbrandt proposed, *Generaloberst* Ewald von Kleist and Field Marshal Erich von Manstein implemented on their own in the areas occupied by Army Groups A and South in February 1943. At the same time OKH and OKW drew up plans for awarding land grants to eastern nationals for meritorious service with the *Wehrmacht*.[22]

In the aftermath of Stalingrad, Riecke grudgingly yielded to what he would later describe as "following the policy of softness, becoming pacifists, even to sabotaging the Führer's political course."[23] On February twelfth he offered to accelerate the conversion rate for farm cooperatives to 20 percent for 1943. For Leibbrandt's subordinate Kinkelin, this merely represented another half-measure; instead he proposed a radical reform in the manner suggested by Walter with an immediate distribution of *kolkhoz* land to the peasants.[24] Leibbrandt would not go this far, but in his official reply to Riecke on March eleventh he urged an increase in the conversion rate to 50 percent in 1943 and 100 percent in the course of 1944.[25]

But Riecke had already fixed the limits of his concessions. During spring 1943 he instituted the awarding of premiums and "bonus-points" for increased buying power as a reward for greater production.[26] At the beginning of March he authorized an acceleration of the agrarian reform in both the *Reichskommissariat* Ukraine and the *Wirtschaftsinspektion Süd* along the lines of his proposals made in February. One out of every five communal farms would be converted to cooperatives during 1943, with priority given to those with the best production; in addition, the small plots adjoining farmsteads for the private use of peasants could be enlarged to a maximum of one hectare (2.47 acres) in at least 10 percent of all communal and cooperative farms during spring 1943, to be extended to another 10 percent in the autumn. Finally, independent family farms were to be granted to a limited number of inhabitants who had distinguished themselves in German service, though "the propaganda treatment of the independent farm should not emphasize it as the ultimate goal" of the agrarian reform.[27]

As tardy and limited as Riecke's 1943 version of agrarian reform was, it nevertheless aroused the opposition of those charged with its execution. In the RKU, Koch's agricultural chief Helmut Körner's efforts to sabotage the reform's implementation brought about a sharp reprimand from even Riecke.[28] One month later the head of the agricultural section of Economic Inspection South found it necessary to issue a general directive that reflected the same command problems that plagued Rosenberg and Koch and Lohse and Litzmann:

It is not the task of the agricultural officer to debate the Agrarian Order but to carry it out. . . . He cannot view the farm co-operative as an indolent and unpopular experiment . . . whose failure would mean no loss as one could return to the collective system; rather he must recognize that the failure of the co-operative would mean a disaster for German agrarian policy in the East.[29]

The point seems to have been taken, as German authorities perceived a clear increase in productivity among peasants working on the farm cooperatives.[30] By June 15, 1943 the number of cooperatives in *Wirtschaftsinspektion Süd* had risen to 1300, or 11.3 percent of the total.[31] The conversion rate in the RKU actually proceeded faster: By May twenty-fifth, 1688 cooperatives had been established, increasing to 2780 (16.8 percent of the total) by August tenth.[32] Dr. Otto Schiller, probably sensing the opportunity of accelerating the reform, proposed on July fifth to convert the remaining *Gemeinwirtschaften* in the coming autumn and winter.[33]

Yet even as conversions increased, the issue of agrarian reform grew increasingly academic. In August 1943, 29 of those privileged Ukrainians who had received private farmsteads offered to return them to German authorities because of the lack of farm labor. Just as likely, these would-be beneficiaries of German rule could read the handwriting on the wall: "The population no longer shows any interest in working with or for German authorities, and in growing numbers are following the directions of bolshevik agents," concluded a German assessment in September.[34]

As a direct complement to the material benefits of farm cooperatives, the formal recognition of peasant land ownership assumed equal importance. The New Agrarian Order had conferred personal property rights only for the garden plots immediately adjoining private farmsteads. On February 15, 1943 Riecke proposed to Rosenberg to grant as private property the strips of land worked by each cooperative's members, heretofore considered only as "land in usufruct."[35] Two months later, with the concurrence of Goering, OKW and OKH, Rosenberg forwarded the plan to Hitler for approval.[36] This measure had probably been thoroughly considered in several quarters, for on the very same day (April twenty-fourth) Hans Frank announced the restoration of individual land ownership to a maximum of 20 hectares (49 acres) in the *Generalgouvernement* district of Galicia.[37]

At the end of May, Hitler gave his consent, and on June third Rosenberg issued the proclamation from Berlin. The "Proclamation Concerning the Introduction of Property in Land of Family Farmers"—its text unchanged from the draft forwarded to Hitler in April—provided that the land allotments granted to native peasants under the New Agrarian Order was "hereby recognized as private property of the family farmers." The measure extended this right to inhabitants temporarily absent from their farms: *Ostarbeiter* working in Germany, prisoners-of-war, even soldiers in the Red Army (as an inducement to desert). In return, of course, the beneficiaries were "obligated to exert the utmost in the new development of agriculture."[38]

The fact of the Proclamation could not mask the differences among German authorities, however, as to its extent and implications. As author of the measure, Riecke never considered it a renunciation of German colonization as control of the state farms and the reserved land of each *Landbaugenossenschaft* (30 percent of each cooperative's total acreage) "fully protected" the needs of future German settlers.[39] Yet at a press conference held by the *Ostministerium*, Otto Bräutigam told 70 newspapermen that the cooperatives' reserved land would be held for the use of repatriated prisoners-of-war and Red Army soldiers.[40] On June fifteenth Rosenberg explained to Sauckel that the property declaration applied to *Ostarbeiter* only insofar as they originated from farm communes and cooperatives; the labor conscripted from Russian cities (the great majority of the *Ostarbeiter*) did not qualify.[41] The full scope of disagreement in the interpretation of the property proclamation gradually emerged in the discussions of the key question: How would the measure be applied?

As Rosenberg rehearsed his announcement, Otto Schiller advised Riecke that the only essential points to clarify concerned the definition of "landed property" (*Bodeneigentum*) and the conditions of its transfer.[42] Riecke's staff drafted a set of implementation provisions by June third which were presented to a conference of *Ostministerium* officials and representatives from interested agencies on June seventh. The discussions produced agreement on 11 basic provisions that reflected Schiller's concerns and safeguarded German interests: The new property owners received hereditary title to the lands described in the proclamation (though only a single individual could claim the inheritance) but were not quite free to dispose of it, as land sales and leases of over three years' duration required the approval of German agricultural authorities. The owner and his family were obligated to work the land regularly, but could utilize the surplus crops however they wished. With minor changes made by Rosenberg after he completed his Ukrainian tour, the final version of the implementation provisions was ready by July thirteenth.[43]

But now the new measure came under attack from a familiar quarter. *Reichskommissar* Erich Koch launched a campaign against the proclamation on July sixth with a letter to Himmler protesting the granting of property to Ukrainians "at a time when a hundred thousand [Germans] in the West have lost their property, and when thousands of German soldiers carry hopes of settlement with them into the areas they have conquered." Koch did not propose revoking the proclamation, merely substituting his own implementation provisions: These withheld the land strips from consideration as private property until after the war while making all sales, leases and inheritances of farmland contingent upon the approval of the civil administration (rather than German agricultural authorities).[44] Himmler forwarded Koch's complaint to Bormann on July thirteenth accompanied by his own "sharpest protest" against a measure he considered "potentially fatal (*lebensgefährlich*) to Germany's political situation today and for all her future."[45] Himmler, who had already locked horns with the *Wehrmacht* over land grants to *Ostruppen*,[46] took his objection to Hitler, who reportedly "grabbed his head and wondered aloud . . . at Rosenberg's lack of political instinct."[47]

The familiar pattern of *Ostpolitik* debate began to repeat when a Rosenberg-Koch meeting on July twelfth produced only a joint appeal for Hitler's judgment,[48] while Bormann advised Rosenberg that the Party Chancellery could not accept the implementation provisions as constituted.[49] Yet this time the substance of the issue proved unequal to the rhetoric it engendered, for it hinged on Koch's misrepresentation of Rosenberg's terms to include a "hereditary farm law more generous to Ukrainians than our own law is to Germans."[50] That this was not true became quickly apparent, as the RSHA and the SS-*Hauptamt* had drafted an alternative set of provisions by July twenty-seventh with only one major change (cancelling an article that protected peasants against foreclosure).[51] During the first week of August Himmler clarified his remaining questions, then authorized Berger to iron out the final details.[52]

Koch, however, would not let go of the issue. Recognizing that only minor differences distinguished the *OMi* from the SS version, he wrote the *Reichsführer* on September second that it must have been through "a misunderstanding" that Himmler had agreed to the measure, that the two of them should again unite in opposition and secure a decision from Hitler.[53] By this time even Bormann had abandoned his resistance, and on September twenty-fourth *Reichskanzlei* chief Hans Heinrich Lammers replied to Koch that he "wished to avoid involving the Führer in this matter" as everyone else concurred in the new provisions. In view of this, "and in the name of Reichsleiter Bormann," he therefore appealed to Koch to withdraw his opposition.[54] But Koch would not be budged and refused to promulgate the property declaration in the *Reichskommissariat* Ukraine, without which the measure was meaningless. One more appeal by Gottlob Berger in mid-October produced no change in the *Reichskommissar*'s attitude; but by then, as Riecke acknowledged, "the suitable moment had slipped away."[55]

Thus the property declaration of June 1943 became the only reform measure of this period to be approved, proclaimed and never enacted. Riecke understandably blamed Koch for this failure, though proper credit should be given here to the Red Army. The property declaration was not too little, but it was too late. Like the accelerated conversion of cooperatives it fell victim to Hitler's gamble at Kursk to regain the military initiative. The impression left with the native population, as Riecke acknowledged, could only be one of dishonesty.[56]

But if the declaration accomplished nothing more than its announcement, its protracted abortion marked a significant episode in National Socialist policy and politics. In this controversy Koch assumed the role of guardian of the *Lebensraum* dream, defying not only *Ostpolitik* reformers but such fellow colonialists as Riecke, Bormann, and Himmler as well. More than yet another example of successful insubordination, Koch's action demonstrated that even Hitler's approval of a measure could not always exact compliance, at least when the führer took little interest in the topic. The elements of pragmatic opportunism and internal competition so characteristic of National Socialist politics played no role here, where one *Gauleiter*'s ideological commitment overruled a consensus for moderation.

A final assessment of German agrarian reform efforts during the 1942/43 period must await additional research into the whole of German agricultural policy in the East. Some observations are in order, however, to establish the context for such an assessment. Germany's gains in foodstuffs from the occupied USSR never matched the Nazi leaders' inflated expectations, and could not even cover the requirements of the German Army in the East; the Reich's imports of Soviet barley under occupation attained its highest levels in 1942 with 120,468 tons, in contrast to nearly 700,000 tons imported in 1940 by commercial agreement.[57] Unlike the rest of occupied Europe, however, German exploitation of the Soviet economy suffered from the ebb and flow of military operations and the "scorched earth'' policies of retreating Soviets in 1941–42 and retreating Germans in 1943–44. Historians generally agree that the 1942–43 period was the only ''normal'' year of occupation for economic purposes.[58] The significance of the eight months from November 1942 through June 1943 in the collection and delivery of agricultural goods vis-à-vis the preceding fifteen and following nine months of occupation is illustrated in Table 2.

The data here do not reflect the true totals, omitting not only the additional *Wehrmacht* deliveries noted, but also the quantities procured by German soldiers and civilians on the black market.[59] The higher production for this period resulted largely from the investments of the *Zentralhandelsgesellschaft Ost* in farm machinery, fuels, chemicals, and breeding livestock.[60] In addition to the vital immediate food contributions to the German Army in Russia, the disproportionate shares of oilseeds (important as fats), poultry, and vegetables for export to the Reich indicate the potential economic value of sustained systematic exploitation. In the fulfillment of delivery quotas, the economic year 1942–43 surpassed the previous year's totals in every major category: grain (2.57 million tons vs. 1.64 million, with a fulfillment ratio of 89.2 percent vs. 80.0 percent), meats (259,000 tons vs. 261,700, but a higher percentage of fulfillment at 81.5 percent vs. 80.4 percent), lard (64,500 tons vs. 44,354, 82.2 percent vs. 73.8 percent), and fats (a lower ratio, 88.4 percent vs. 92.0 percent, but double the total, 184,500 tons against 81,919).[61]

As far as can be determined, the incomplete agrarian reform that occurred probably contributed little to this increased productivity. The significance rather lies in the determination to integrate the Ukrainian peasant into the exploitation of his own land. Just as the ZHO imported tractors to improve seeding and harvesting, so Riecke employed concessions to secure the collaboration of those needed to operate the machinery. With an expanded private plot for his own use, parceled farmland whose surplus crop he could dispose as he wished, and (but for Koch) legal title to the land, the Ukrainian farmer at last shared a material stake in the German system. For its part the Reich encouraged greater productivity and counteracted peasant dissatisfaction; though Riecke would doubtless have denied it, he had revised National Socialist agrarian policy to accommodate a traditional liberal reform.

Riecke perceived the first fruits of his policy in the 1943 autumn planting, ''the best in ten years,'' and eagerly anticipated a rich harvest in 1944.[62] The Red Army prevented the fulfillment of this prediction, but it also spared German authorities the future conflict inherent to their policy's contradictions. How, for example, could the reforms be reconciled with long-range German colonization? The inhabitants of the state farms and machine tractor stations remained condemned to vassalage, while the reservation of land on the cooperatives for German settlers raised the prospect of extreme tensions in the post-war staking of claims. Nor did the reforms redress the abuses committed by agricultural officials, which continued despite *Wi-Stab-Ost*'s directives to the contrary: the occasional transfer of a notorious offender hardly reflected just punishment to

Table 2

Production and Deliveries of Agricultural Goods in the Occupied USSR, 1941–1944 (in thousands of tons and percentages)

	Total Volume			Deliveries to Wehrmacht			Deliveries to Reich*		
	Aug.41–Oct.42	Nov.42–Jun.43	Jul.43–Mar.44	Aug.41–Oct.42	Nov.42–Jun.43	Jul.43–Mar.44	Aug.41–Oct.41	Nov.42–Jun.43	Jul.43–Mar.44
Grains	3813.9 47.7%	2639.8 28.8%	2698.2 29.5%	1429.9 35.3%	1499.4 37.0%	1120.7 27.7%	696.9 36.6%	173.7 9.9%	890.2 50.5%
Meats/Livestock	399.0 53.3%	251.6 33.6%	97.6 13.1%	231.9 56.3%	111.4 27.0%	68.6 16.7%	49.7 74.6%	12.0 18.0%	4.9 7.4%
Hay	646.5 25.8%	1082.7 43.2%	778.4 31.0%	501.3 27.6%	688.8 37.9%	626.4 34.5%	---- ----	---- ----	---- ----
Poultry	3.5 20.0%	10.4 59.8%	3.5 20.2%	2.8 35.5%	3.7 46.8%	1.4 17.1%	0.7 10.1%	5.2 78.8%	0.7 10.1%
Oilseeds	222.85 23.4%	552.3 58.0%	176.95 18.6%	5.3 25.6%	10.1 48.5%	5.4 25.9%	166.6 23.2%	414.1 57.6%	138.4 19.2%
Vegetables	77.7 19.8%	118.1 30.1%	196.7 50.1%	35.8 16.6%	45.3 21.0%	134.75 62.4%	0.45 45.8%	2.8 37.3%	1.25 16.9%

Source: Extracted from data in "Vierter Arbeitsbericht der Zentralhandelsgesellschaft Ost (Berichtszeit 1.11.1942 bis 30.6.1943)," Anlage 7, and "Fünfter Arbeitsbericht der Zentral-handelsgesellschaft Ost (Berichtszeit 1.7.1943 bis 31.3.1944)," Anlage 1, T-84/75/1362752-756, 1362827-833. Totals omit requisitions carried out directly by German military forces, esti-mated at an additional 20 percent of the Wehrmacht totals.
*Approximately 600,000 tons of grains shipped to the Reich were re-exported for use by the army in Russia.

his victims.[63] The efforts of Riecke and his staff to employ a pragmatic approach to achieve a visionary concept was probably doomed from the start; in his recognition of this Koch appears more a realist than Riecke. Agrarian reform, however, revealed a vulnerability of Nazi ideology to economic realities, a condition that would be tested in other aspects of German economic policy.

NOTES

1. See Brandt, et al., *Management*, pp. 57–58, 621–40; A. A. Annikeev, "Die marxistische Historiographie über die Agrarpolitik des deutschen Faschismus im Zweiten Weltkrieg," *Zeitschrift für Geschichtswissenschaft*, Vol. XXVI, no. 7 (1978): 629–34, and N. I. Sinizyna, W. R. Tomin, "Das Scheitern der faschistischen Agrarpolitik in den okkupierten Gebieten der UdSSR (1941–1944)," *Sowjetwissenschaft Gesellschaftswissenschaftliche Beiträge*, 1966, Heft 11 (November), pp. 1190–99.

2. "Zur Neugestaltung der Agrarordnung während der Übergangszeit: Entwurf in grossen Zügen, von Prof. Dr. Dr. M. Achmeteli [sic]," n.d. (receipt stamp dated June 17, 1941), T-77/344/1181863–1957.

3. See V. L. R. Grosskopf, "Sitzung im Aussenpolitischen Amt am 29. Mai 1941 über Ost-Fragen," T-120/270/339/198850–858; and V. A. A. beim AOK 17 Hptm. Pfleiderer, "Aufzeichnung," October 14, 1941, T-120/285/430/219049–058.

4. See Brandt, *Management*, pp. 93–101, 655–70, and Otto Schiller's *Ziele und Ergebnisse der Agrarordnung in den besetzten Ostgebieten* (Berlin: Reichsministerium für die besetzten Ostgebiete, 1943), passim; the merits of the "farm co-operative" are debated by Otto Schiller, "The Farming Co-operative: A New System of Farm Management," *Land Economics*, Vol. XXVII, no. 1 (February 1951): 1–15, and Karl Brandt, "Otto Schiller's 'Farming Cooperative': A Critical Appraisal," *Land Economics*, Vol. XXVII, no. 2 (May 1951): 102–07.

5. Interrogation of Hans-Joachim Riecke, July 25, 1945, War Department Historical Commission (Shuster Commission), RG 165, NA.

6. Dr. Kurt Schünemann, "Erfahrungsbericht: Agrarordnung," September 17, 1943, T-77/95/820624; and Prop. Staffel Taurien, "Bericht über mittelalterliche Gerichtsbarkeit des La-Führers Dienstmeier in Gawrilowka," June 30, 1943, EAP 99/158, MR 281, RG 242, NA.

7. M.V.O.R. Dr. Kurt Ketter, "Erfahrungsbericht: Agrarordnung," October 15, 1943, T-77/95/820515–519.

8. Wi In Nord, *Zwei Jahre Kriegswirtschaft im russischen Nordraum* (Pleskau: Wi In Nord, September 1, 1943), pp. 30–32.

9. See "Fünfter Arbeitsbericht der Zentral-Handelsgesellschaft Ost, Berichtszeit 1.7.1943 bis 31.3.1944," T-84/75/1362777–787.

10. Fleischhauer, *Dritte Reich*, pp. 179–82.

11. SS-Oberführer Meyer, "Vermerk über den Vortrag beim Reichsführer am 19.II.42 im Führerhauptquartier," February 23, 1942, Document NG-1118, RG 238, NA.

12. KTB des Wi-Stab-Ost, June 25, 1943, "Rückblick zum KTB der Chefgruppe La über das 1. Halbjahr 1943," T-77/1089/1205.

13. Riecke, "Umstellung der landwirtschaftlichen Erfassungs- and Steuerpolitik," July 10, 1943, T-77/594/1775821–827 and Sinizyna and Tomin, "Scheitern," p. 1196.

14. See Wi-Stab-Ost/I/Ic, "Auswirkungen der Banden," May 22, 1943, T-

77/1090/263–77, and Alexander Pronin, "Guerrilla Warfare in the German-occupied Soviet Territories 1941–1944" (unpublished Ph.D dissertation, Georgetown University, 1965), pp. 161–70.

15. M. V. R. Karl Keller, "Erfahrungsbericht: Arbeiterfragen," October 15, 1943, T-77/95/820521, and this writer's "Reckoning the Cost of People's War: The German Experience in the Central USSR," *Russian History*, Vol. IX, Pt. 1 (1982): 27–48.

16. Brandt, *Management*, p. 99; Lazar Volin, "The 'New Agrarian Order' in Nazi-invaded Russia," *Foreign Agriculture*, Vol. VII, no. 4 (April 1943), p. 83.

17. See Brandt, *Management*, pp. 57–58, 632–36.

18. "Stand der Bildung von Landbaugenossenschaften in der Ukraine (RKU u. Wi In Don-Donez) am 1.12.1942," T-77/1089/720. The breakdown was 1318 out of 16,193 (8.1 percent) in the RKU and 877 out of 11,463 (7.6 percent) in Economic Inspection South.

19. Wi-Stab-Ost, Chefgruppe La, "Niederschrift über die Besprechungen mit den KVVCh der Chefgruppe La," December 30, 1942, T-77/1089/410–12.

20. Paul Walter, "Vorschläge zur besseren Ausnutzung der besetzten Ostgebiete im Interesse unserer Kriegsführung," December 2, 1942, T-454/98/109–117, with additional correspondence on T-454/98/106–07, 118–27.

21. Leibbrandt to Meyer, "Behandlung der Landbevölkerung in den ehemals sowjetischen Gebieten," December 17, 1942, T454/93/155–58.

22. See Chapters 9 and 11, below.

23. Riecke to *Staatssekretär* Klopfer, July 19, 1943, T-175/20/2524296.

24. Kinkelin to Leibbrandt, "Stellungnahme zu der Vorlage der Chefgruppe Ernährung und Landwirtschaft," February 19, 1943, Folder R-361, ML 473, RG 242, NA.

25. Leibbrandt to Riecke, "Übertragung des Bodeneigentums an die einheimischen Bauern der besetzten Ostgebiete," March 11, 1944, T-454/93/76–78.

26. "Die gute Leistung wird belohnt," in *Deutsche Ukraine-Zeitung*, May 28, 1943, p. 3, and SD *Meldungen* Nr. 52, T-175/236/2725871.

27. Wi In Süd/Chefgruppe Landwirtschaft, "Chefgruppenbefehl Nr. 64: Durchführung der Agrarordnung im Jahre 1943," March 4, 1943, T-77/1104/1297–1304; "Richtlinien für die Durchführung der Grundsätze zur Agrarordnung im Jahre 1943 im Gebiet des RKU," T-454/93/000069–73.

28. Dallin, *German Rule*, p. 346.

29. Wi In Süd/Chefgruppe Landwirtschaft, "Durchführung der Agrarordnung," May 27, 1943, T-77/1105/561–62.

30. See Wirtschaftsstab Ost, Stab Abt. I./Id, "Die wirtschaftliche Lage in den besetzten Ostgebiete: Monatsbericht (1.4–30.4.1943)," May 17, 1943, T-77/1090/233; Riecke interrogation, July 25, 1945, RG 165, NA.

31. Wi In Süd/I/Id, "Lagebericht für Juli 1943," T-77/1106/000040.

32. RKU/E II b, "Zusammenstellung der im RKU-Gebiet vorhandenen Landbaugenossenschaften" (25.5.1943)," and "Stand der Landbaugenossenschaften," September 2, 1943, T-454/93/000045, 000010.

33. Otto Schiller, "Endgültige Abschaffung des Kolchossystems in der Ukraine," July 5, 1943, T-454/93/000003–005.

34. Maj. O. W. Müller, "Bericht Nr. 8/43," August 26, 1943, T454/102/811; Wi In Süd/Id, "Lagebericht für September 1943," T77/1106/127.

35. KTB Wi-Stab-Ost, February 15, 1943, T-77/1089/518.

36. Rosenberg to Hitler, April 24, 1943, T-454/100/426–29.

37. Mekarski, "Südostgebiete Polens," pp. 402–03.

38. Compare Brandt, *Management*, pp. 670–71, and Rosenberg to Hitler, T-454/100/428–29.

39. Wi-Stab-Ost, "Rückblick zum KTB der Chefgruppe Landwirtschaft über das 1. Halbjahr 1943," T-77/1089/1205.

40. Bräutigam, *So hat es*, p. 602.

41. Rosenberg to Sauckel, June 15, 1943, T-454/30/575.

42. Otto Schiller, "Vermerk über Eigentumserklärung," June 2, 1943, file EAP 99/1207, RG 242, NA.

43. See: Riecke, "Einführung des bäuerlichen Grundeigentums," June 3, 1943; "Entwurf: Richtlinien zur Durchführung der Proklamation," and Chefgruppe Landwirtschaft to Bräutigam, "Durchführungsbestimmungen," July 13, 1943, all in file EAP 99/158, MR 281, RG 242, NA.

44. Koch to Himmler, July 6, 1943, and accompanying "Vorschlag des Reichskommissars betr. Durchführungsbestimmungen," T-175/20/2524319–336.

45. Himmler to Bormann, July 13, 1943, T-175/20/2524317.

46. See below, Chapter 11.

47. Dr. Kinkelin, "Vermerk," July 19, 1943, file EAP 99/1218, RG 242, NA.

48. "Materialsammlung zur Geschichte Wi-Stab-Ost," p. 279, Document 3013-PS (Weizsäcker Pros. Exhibit 1060), RG 238, NA (hereafter "Materialsammlung").

49. Ibid., and Ostministerium Hauptabteilung I, "Vermerk" July 22, 1943, file EAP 99/158, MR 281, RG 242, NA.

50. Koch to Himmler, July 6, 1943, T-175/20/2524319, and Kinkelin "Vermerk," file EAP 99/1218.

51. Berger to Himmler, "Ausführungsbestimmungen," July 28, 1943 (with accompanying appendices), T-175/20/2524282–288.

52. "Materialsammlung," RG 238, NA.

53. Koch to Himmler, September 2, 1943, T-175/20/2524278–280.

54. Lammers to Koch, "Durchführung der Deklaration über das landwirtschaftliche Grundeigentum," September 24, 1943 T-175/20/2524255–268.

55. Berger-Koch exchange, October 14 and 19, 1943, T-175/20/2524248–249; "Materialsammlung," RG 238, NA.

56. "Materialsammlung," RG 238, NA.

57. See the discussion in Brandt, *Management*, pp. 145–49, and "Die kriegswirtschaftliche Beitrag Osteuropas," pp. 25–29, T-84/72/135869–702.

58. Brandt, *Management*, p. 148, Dallin, *German Rule*, p. 369.

59. See Chapters 2 and 11, this volume.

60. See Brandt, *Management*, pp. 142–43.

61. See Müller, *Besatzungspolitik*, pp. 264–65, and Dallin, *German Rule*, pp. 373–75.

62. Riecke interrogation, July 25, 1945, RG 165, NA.

63. See, for example, Hauptabteilung II (von Allwörden) to Rosenberg, September 10, 1943, and Koch to Rosenberg, September 22, 1943, EAP 99/158, MR 281, RG 24, NA.

8

GERMAN ECONOMIC POLICY: THE EXPLOITATION OF SOVIET RAW MATERIALS AND LABOR

Agrarian reform offered but one example of the conflicting currents within German economic policy during the first half of 1943. The *Blitzkrieg* goals of maximum immediate exploitation, dismantlement of the Soviet industrial base and eventual colonization were superseded, though not abandoned, by the necessity of mobilizing the occupied industrial economy for a protracted global conflict.[1] German authorities clashed over economic priorities and the political desirability of increased native cooperation while German private industry staked out its own claims in the East. In the absence of any coordinated policy, reform in the economic sphere fragmented into specific efforts within limited areas, where improved treatment was directly linked to increased productivity.

Only one effort at a general economic reform appears to have been attempted. In January 1943 the *Ostministerium*'s Dr. Otto Kinkelin urged political reform through economic policy in a proposal to Goering, arguing for improvements in the recruitment and treatment of *Ostarbeiter*, acceleration of the agrarian reform, and increased food rations for the population. Though these suggestions were endorsed by Paul Körner, Goering's own state secretary of the *Vierjahresplan*, the *Reichsmarschall* categorically rejected any program of economic concessions on April 28, 1943. Goering got no further with his own plans, however, to consolidate his control of the industrial economy. Throughout this period Goering sought to establish a "Central Planning East" directorate under Paul Pleiger, director general of the Mining and Smelting Corporation East (*Berg- und Hüttenwerksgesellschaft Ost* or BHO) and chairman of the managing board of the *Herman-Goering-Werke*, but the plan foundered without the approval of all the many authorities involved.[2]

THE ROLE OF GERMAN INDUSTRY

In the autumn of 1942 the role of German private industry in the economic exploitation of the occupied USSR was in the process of expansion. Supported by Speer, German firms assumed increasing responsibility for the reconstruction of industrial facilities destroyed in combat or by Soviet "scorched earth" measures. The key region was the rich Donetz basin in southeastern Ukraine, where valuable resources of coal, iron ore, and manganese figured prominently in the battle of production, while the establishment of munitions plants in the area (the "Iwan-Programm") supplied the *Wehrmacht* with ammunition at a fraction of the transportation costs and delays involved in shipping the same material from Germany. Economic planners still held fast to their original position that the post-war economy in the East belonged to the colonizer-veteran, but Goering assured industrialists "they may, however, be confident that they will receive preference later."[3]

Though the monopoly corporations opened the door to German private enterprise, they could not always guarantee a profit. During the peak of its activity the Central Trade Corporation East (ZHO) included participation by some 250 German food and agricultural businesses, most of them small- to medium-sized firms, but their interest waned as difficulties increased.[4] The prospects were far better for the industrial giants, who could challenge or circumvent the monopoly corporations when necessary. I. G. Farben, for example, won from the Reich Economics Ministry the exclusive right to Soviet manufacturing methods in the production of synthetic rubber.[5] The BHO allowed German firms to stake claims to specific plants through the device of "sponsorship": the Krupp concern, whose ambitious plans in the East were known to their rivals,[6] thus assumed control of the Asov Steelworks in Mariupol.[7]

The occupied population had no illusions as to the motives of German business. In Estonia, where the owners and shareholders of banks and department stores found they could not recover their former property, the German business abbreviation "GmbH" ("*Gesellschaft mit beschränkter Haftung*," company with limited liability) was commonly translated as "Greift mit beiden Händen!" ("Grab with both hands!").[8] The reciprocal perspective of German business was expressed by an I. G. Farben official who, after completing a tour of the occupied East in December 1942, remarked that "the Russians . . . if they are no longer under the influence of the Jews and the Commissars, are to be considered big children."[9] No less important was the antagonistic attitude of business executives toward any attempted regulation by the Reich, as expressed by one BHO official: "We had to defend ourselves in the Ukraine against the effects of a governmental planned economy, part civilian, part military, and always keep before our minds the ultimate purpose of the BHO,"[10] apparently referring to the reservation of Soviet industrial facilities to German industrialists.

And, on the basis of war production, German business could justify its claim. The evacuation of machinery and devastation left behind by the retreating Soviets

Table 3
Output of Raw Materials in the Donetz Region, 1942–1943 (in thousands of tons)

	Month	Bituminous Coal	Manganese Ore	Iron Ore
1942	October	240	94	--
	November	306	88	--
	December	392	95	--
1943	January	424	79	--
	February	182	79	--
	March	256	103	--
	April	250	107	9
	May	305	121	27
	June	394	125	73
	July	456	138	117

Source: Wi-Stab-Ost/Stab. Abt. I/Ic,
"Monatsbericht Wi Stab Ost vom. 1.-31.7.1943,"
T77/1090/814-16.

required a massive reconstruction effort (the BHO spent RM 25 million on machinery and equipment for the Donetz coal mines alone through 1942) that only began to bear fruit in the second year of occupation (by December 1942 electric power facilities in the Donetz region operated at only 5 percent of their prewar capacity).[11] The results, then, began to show: coal output rose from 6000 tons in February 1942 to 60,000 tons three months later and 90,000 tons in August.[12] Except for a late winter interruption caused by the Soviet advance, production in the Donetz accelerated significantly throughout the period October 1942–July 1943 (see Table 3).

In the case of manganese, the quantities yielded by Nikopol proved of immediate strategic value: Soviet manganese ore supplied 40 percent of the total German consumption from July–December 1941, rising to 126.6 percent for the second half of 1942 and 112.7 percent for the first six months of 1943.[13] More significant was the potential for the future, with the restoration of the great hydroelectric dam at Zaporozh'e on the Dnepr River on January 6, 1943.[14] Economic experts anticipated monthly coal production in the Donetz basin to rise to 900,000 tons per month by the end of 1943 and 1.5 million tons per month one year later.[15]

Though these anticipated gains were never attained, the significance of the actual contributions for the Eastern Front exceeded their numbers. The coal of the Donetz basin cut down enormously on the fuel costs involved in supplying the *Wehrmacht* in Russia: to ship a thousand tons of coal from Upper Silesia to Rostov by rail required the expenditure of an additional 500 tons.[16] By summer 1943 German railway traffic in the East depended on Ukrainian coal for 30 percent of its fuel supply.[17] Above all, coal production furnished the foundation for other heavy industries of immediate value to the German war effort. Iron and steel works in the Ukraine were producing six thousand tons monthly by July 1943, and the munitions factories scheduled to begin production under the "Iwan-Programm" in September 1943 were expected to provide over a million rounds of artillery ammunition monthly by the end of 1944—more than half of the requirements for the German Army in Russia.[18]

The Donetz was not the only economically valuable area for German business. In Estonia the *Baltische Öl GmbH*, a subsidiary of the monopoly corporation *Kontinentale Öl A.G.*, assumed control of the shale-oil industry, important especially as a source of fuel oil for the German Navy. From a monthly level of 20,000 tons in November 1941 production rose to an average of nearly 125,000 tons from July to September 1943; peak productivity was attained in December (140,000 tons) before Soviet advances forced the evacuation of the easternmost plants.[19]

The growing economic power of German industry in the East implied an increasing political influence that offered some advantages to over 60,000 inhabitants employed by the BHO at the end of 1942.[20] Backed by Reich Armaments Minister Speer, the BHO secured in spring 1943 the exemption of its workers from the labor drafts of the army and *GBA* Sauckel.[21] In February 1943, when the Gestapo arrested the Russian engineers and department chiefs of a bridge construction plant at Stalino, the plant management and the BHO arranged their release within eight days. An SD officer's attempt to establish a security position for himself at the Makeyevka foundry was foiled by the company management.[22]

Confronted with a labor shortage, the BHO undertook a number of employee-welfare measures usually linked to higher productivity. Pleiger tried to supplement native workers' food rations by the establishment of factory canteens and the allocation of garden plots of 500 to 2000 square meters (depending on family size) for the growing of vegetables.[23] An improvised bonus system distributed clothing, shoes, furniture, and wristwatches to employees.[24] By the end of June 1943 a premium system had been instituted throughout the BHO that rewarded performance with cash payments of up to one *Reichsmark* per worker per day, and more commonly, extra rations of tobacco, food, and beer.[25] On August 1, 1943 the BHO introduced a general health and accident insurance program for employees, together with a provision for the granting of paid leave (six workdays for all employees with at least one year's experience, up to 12 days' leave for employees with high performance ratings).[26]

But none of these "benefits" altered German industry's basic exploitation of Soviet labor. The BHO's own directors provided a measure of this exploitation during a conference on March 31, 1943 when they acknowledged that a Russian miner worked at about 50 to 60 percent of the capacity of his German counterpart, yet received only one-eighth of the latter's wages.[27] In an article published in the *Breslauer Neuester Nachrichten* on August 27, 1943 a German journalist defended concessions to Russian workers with a guarded criticism of German policy. After touring the Donetz area the writer reported that workers' wages and food rations were far too low: "These were no conditions upon which reasonable living conditions and thus in turn work or economy can be built." This accompanied a favorable portrait of Ukrainian workers as clean, hard-working, and capable of bearing "any severity but who appreciate fair treatment and justice above all."[28] That such concessions had to be justified in a controlled press underscores the exploitative nature of the relationship between German business and Russian labor.

Insufficient data precludes any firm conclusions as to employee morale or productivity under the BHO. The concessions described above have been termed "a greater success than expected," to which the higher coal production in autumn 1942 can be seen as a "direct response" by native labor.[29] The reconstruction of the Donetz industrial economy alone has been interpreted as a stabilizing factor of occupation, undercutting support for Soviet partisans and buttressing Ukrainian nationalism.[30] Some employees did choose to accompany the Germans in retreat and relocated to other factories in Germany; others engaged in outright sabotage of industrial equipment.[31] The *Wirtschaftsinspektion Süd* reported in February 1943 the widespread growth of passive resistance, resulting in an absentee rate of 30 to 40 percent among the personnel employed in Stalino's factories.[32] What is indisputable, however, is that during its brief history the BHO provided the German war effort valuable raw materials and offered German business a tremendous opportunity for the future, all at minimal cost in consideration for its workers. In this, German industry matched the exploitation of Russian coal in the Donetz with the exploitation of Russian labor in the Reich.

THE *OSTARBEITER*[33]

Even before Germany's conversion to a total war footing, economic authorities recruited Russian miners for work in the Ruhr coal mines. The first mass use of Eastern labor in Germany in early 1942 still relied upon volunteers, but with Fritz Sauckel's appointment as "Plenipotentiary General for Labor Allocation" (GBA) in late March 1942, conscription by force became the rule. In Kiev, for example, all unemployed able-bodied inhabitants in a cordoned-off district were rounded up in September 1942. By July 10, 1942 *Ostarbeiter* comprised 697,000 of the 3,159,000 foreign workers in the Reich, an increase of 170 percent over the number employed less than two months before.[34] But the costs were considerable in the disastrous political effects of labor conscription among the occupied population.

Sauckel, another old party member and *Gauleiter* (Thuringia) considered by Goebbels as "one of the dullest of the dull," possessed no special qualifications for his task and could not himself explain his selection after the war.[35] In the autumn of 1942 Hitler strengthened his authority with the ability to issue orders directly to civil and military administrations and appoint delegates to ensure compliance.[36] Yet to exercise this power Sauckel had to rely upon a patchwork of borrowed offices and informal alliances. For field personnel Sauckel drew on the Reich Ministry of Labor, while the administrative superstructure was supplied by the *Ostministerium*'s labor department. Transportation of the *Ostarbeiter* to the Reich fell under the jurisdiction of the *Reichsbahn*, the official railway authority; security remained the province of the SS and police; and the feeding and general treatment of the workers was shared by the Ministry of Agriculture, the Nazi party Labor Front, and private industry.[37] Concealed behind this jumble of authorities was the growing power of Armaments Minister Speer, who cooperated closely with Sauckel to assure a full labor supply for German armaments.[38]

The confused division of bureaucratic responsibilities, Sauckel's determination to meet his quotas at all cost and the early prevalence of the *Untermensch* mentality among many Germans combined to create atrocious conditions for the *Ostarbeiter* from the moment of conscription through every day's work in Germany. Throughout the autumn of 1942 criticism mounted on these issues in official circles. The *Ostministerium*'s "Central Office for Members of Eastern Nationalities," one of the very few organs that permitted even a minimal representation of popular grievances, catalogued the errors of German policy in a lengthy memorandum of September thirtieth: indiscriminate manhunts to meet quotas, separation of families, poor food, inadequate clothing and housing, low pay and demeaning treatment, not to mention complete disregard for matching workers' skills with job selection and the conscription of tens of thousands unfit for labor who could only be shipped back.[39] In October German Army field officers and the OKW/WPr propaganda staff also warned the civil administration that the use of slave labor carried potentially disastrous consequences, that "before everything, the treatment of the *Ostarbeiter* in the Reich is decisive."[40]

Even as these protests were made, Sauckel notified Rosenberg and Koch of the new labor quotas for the RKU of 225,000 by December 1, 1942 and another 225,000 by May 1, 1943.[41] Rosenberg himself now began to argue the eastern workers' plight at a Labor Front conference in November, when he criticized the transportation and food provided the *Ostarbeiter*.[42] On December twenty-first Rosenberg wrote the GBA on behalf of improved medical facilities and against the use of indiscriminate force in recruiting labor.[43]

Sauckel, apparently sensitive to these criticisms, defended himself before a meeting of his labor recruitment staffs in Weimar on January 6, 1943. The GBA issued a double standard for his subordinates: workers must be accorded humane and correct treatment after their arrival in Germany ("I will not tolerate men being treated badly"), but procuring more labor for Germany remained the "iron law" for 1943 ("We shall lay aside the last scraps of our sentimental humanitarianism").[44] Sauckel thereby fixed the dual emphasis of *Ostarbeiter* policy in 1943, improved treatment on the job and accelerated exploitation of manpower in Russia.

The labor press-gangs implemented Sauckel's directives in full accordance with the desired spirit. Incidents such as the rounding-up of a crowd as it exited a movie theater united even the army and *Reichsführer* Himmler in protest.[45] As spring approached, Sauckel cast about for still more workers. On March seventeenth, less than two weeks after Hitler expanded this power with direct authority over regional labor offices and the formal annexation of the *Ostministerium's* labor department,[46] Sauckel notified Rosenberg of the need to draft 1 million more *Ostarbeiter* over the next four months.[47]

Several of the army commanders balked at the new directive. Army Group A's Field Marshal von Kleist openly challenged Sauckel by prohibiting all but voluntary recruitment of *Ostarbeiter* in his sector.[48] At the same time General Erich Friederici, in command of the Army Group South Rear Area, issued the same prohibition on the grounds that the inhabitants were more urgently needed for constructing field fortifications and roads for the army.[49] Sauckel protested directly to Hitler on March tenth as the *Wi-Stab-Ost* countermanded von Kleist and directed full compliance with the GBA's quotas.[50]

Yet the army successfully evaded or ignored this task. Though individual armies and corps dutifully ordered the evacuation of whole populations to the Reich for labor, the *Wehrmacht* allocated itself first priority in labor duties.[51] For the first quarter of 1943 only 27,375 *Ostarbeiter* traveled to Germany from the military areas. This total increased to about 65,000 for the next quarter, but still fell far below Sauckel's quotas (23,875 instead of the required 90,000 for May 1943) and those furnished by the *Reichskommissariate* (23,875 vs. 109,919 for May 1943). Even during the strategic retreats of July–September 1943 the army supplied only 50,337 of the 232,762 *Ostarbeiter* procured for that period.[52] In contrast, the *Wi-Stab-Ost* reported over 8.2 million Russian civilians employed in the military government areas for the first half of 1943.[53]

The Baltic states also evaded the worst of Sauckel's demands. When the GBA visited Riga in April 1943 he announced a labor quota of 183,000 for the *Reichskommissariat* Ostland over the next four months, disproportionately allocated among "White Russia" (130,000), Lithuania (40,000), Latvia (10,000) and Estonia (3000), the latter limited to female labor to facilitate recruitment for the SS Baltic legions.[54] But a combination of partisan disruption, transportation difficulties and official recalcitrance produced a total of only 63,599 workers for the entire period of January 1–November 30, 1943.[55]

The difference was partially compensated in slave labor from the *Reichskommissariat* Ukraine. Rosenberg complained to Sauckel on several occasions about the press-gang methods used in recruitment, but the GBA's expanded authority allowed him to bypass the eastern minister.[56] When Sauckel raised the issue himself with *Reichskommissar* Koch he was brusquely told, "I am willing to supply labor to you. How I do that is none of your business, and I don't want to be advised about it."[57] Supply bodies Koch certainly did, over 1.5 million in the course of the occupation; every household in the Ukraine experienced the loss of family or friends to the press-gangs. Worst hit were the cities: *Generalbezirk* Kiev lost 440,000 workers to Germany out of a population of 4.5 million by summer 1943, sparking protests by SD officers that new labor demands in July jeopardized the collection of the harvest.[58]

As a result, Sauckel secured 291,214 Eastern workers for the first six months of 1943, the largest contribution of any German-occupied or allied country to the German war industry.[59] But if labor requirements precluded a reform of recruiting methods, material improvements in the treatment of the *Ostarbeiter* in Germany assumed growing significance for German officials. An investigation commissioned by Sauckel in December 1942 revealed that far too little attention was being paid to *Ostarbeiter* welfare, with direct implications for work productivity.[60]

By summer 1943 some 1.7 million *Ostarbeiter* (more than one of every four foreign workers in the Reich) were laboring on German farms and in German factories.[61] Wages followed a series of guidelines issued June 30, 1942 that minimized purchasing power and protected German workers from competition: the labor that earned a German worker 3.50 RM per day provided an *Ostarbeiter* 2.30 RM, of which 1.50 was deducted to cover the cost of his room and board, while his German employer paid a tax of 1.10 RM for the same work (to discourage business from a tempting reliance on cheaper labor). Averaging 12 RM per month, the eastern worker received neither fringe benefits, paid leave, overtime, nor access to his pay accounts, but his employer could deduct from his pay the costs of clothing provided him and transportation to and from work.[62] The *Ostarbeiter* received smaller food rations than other foreign workers, wore degrading "Ost" badges over their breasts, and could not fraternize with Germans or other foreign workers after hours.[63]

The increased numbers of *Ostarbeiter* aggravated the poor housing and sanitary conditions common to the work camps. The senior German doctor responsible for Krupp's camps in Essen later described how 1200 workers were crowded into an old school with only ten children's toilets available, and how tuberculosis, malnutrition, and skin disease were so common as to reduce medical treatment to only the worst cases. These conditions deteriorated even more in the spring of 1943 with increased Allied bombing.[64] Deaths among the *Ostarbeiter*, primarily to tuberculosis, averaged 1268 per month through the first nine months of 1943.[65]

Yet despite this treatment they astonished their masters with a high rate of production. By mid-April 1943 Sauckel's own studies of this question had concluded that the *Ostarbeiter* averaged 80 percent of the productivity of their German counterparts, persuading the GBA to increase the measures already underway to improve their condition.[66] A subsequent study by the German Labor Front similarly linked productivity to material improvements and increased self-responsibility on behalf of the *Ostarbeiter*.[67]

The economic motive thus provided a strong incentive for improvement. This, however, cannot be seen as the only force for change in German policy. The prolonged contact between Germans and Russians in the factories and on the farms had done much to overcome Nazi ideology. In its surveys of German public opinion in mid-April 1943, the SD reported that the *Ostarbeiter* had impressed Germans with their religious beliefs, technical know-how, literacy, personal morality and willingness to work not based on punishment, attributes that contradicted the propaganda image of the Russian *Untermensch*.[68] The evidence moreover suggests that the *Ostarbeiter* developed a favorable attitude toward their German co-workers, at least in comparison with French and Italian workers in Germany.[69] Recognition of these attitudes contributed to the revision of policy.

Propaganda Minister Goebbels signaled the change in his decree of February 15, 1943 to the *Gauleiters*, calling for greater consideration of the eastern peoples.[70] On March tenth Goebbels addressed representatives of the various Reich ministries with a program for raising *Ostarbeiter* living standards: food rations to be raised to the same level as other workers, wages to be increased on a par with Polish workers, and physical mistreatment of workers to be banned. The last point, however, was vetoed by Sauckel's and Himmler's representatives, revealing the central problem of concurrence on any attempted reform for the eastern workers.[71] The subject of a follow-up conference on March twenty-seventh was the necessary reeducation of German supervisors in all fields, followed shortly thereafter by the distribution of several pamphlets and handbooks throughout the Reich.[72]

In the area of wages and compensation, Sauckel did attempt to improve the situation. On March 30, 1943 he met with representatives from the ministries and the Nazi party to propose more humane treatment of eastern workers, though noting that it was not yet possible to raise their pay to that of Polish laborers.[73] That same day the Reich Labor Ministry finally issued an *Ostarbeiter* accident insurance program (none had applied previously), but which paid injured workers and survivors only benefits, not pensions, and left all determinations to Reich authorities for qualification.[74] On April fifth Sauckel released a new set of regulations on wages that lowered withholding taxes and permitted (but did not require) German businesses to pay bonuses for outstanding work and lower deductions for room and board.[75] The ensuing adjustments of wage scales could improve earnings by as much as one-third: in June 1943 the same *Ostarbeiter* who was paid 2.30 RM per day previously found his daily wage raised to 2.94 RM, of which he actually received 1.14 RM (vs. 0.80 RM prior to April).[76] Sauckel expanded this on July twenty-third with a provision that rewarded excellent performance with a rebate of 20 percent of an eastern worker's tax withholdings for the first year's employment and 30 percent for two years' performance.[77]

Simultaneously the Nazi party Chancellery, the Propaganda Ministry and the RSHA approved a memorandum for party leaders on the *Ostarbeiter* question, dispatched by Bormann on May 5, 1943. The directive forbade physical abuse and insisted upon improved food rations, sanitary living conditions, adequate clothing and increased recreational opportunities as binding for future policy.[78] In June, Sauckel and the German Labor Front established a central inspection agency for *Ostarbeiter* facilities in the Reich, empowered to correct conditions on the spot.[79] The next month Sauckel finally determined that eastern workers were entitled to ten-day vacations within Germany for those in their second year of labor service and 14-day leaves for those in their third year.[80]

The changes in *Ostarbeiter* policy 1943 marked not only a significant improvement, but a transition from colonial slavery to conventional industrial exploitation of labor. Yet even the new measures suffered from a reliance upon wartime conditions (Allied bombing greatly impeded the construction of adequate housing) and the goodwill of German employers.[81] Ironically, measurable changes in wages and benefits did not carry over into the symbols of bondage. Goebbels' efforts to abandon the use of the ''Ost'' badge for eastern workers failed against opposition from Himmler and the leadership of the National Socialist Women's Organization, apparently concerned at the prospect of increased fraternization.[82] The *Ostarbeiter* were denied the protection of the law and equal status with all other foreign workers.

Ostarbeiter productivity nevertheless remained high. A 1944 study by Speer's ministry concluded that Russian men worked at 60 to 80 percent capacity of their German counterparts—higher than that for the Italians, Dutch, Danish, and Balkan nationalities—while Russian women rated the highest of all foreign labor at 90 to 100 percent.[83] The improvements initiated in 1943 may have contributed to this, though the extent cannot be known. The extension of employee welfare, however, fell far short of agrarian reform or self-government as it sought only to ameliorate a policy whose exploitative character was unquestioned. ''Medieval coercive measures,'' as described by critical German officers, continued as the standard of labor recruitment in the East through the autumn of 1943.[84] The *Ostarbeiter* played a major role in the growth of the German war economy from 1942 to 1945, but at an incalculable political cost in the attitudes of the occupied population; in this they represented the price paid by economic mobilization at the expense of *Ostpolitik* reform.

GERMAN ECONOMIC POLICY IN RUSSIA, 1942–43: AN ASSESSMENT

Historians have judged German economic policy in the USSR a failure, with the total contribution of the region to the German war effort amounting to only one-seventh that of occupied France.[85] Though such a comparison overlooks several factors (duration of occupation, disruption caused by concurrent military operations in the East, and above all the costs necessitated by the total reconstruction of the Soviet industrial economy), the conclusion may be valid as a summary assessment. It is inapplicable, however, to the first half of 1943. The gains in agricultural productivity have already been discussed. Most significant, the efforts of German business in the restoration of industrial productivity were just beginning to pay off. The production of key raw materials, after a period of gradual increases, hit high gear in the first quarter of 1943. (See Table 4.)

Table 4

Production of Key Raw Materials in the Occupied USSR, July 1941–April 1943

Raw Material	Production (tons) Jul 41–Dec 42		Production (tons) Jan–April 43	
	Total	Per Month	Total	Per Month
Bituminous coal	1,770,000	98,333	1,108,750	277,187
Brown Coal	280,000	1556	137,697	34,424
Iron ore	0	--	8672	2168
Mineral Salt	43,260	2403	19,571	4893
Shale oil	54,000	3000	27,268	6817
Manganese ore	642,000	3567	366,359	91,590
Phosphorite	3000	167	4560	1140
Mercury	35	2	307	77

Source: Wi-Stab-Ost/Chefgruppe W, "Produktionsstatistik: Erzeugung wichtiger industrieller Rohstoffe und Fertigwaren in den besetzten Ostgebieten," June 17, 1943, T-77/1089/1295-96.

To the growing production in raw materials and foodstuffs must be added the labor contributions of the *Ostarbeiter*, whether on the assembly lines or in jobs that freed German males for military service. The German achievement in economic mobilization for this period was extraordinary: using as a base January–February 1942 = 100, the index of armaments production rose to 182 by January 1943 and to 232 in May, the highest monthly total to that point in the war. Production of tanks rose from an index of 210 in March to 289 in April and 465 in May, increases that were never matched.[86] This provided Hitler the armor necessary to launch his all-out offensive at Kursk in July. Moreover, the reliance on slave labor freed roughly 1 million German workers for military service during the first half of 1943.[87] Mobilization's successes also allowed the regime to again postpone changes in social policy, maintaining consumer goods production and keeping more German women in the home instead of at the factory.[88]

"Total war" mobilization, however, exacted a price. In the East, German economic policy in 1942–43 signified the integration of Soviet natural and manpower resources into the German industrial economy—a more moderate process than Hitler's planned depopulation of Soviet cities, but which equally undermined *Ostpolitik* reform through the use of slave labor and German control of Soviet industry. In the context of this increasingly profitable economic policy, reform served as the handmaiden to exploitation: denunciations of press-gang excesses did not question labor recruitment needs, while material concessions were enacted to boost productivity. The silence of German officials on reform of *Ostpolitik*'s economic foundation derived from a shared assumption of German domination. Any post-war settlement favorable to the Axis would have reflected this reality and so determined the basis of any future eastern policy.

Yet in its immediate significance economic mobilization provided the means by which Germany rebuilt her strategic reserves in the aftermath of Stalingrad. Through a more rational and systematic exploitation of Soviet resources, Germany significantly increased industrial production in the occupied areas and simultaneously expanded the use of eastern labor in German factories and on German farms. The integration of Soviet agriculture, industry and labor within the German war economy thus paid handsome dividends in the first half of 1943. The implications of this development for a *Lebensraum*-oriented vision of the future eastern territories do not appear to have been considered, perhaps out of recognition of their essential incompatibility. Germany would have no future in Russia, however, until she at least mastered the areas she already occupied; and the German Army had already learned that brute force was not enough in the lands under its control.

NOTES

1. For an example of what can be done in this field, see Alan S. Milward, *The New Order and the French Economy* (Oxford: Oxford University Press, 1970).

2. See the author's "The Politics of Illusion and Empire: The Attempts to Reform German Occupation Policy in the U.S.S.R., Autumn 1942–Summer 1943" (unpublished Ph.D. dissertation, University of Maryland, 1985), pp. 231–35.

3. See Gibbons, "Soviet Industry," pp. 155–73; compare Goering's views safeguarding veterans' future rights in Müller, *Besatzungspolitik*, pp. 250–54, and his decree of November 2, 1942, "Wirtschaftseinsatz Ost," Document NI–6732, *NMT*, VIII, 280–82.

4. Köller, "Zur Rolle," in *Der deutsche Imperialismus*, Bd. 4, pp. 23–42.

5. Otto Ambros, I. G. Farben A. G. to the Reich Ministry of Economics, July 3, 1942, Document NI–4971, *NMT*, VIII, 282–84.

6. See Dr. Küttner, "Notiz für Herrn Flick: Expansionsbestrebungen der Firma Krupp," June 26, 1942, Document NI–3101, RG 238, NA.

7. See Dietrich Eichholtz, *Geschichte der deutschen Kriegswirtschaft 1939–1945*, Bd. II (Berlin: Akademie-Verlag, 1985), pp. 466–68.

8. Oskar Angelus, "Denkschrift," March 15, 1943, BA: R 6/76.

9. Dr. Gerhard Fuerst, Report of lecture tour at the Eastern Front, December 1942, Document NI-8995, *NMT*, VIII, 505.

10. Affidavit of Dr. Heinrich Kuhlmann, June 11, 1948, Pleiger Defense Exhibit 211, RG 238, NA.

11. "Extract from the Report on the Activities of the Berg- und Hüttenwerksgesellschaft Ost m.b.H. for the year 1942," Document NI-4332, RG 238, NA.

12. Riedel, *Eisen and Kohle*, pp. 320–21.

13. Jörg-Johannes Jäger, *Die wirtschaftliche Abhängigkeit des Dritten Reiches vom Ausland* (Berlin: Berlin Verlag, 1969), p. 205.

14. "Materialsammlung zur Geschichte Wi-Stab-Ost," pp. 177–76, Document 3013-PS, RG 238, NA.

15. V.O./"W" Stab to Wi-Stab-Ost/ChefQu, August 19, 1943, T-77/1090/1024.

16. Pleiger testimony of April 21, 1948, *U.S.A.* vs. *Krupp et al.*, Eng. transcript, p. 5675, RG 238, NA.

17. V.O./"W" Stab to Wi-Stab-Ost/ChefQu, August 19, 1943, T-77/1090/1024.

18. Ibid., T-77/1090/1025, and Wi-Stab-Ost/Abt. Rü, "Beitrag zum KTB für die Zeit vom 10.–17.9.1943," September 17, 1943, T-77/1090/586.

19. See Czollek, *Faschismus*, pp. 94–102; KTB Min. Öl.Kdo. Estland/Gruppe "W," "Rückblick," October 8, 1943, T-77/690/1899311.

20. Riedel, *Eisen*, p. 321.

21. See Willi A. Boelcke, ed., *Deutschlands Rüstung im Zweiten Weltkrieg: Hitlers Konferenzen mit Albert Speer 1942–1945* (Frankfurt am Main: Akademische Verlagsgesellschaft Athenaion, 1969), pp. 99, 135, 243–44, 256.

22. Affidavits of Richard Smieja, June 24, 1948, and Gerhard Schypulla, April 10, 1948, Pleiger Defense Exhibits 248 and 227, RG 238, NA.

23. Riedel, *Eisen*, pp. 318–19; Artur Schildkötter, "Commercial Report of the Asov-Works, Mariupol," January 15, 1944, Pleiger Defense Exhibit 222, RG 238, NA.

24. Riedel, pp. 319–20.

25. "Ergebnisse der 42. Sitzung der Zentralen Planung am 23. Juni 1943, 16 Uhr," T-83/76/3447858–859.

26. Schildkötter, "Commercial Report," Pleiger Defense Exhibit 222, RG 238, NA.

27. Der Vorsitzende des Verwaltungsrats der B.H.O., "Protokoll über die Verwaltungsratsitzung der Berg- und Hüttenwerksgesellschaft Ost m.b.H. unter dem Vorsitz des Herrn Staatssekretär Körner am 31.3.1943 um 16.00 Uhr," Document NI-5261, RG 238, NA.

28. "General Conditions in the Ukraine in the Third Quarter of 1943 as Reflected in the German-controlled Press," February 10, 1944, file 860E.00/179, RG 59, NA.

29. Gerber, *Staatliche Wirtschaftslenkung*, p. 131; Brandt, *Management*, p. 126.

30. See Gibbons, "Soviet Industry," p. 196.

31. Compare Schypulla affidavit, Pleiger Defense Exhibit 227, RG 238, NA, and *IVOVSS*, III, pp. 482–86.

32. "Lagebericht Wi In Süd, Februar 1943," T-77/1105/000080.

33. The standard works remain Homze, *Foreign Labor*, and Hans Pfahlmann, *Fremdarbeiter und Kriegsgefangene in der deutschen Kriegswirtschaft 1939–1945* (Darmstadt: Wehr und Wissen Verlagsgesellschaft m.b.H., 1968).

34. Pfahlmann, *Fremdarbeiter*, pp. 44–52, 131–35. The *Ostarbeiter* total excludes 30,000 workers from the Baltic states and 119,000 Ukrainians from Galicia in the Government-General.

35. Goebbels, *Diaries*, p. 325; Sauckel testimony, *TMWC*, XIV, 618.

36. "Erlass des Führers zur Durchführung des Erlasses über einen Generalbevollmächtigten für den Arbeitseinsatz," September 30, 1942, Document 1903-PS, *TMWC*, XXIX, 93–94.

37. Bräutigam, *Überblick*, pp. 91–92; Sauckel testimony, *TMWC*, XV, 8–18, 26–35, 45–47.

38. See Speer, *Inside*, pp. 292–95, and Homze, *Foreign Labor*, pp. 104–07.

39. Zentralstelle für Angehörige der Ostvölker, "Gegenwärtiger Stand der Ostarbeiter-Frage," Document 084-PS, *TMWC*, XXV, 161–79.

40. Oberlt. Theurer to RmfdbO Hauptabt. I, "Behandlung ukrainischer Facharbeiter," October 7, 1942, Document 054-PS, *TMWC*, XXV, 101–10; Oberkommando der Wehrmacht, WFSt/WPr, "Behandlung der Ostarbeiter," October 22, 1942, EAP 99/158, MR 281, RG 242, NA.

41. Sauckel to Rosenberg, October 3, 1942, Document 017-PS, *TMWC*, XXV, 72–3.

42. Extracts from Document USSR–170, *TMWC*, XV, 168, 170.

43. Rosenberg to Sauckel, December 21, 1942, Document 018-PS, *TMWC*, XXV, 74–79.

44. Sauckel, "Totaler Arbeitseinsatz für den Sieg: Kernsätze aus einer Rede anlässlich der ersten Tagung der Arbeitseinsatzstäbe (6. Januar 1943, Weimar)," Document Sauckel-82, *TMWC*, XLI, 225–28.

45. Sauckel testimony, *TMWC*, XV, 188–9; Himmler to Sauckel, March 11, 1943, T-175/71/2588149.

46. See Homze, *Foreign Labor*, pp. 159–60.

47. Sauckel to Rosenberg, March 17, 1943, Document 019-PS, *TMWC*, XXV, 79–81.

48. Oberkommando der Heeresgruppe A/Ia, "Behandlung der Zivilbevölkerung im Operationsgebiet," February 17, 1943, T-311/165/7217477.

49. Quoted in "Aktenvermerk über die am 10. März 1943 stattgefundene Besprechung mit KV-Chef Staatsrat Peuckert in Rowno," Document 3012-PS, *TMWC*, XXXI, 488.

50. Sauckel to Hitler, March 10, 1943, Document 407-II-PS, *NCA*, III, 389–90; Dallin, *German Rule*, pp. 441–42.

51. See, for example, Müller, *Besatzungspolitik*, pp. 308–18.

52. Statistics are taken from "Anlagen zum Kriegstagebuch Wi-Stab-Ost," T-77/1089/639, 1045 and T-77/1090/343, 363, 522.

53. Pfahlmann, *Fremdarbeiter*, p. 142.

54. R.K.O./Abt. Arbeitspolitik und Sozialverwaltung, "Abgabe von Arbeitskräften aus dem Ostland in das Reichsgebiet," May 3, 1943, Document 2280-PS, *TMWC*, XXX, 101–04.

55. Czollek, *Faschismus*, p. 174.

56. Sauckel testimony, *TMWC*, XV, 13–15; Homze, *Foreign Labor*, pp. 159–60.

57. Sauckel interrogation, September 28, 1945, RG 238, NA.

58. Armstrong, *Nationalism*, pp. 124–25; Der Kommandeur der Sicherheitspolizei und des SD, "Vermerk: Besuch Gauleiter Sauckel in Kiew," April 24, 1943, and "Arbeitseinsatz von Ukrainern im Reich," July 1943, T-454/94/920–23, 933–34.

59. "Bericht des Generalbevollmächtigten für den Arbeitseinsatz über die Aufgaben und Ergebnisse auf dem Gebiet des Arbeitseinsatzes vom. 1. Januar bis 30. Juni 1943," p. 20, T-175/71/2588099.

60. KTB Wi-Stab-Ost, December 10, 1942, T-77/1088/1036.

61. Pfahlmann, *Fremdarbeiter*, pp. 138–46; Eichholtz, *Kriegswirtschaft*, pp. 243–45.

62. See Lemkin, *Axis Rule*, pp. 556–62; and Homze, *Foreign Labor*, pp. 170–71.

63. Pfahlmann, *Fremdarbeiter*, pp. 196–206; Homze, *Foreign Labor*, pp. 272–73.

64. Affidavit of Dr. Wilhelm Jaeger, October 15, 1945, Document D–288, *NCA*, VII, 2–7.

65. "Anlagen zum Kriegstagebuch Wi Stab Ost" (April 1–September 30, 1943), T-77/1090/000014, 000046, 000065.

66. Wi-Stab-Ost/Chefgruppe Arbeit, "Beitrag zum KTB für die Zeit vom 17. bis 23.4.1943," April 22, 1943, T-77/1089/1314.

67. "Arbeitseinsatz der Ostarbeiter in Deutschland," May 1943, Document NG-2171, RG 238, NA.

68. SD *Meldungen aus dem Reich* Nr. 376, April 15, 1943, T-175/265/2759264–273.

69. See Heinz L. Ansbacher, "The Problem of Interpreting Attitude Survey Data: A Case Study of the Attitude of Russian Workers in Wartime Germany," *Public Opinion Quarterly*, Vol. XIV, no. 1 (Spring 1950); 126–38.

70. See Boelcke, *Secret Conferences*, pp. 331–32, 338.

71. "Vermerk über die Besprechung im Reichsministerium für Volksaufklärung und Propaganda am 10. März 1943," Document 315-PS, *TMWC*, XXV, 346–50.

72. See "Aus Geheimakten: Zur Ostarbeiterfrage," file D.A.I. 188, T-81/412/5157239–242; and Homze, *Foreign Labor*, pp. 173–75.

73. "Vermerk," April 2, 1943, Document 021-PS, RG 238, NA.

74. "Verordnung über die Unfallversorgung der Ostarbeiter vom 30. März 1943," Koerner Defense Exhibit Nr. 255, RG 238, NA.

75. See U.S. Legation, Stockholm, "Employment Conditions in the Reich," May 26, 1943, OSS R & A report No. 39327, RG 226, NA.

76. Bezirksgruppe Steinkohlenbergbau Ruhr, "Wage Register for East-laborers," June 30, 1943, Document NI-1977, RG 238, NA.

77. Pfahlmann, *Fremdarbeiter*, p. 163.

78. NSDAP Kanzlei, "Merkblatt über die allgemeinen Grundsätze," May 5, 1943, Document 205-PS, *TMWC*, XXV, 298–301.

79. Homze, *Foreign Labor*, pp. 269–70.

80. Wi-Stab-Ost//Chefgruppe Arbeit, "Beitrag zum KTB: 19.7.1943," July 23, 1943, T-77/1090/000021.

81. Homze, *Foreign Labor*, pp. 270–87.

82. Boelcke, *Secret Conferences*, p. 338; Bräutigam, *Überblick*, pp. 93–94; Wi-Stab-Ost/Chefgruppe Arbeit, "Beitrag zum KTB: 17.7.1943," T-77/1090/000021.

83. See the studies quoted in Homze, *Foreign Labor*, pp. 259–61.

84. Reports of Lieutenant Adolf Aumann, August 27, 1943, and Lieutenant Erbsloeh, September 5, 1943, Documents NO-2008, NO-2009, *NMT*, XIII, 1040–43.

85. For example, Dallin, *German Rule*, pp. 406–08; Alan S. Milward, *War, Economy and Society 1939–1945* (Berkeley/Los Angeles: University of California Press, 1979), pp. 164–65, 260–65.

86. Alan S. Milward, *The German Economy at War* (London: The Athlone Press, 1965), pp. 192–93.

87. Burckhart Mueller-Hillebrand, *Das Heer 1939–1945*, Bd. III (3 vols.) (Frankfurt am Main: E. S. Mittler & Sohn, 1969), p. 109.

88. See Homze, *Foreign Labor*, pp. 100–02, and the USSBS study "Effects of Strategic Bombing on the German War Economy," pp. 34–35, 131.

9

CONDITIONS IN THE AREAS UNDER GERMAN MILITARY GOVERNMENT

In contrast to the Reich commissariats, there were no personal clashes over policy goals in the areas governed by the German military. Here, where ideology had always taken a back seat to pragmatism, army supporters of *Ostpolitik* reform tested their ideas on the roughly 20 million Soviet citizens under military government. Granted Hitler's veto of a policy change in December 1942 and the priority of strictly military requirements, their efforts constituted a holding action until circumstances permitted a return to the issue of a general reform.

The organization of military government followed a pattern of successive strata behind the front lines, collectively termed the *Operationsgebiet* or "zone of operations." The immediate area of the front to a depth of 15–25 kilometers comprised the combat area (*Gefechtsgebiet*), behind which lay the "army rear area" (*Rückwärtiges Armeegebiet*, or *Korück*) extending perhaps 50 kilometers behind each German army along the front. An "army group rear area" (*Rückwärtiges Heeresgebiet*) formed the final layer of military administration for each army group, to a depth of up to one hundred additional kilometers. Within these areas military government was organized into regional offices (*Feldkommandanturen*) responsible directly to the *Korück* or one of the security divisions operating in the *Heeresgebiet*; the regional offices in turn were divided into *Kreiskommandanturen* for rural districts and *Ortskommandanturen* for towns. In the autumn of 1942 a reorganization provided each army group with its own military government headquarters, signifying the increased role of military government as a command issue.[1]

The primary duties of the rear area commands lay in the maintenance and protection of the logistics and communications networks that serviced the front lines. In its relations with the occupied population, "the German Army was only interested in the maintenance of quiet," thus allowing the inhabitants a qualified freedom.[2] Local German military government officials retained considerable discretion in policy issues, as one official account observed: "It was no time to await the orders and detailed formal directives of upper echelons . . . things had to be largely improvised."[3] In consequence, a degree of power impossible in the *Reichskommissariate* devolved upon the native mayors and *raion* chiefs, extending even to aid to escaped prisoners-of-war with the acquiescence of the *Feldkommandantur*.[4]

The reformers also found their task facilitated by the relatively favorable disposition of the population toward the ordinary German soldier. Initially, many of the latter were hostile toward a native population whose poverty seemed to confirm the *Untermensch* stereotypes of Nazi propaganda.[5] But prolonged social contact broke down many barriers and established amicable, and often intimate, relationships.[6] German soldiers also proved to be good customers: where Russian farmers received only 0.10 RM for each egg delivered to German economic authorities, the *Landser* paid 1.0–1.5 RM for the same product on the black market.[7] Army discipline enjoined a correct treatment of civilians, a quality much less evident among the elite *Waffen*-SS units.[8] The popular response is evident in post-war surveys among Soviet refugees who decisively rated *Wehrmacht* front line troops as the best-behaved representatives of the occupation.[9]

During the spring and early summer of 1943 German military commands attempted several measures to increase the average German soldier's political awareness of his position in Russia. Army Group Center attempted to redress a long-standing problem when it encouraged instruction in the Russian language throughout the command, and required a working knowledge of Russian for all military government officials in direct contact with the population.[10] Army Group North, following a suggestion by Rosenberg and OKW/WPr, declared a major holiday in the region under its control on June 22, 1943, the second anniversary of the German invasion, with church services, speeches, concerts and other festivities to encourage fraternization.[11] The previous month the Fourth Army distributed a pamphlet on "The German Soldier and His Political Tasks in the East." The directive emphasized that the "most acute task" involved winning over the Russian population, yet continually lapsed into paternalistic stereotypes ("The Russian is childlike, that is he acts upon his emotions rather than his intellect").[12]

But reactions to these measures demonstrated the lack of consensus within the *Wehrmacht* on the necessity of Russian support. One of Fourth Army's divisions strongly criticized the pamphlet as "pretending the Russian to be the equal of the German," and suggested that this policy could be justified to the average soldier only on the basis of military necessity.[13] Some officers were openly hostile to the political views behind these measures. The chief intelligence officer of the Eighteenth Army expressed this antagonism in the traditional context of the "nonpolitical" German officer in June 1943:

These political questions are of decisive importance. We as soldiers, however, have no policy to conduct. . . . [and] may do nothing else but carry out the orders and directives given us as best as we can. . . . There are naturally many who believe that it is now time to say what should be done with the Russians. But we are not empowered to intervene in matters of high policy.[14]

Yet political matters could not be avoided in an occupied area, and every day German commanders confronted policy decisions in the treatment of the population. *Ostpolitik* thus devolved upon German officers on the scene, whose political attitudes assumed major significance. Those disposed toward reform could rely upon Wagner, Altenstadt, and Stauffenberg for support at OKH, but it was within the *Operationsgebiet* that the gains would have to be made. And as the aborted alliance with Rosenberg strengthened the centrifugal impetus of the reform movement, so the pressure of events and adaption to local conditions further fragmented reform efforts.

For the northernmost area under military government, reform was less a political strategy than improvised pragmatism. The operations zone of Army Group North, forming a quadrilateral from the south shore of Lake Ladoga to just north of Velikiye Luki, thence west to the border of *Reichskommissariat* Ostland and north to the Gulf of Finland, featured swamps, forests, and just enough farmland to support a population of about 1.26 million.[15] Nearly all of these were ethnic Russians who, unlike their neighbors in the Baltic states, greeted the Germans in 1941 without enthusiasm. To minimize problems and solicit local cooperation, *Heeresgruppe Nord* officials offered numerous concessions: the restoration of the Russian Orthodox Church, an elementary school system, and open markets for the sale of goods.[16]

These measures reflected favorably on the army group's administration of the North so that even Vlasov remarked after a brief tour that ''no other area he had visited left such a positive impression of the activity of German military government.''[17] Behind these appearances, however, lay a grimmer reality. In April and May 1943 the *Ostministerium* representative to army group headquarters strongly criticized the military's handling of civil affairs, particularly their failure to supplement the population's food supplies and inadequate pay for Russian schoolteachers.[18] The mortality rates more accurately reflected living conditions: in four *raions* of the operations zone, 201 births were registered against 698 deaths in late 1942.[19] Military courts duly opened criminal proceedings against 27,000 peasants for failing to meet their delivery quotas, though it was recognized that 24,000 of them possessed only a single cow after requisitions.[20] When Russian village chiefs requested permission to organize a militia for protection against Soviet partisans, German military authorities turned them down.[21] In short, the foundation of pragmatic reform remained true to an October 1942 directive of the Eighteenth Army: ''[T]he indigenous administration is not an end in itself, but only a means to the full utilization of all additional assistance of the conquered land for the *Wehrmacht*'s tasks.''[22]

By contrast, the area of Army Group Center offered a blend of reform by the most basic pragmatism and most radical political alternatives. The region also featured swampy woodland, yet included several major cities and a population of about 6.2 million in early 1943. In a 77,000-square-mile area that sustained the bulk of the Soviet partisan bands, the German military presence was necessarily limited to the protection of the major supply routes and occasional anti-guerrilla sweeps of the countryside. A number of villages removed from the main roads spent over two years under occupation without ever seeing a German soldier. One result was the establishment of several semi-independent forest "republics" under Russian leaders, tolerated and armed (in contrast to Army Group North) by local army authorities to fight off partisans and deliver food quotas, thus preserving German power without German supervision. The largest of these areas, located in the Lokot' district south of Bryansk, acquired notoriety for its leader Bronislav Kaminsky.[23]

But the distinguishing characteristic of reform here lay in the radical plans of a group of officers serving on the army group headquarters staff. Including Lieutenant Fabian von Schlabrendorff (aide to the Operations Section), Colonel Rudolf-Christoph von Gersdorff (Army Group Intelligence officer), and especially Lieutenant-Colonel Henning von Tresckow (Army Group Operations officer), they pushed a reluctant Field Marshal Günther von Kluge along the path of reform. Tresckow had sought to bring about basic changes in policy since the autumn of 1941, and had established anti-Soviet Russian units which, unlike other *Osttruppen*, were officered by Russians.[24] But by March 1943, he and his associates had gone far beyond *Ostpolitik* reform in plotting Hitler's assassination and a military coup. Though the attempt, made during Hitler's visit to Smolensk on March 13 (and involving Cossack cavalry in German service), failed, it at least demonstrated that Tresckow had no illusions as to the root of Germany's problem.[25]

Yet Tresckow's influence could only reach so far. Many of his colleagues shared his views on the need for improved treatment of the population, but the anticipated political future to be won by this cooperation remained a one-sided relationship. This is illustrated in an otherwise perceptive analysis prepared on Christmas Day, 1942, by a staff officer of the Army Group Center Rear Area. The author diagnosed the sources of popular discontent as well as "the main problem . . . the lack of uniform political approach to the treatment of the Russian people." Among his recommendations, however, he proposed only a system of autonomy "somewhat in the manner of the Protectorate [of Bohemia-Moravia]," as the basis for "the erection of a new Russia."[26]

Ambivalence and ambiguity similarly characterized the views of the various German armies constituting the army group. The Third Panzer Army in February 1943 urged concessions to the "national sentiments and rights" of the populace through the establishment of a "Great Liberation Council" to negotiate with the Reich government.[27] A Second Army memorandum in May criticized "half-measures" and proposed an accelerated land reform and increased autonomy, yet added the condescending expectation that "the Russian must know what place he will occupy in the future Europe. He will gladly do this under German leadership, but not as a slave. . . . "[28]

The blend of pragmatism, activism and ambivalence shaped the character of *Ostpolitik* reform in Army Group Center. Recognizing the benefits of Kaminsky's district, military government officials established a higher level of native administration, the *Bezirksverwaltung* ("district administration") to include several *raions* as a civilian counterpart to the *Feldkommandantur*. The army group extended this in a draft proposal to the Army High Command in January 1943 for a codification of native jurisdiction, but OKH delayed the authorizing directives until May and the issue was soon overtaken by events.[29] Another draft proposal in February recommended the establishment of a sickness insurance program for Russians performing labor duties for German forces, to be administered and financed by the native authorities.[30]

Army Group Center also rebuilt the educational system in its sector during the first half of 1943. By July, 4000 primary schools had reopened for an enrollment of 500,000 children, though supply shortages forced some students to rely upon the margins of occupation newspapers for notepaper. Specialized schools were also established for agriculture, education, medicine, and technical skills. The population responded favorably to these measures, but might have been less enthusiastic had they read one military government officer's description of educational planning: Fearful that "too many schools might mobilize an undesirable intellectual class," the number of secondary schools was limited and requirements for student advancement instituted "with preference given to children whose parents served the German cause."[31]

The regions of the southern USSR under German military government differed greatly from those to the north. While most of the front remained stable through the autumn and winter of 1942–43, the southern flank proved the most fluid of all sectors as the new German conquests of September were retaken in January. The topography varied from the rolling farmlands of the Ukraine and the industrial Donbas basin to the mountains of the Caucasus. The population differed, too, in both ethnic variety (Russians, Ukrainians, Cossacks, the Turkic peoples of the Caucasus and Crimea) and numbers: in October 1942, the army group rear area of *Heeresgruppe* B alone included nearly 8 million inhabitants.[32] Moreover, the opportunities for policy reform were enhanced by Rosenberg's fixation on the ethnic minorities and Hitler's disinterest in the Caucasus beyond control of its oil. For these reasons, the area most briefly occupied by the German Army became the showcase of *Ostpolitik* reform.

The North Caucasus fell under German control in the late summer of 1942, as Army Group A drove on towards the oilfields of Grozny and Baku. The Islamic inhabitants of the region took full advantage of the withdrawal of Soviet authority, establishing governing bodies and beginning the redistribution of collectivized property. German commanders ordered their troops to treat the Caucasian peoples as "friendly peoples" and assure their rights to private property and religious freedom.[33] Even Himmler concurred with this view, proposing the establishment of "Independent Caucasian Protectorates" for the region as early as July 1942.[34]

To take full advantage of this opportunity, *Ostpolitik* reformers assumed direct responsibility to implement the new policy. *Ostministerium* reformer Dr. Otto Bräutigam, with several years' consular experience in the Caucasus, was nominated by OKH Quartermaster-General Wagner as liaison officer to *Heeresgruppe* A. Stauffenberg at OKH secured the services of General Ernst Köstring, the Russian-born former military attaché to Moscow, as "governor-general" of the area with reform advocate Lieutenant Herwarth von Bittenfeld as his deputy. Dr. Otto Schiller, architect of the agrarian reform, was responsible for its execution in the North Caucasus. Dr. Theodor Oberländer was already there as the commander of the *Abwehr*'s "Bergmann" unit. With a sympathetic army group commander in *Generaloberst* Ewald von Kleist, the reformers wasted no time in putting their ideas into practice. They restored freedom of worship to Russian Orthodox and Moslem alike; prohibited the conscription of forced labor; initiated the planned conversion of collectives to farm cooperatives at a rate of 30 to 40 percent for the first year, and even recognized the existing ruling committees in the Karachai and Kabardino-Balkar areas as the legal governments for the occupied population.[35]

Further to the rear, the German military accorded the inhabitants similar favorable treatment. In the Kalmyk steppe to the northeast, a screening force of motorized infantry commanded by a knowledgeable *Abwehr* officer cultivated the good will of the Kalmyks, a people of Mongolian stock and Buddhist faith. The temples were reopened and the local administration, though appointed by the occupiers, enjoyed considerable autonomy. Requisitions of cattle (the basis of the region's economy) were orderly and usually coordinated with Kalmyk authorities, and in December 1942 the agrarian reform began to restore private farmland. In return, the Kalmyks supplied 3000 expert cavalrymen to the Germans.[36]

In the Kuban steppe further west, Army Group A overstepped its authority in a planned experiment in self-government for the Cossacks. In September 1942 Altenstadt's section of OKH authorized the establishment of an "experimental area" for limited self-government in six *raions* with a population of 160,000, roughly half of whom were Cossacks. Six days later Army Group A issued its own directives that far exceeded these guidelines: OKH's proposed gradual transition from the Soviet administrative structure was abandoned in favor of an immediate restoration of the traditional Cossack *Hetmanate*, with economic gains subordinated to political cooperation.[37] In November the army group proposed the experiment's expansion to the rest of the Krasnodar area, producing rumors of an independent "Cossack republic" that were quickly repudiated by a surprised OKH as "absolutely unfounded."[38]

Another latent problem began to take form in the mountain district to the south. In November 1942, Army Group A acknowledged the right of the Karachai "government" to hold in trusteeship the property formerly owned by the Soviet state. The reformers sought to expand this with a formal recognition, duly granted by Kleist, of the Karachai people's trusteeship of the mineral resources and forestry on their land. This was too much for the economic inspection officer attached to the army group, who protested the order and appealed to higher authority. When Bräutigam requested support from the *Ostministerium*, he received a curt refusal on the grounds of "basic considerations and ensuing consequences for other [occupied] areas."[39]

The issue reflected the contradiction inherent to the reform efforts, political concessions without economic control. During the initial planning for the occupation of the Caucasus in June 1942, the agricultural section of *Wi-Stab-Ost* specified that the dissolution of the *kolkhozy* be limited to the mountain districts, that is, the least productive agricultural areas; in the more fertile plains of Krasnodar, Stavropol, and the Kalmyk, the restoration of private farming land would be delayed until spring 1943 at the earliest.[40] OKH recognized this in September 1942 when it excluded a return to the traditional Cossack forms of land ownership in the "experimental area" due to the requirements of the German war economy.[41] Only the precipitate retreat of German forces from the Caucasus forestalled the development of these contradictions into problems. Within two weeks after the Eastern Ministry denied Bräutigam's request for support, Army Group A began a withdrawal to avoid being cut off by Soviet forces advancing from Stalingrad. By mid-February the Germans held only a bridgehead on the Taman peninsula.

The brevity of the occupation renders any assessment of German policy in the North Caucasus problematic. The internal contradictions became academic before they could fully develop; the attitudes of the population did not have time to crystalize; and the "scorched-earth" policy that characterized so many retreats in the East negated much of the reformers' efforts. A moderate policy was not in any case extended to Jews and the incurably ill, who were murdered as elsewhere in the USSR.[42] In reflecting on this period, an officer who had commanded Turkic units later considered that many Germans erred in "transplanting their own exaggerated nationalistic feeling into the minds of the members of the Caucasian and Turkic peoples" as the basis for collaboration.[43] The North Caucasians, in contrast to the Crimean Tatars and Kalmyks, offered few volunteers to German service (excluding those recruited from prisoner-of-war camps) and perhaps 8000 chose to accompany their erstwhile conquerors in retreat. Given the large numbers of Slavic inhabitants of the region who enjoyed none of the privileges extended to the minority nationalities, popular attitudes toward the occupation were likely much less favorable than German reformers imagined.[44]

The latter, however, returned from the Caucasus with a sense of vindication for their ideas, which they now applied to adjacent areas under military government. Though his army group now governed only the Kuban bridgehead and the Crimea, Kleist issued a directive on February 17, 1943 that incorporated an ambitious 15-point program for reform. Beginning with the instruction that the inhabitants were to be treated "as allies" (*Bundesgenossen*), Kleist called for the conversion of 50 percent of farm collectives to cooperatives during 1943, forbade the delivery quotas for agricultural products to exceed 80 percent of the total harvest, reserved 20 percent of locally produced consumer goods for the population, prohibited the use of force to recruit *Ostarbeiter*, and promoted the growth of deregulated civilian markets, public education, freedom of worship, and cultural institutions.[45] Kleist must have lobbied among his colleagues as well, for only nine days later a similar order was issued by Field Marshal Erich von Manstein, commander of Army Group South. Manstein's directive differed in terminology and specifics ("friends and comrades-in-arms" replaced "allies," and the cooperative conversion rate was reduced to "at least an additional 20%" for 1943), but the intent clearly remained the same.[46]

But once again the reform issue touched the raw nerve of economic policy as the agricultural section of *Wi-Stab-Ost* cried out in protest. The head of the section, *Ministerialdirektor* Hans-Joachim Riecke, caustically wrote Kleist on March 11th that his program was "simply impossible" because of wartime necessities. Riecke rejected any reservation of consumer goods and food harvests for the inhabitants when the German Army in Russia was obliged to live off the land.[47] In preparing a reply, Kleist did not back away from his proposals, yet did not question Riecke's premise.[48]

Kleist rested his defense on the example of the Crimea, the scenic peninsula that only the previous summer was being prepared for German colonization.[49] German policy again favored a minority nationality, the Crimean Tatars who comprised nearly a quarter of the population. From the beginning of the Crimean occupation German forces organized and armed Tatar militia units totalling 20,000 men for use against Soviet partisans.[50] As in the Caucasus, religious and cultural concessions were accompanied by increased self-government, and even Riecke granted the Crimean Tatars a cooperative conversion rate of 40 percent for 1943, double that of their Russian and Ukrainian neighbors.[51] During the winter of 1942–43, the army and the SD cooperated in setting up a "Central Moslem Committee" in Simferopol in recognition of Tatar cultural autonomy.[52] And at least one of Kleist's proposals proved a major success: the introduction of an open market for surplus food products at the end of 1942 so increased food supplies to the cities that German authorities deregulated all agricultural products except meats in May 1943. In Simferopol, where death by starvation had increased 100 percent from January to February 1942, food prices declined markedly through the summer of 1943.[53]

Even as events seemed to vindicate Kleist's program, however, the conflicting policies of rival authorities eroded its effectiveness. In January 1943 the *Ostministerium*, granting priority to the minority nationalities, established a "Crimean Tatar Main Office" and dispatched to the Crimean two strongly nationalist Tatar emigrés. Though their trip was approved by OKH and both were elected members of the Simferopol Moslem Committee, local army and SD authorities considered a Tatar nationalist program unrealistic, which could only raise false political hopes among Tatars and alienate the bulk of the peninsula's population. When Army Group A received numerous petitions for support of this program— including Tatar domination of the native administration and repression of the Slavic inhabitants—it forbade any further activity by emigrés in the Crimea. The ensuing policy debate that continued through the remainder of the occupation soured relations between the army and Tatar political leaders. Nor could the military look to the Slavic inhabitants for support, where Kleist's inability to block Sauckel's conscription of thousands of workers in spring 1943 precluded any substantial cooperation.[54]

The Crimea in many ways presents a microcosm of *Ostpolitik* in the occupied Soviet Union. It offered an opportunity to each of the three variants of Eastern policy, Hitler's colonization plans, Rosenberg's nationalities concept and the army's belief in a general reform and all had begun to be implemented. But the realities of wartime conditions denied each the full chance their champions desired and exposed the contradictions within German policy. Field Marshal von Manstein anticipated Hitler's own verdict on *Ostpolitik* reform when he wrote on May 9, 1943: "Of course it would be a big help to us if we could mobilize both Russians and non-Russians and use them against the Bolsheviks on a large scale. The most difficult question will always be what task to assign them, since their interests are opposed to ours and in the last analysis are bound to diverge."[55]

Manstein's observation pertained not only to the larger political issues but to the daily requirements of sustenance. Perhaps the most important of the many paradoxes characteristic of *Ostpolitik* lay in the German Army's relationship to occupation policy: Though the most liberal institution in its political views, the *Wehrmacht*'s food requirements demanded the utmost exploitation of Russian foodstuffs and livestock. And whereas the benefits of military government affected perhaps one of every three inhabitants, the entire occupied population paid the price of feeding the German Army. The priority of this effort was beyond question: Kleist's own army group rear area in August 1942 faithfully echoed Hitler's order to provision the army from the land as "the highest commandment of the hour," "to be carried out under any, even the most difficult circumstances."[56]

To their credit, Manstein and especially Kleist did their best to improve the civilian population's food supply. For Easter 1943, Army Group South distributed extra rations of 500 grams of millet or buckwheat and 300 grams of salt per person in its area.[57] Kleist secured from *Wirtschaftsinspektion Süd* a 40 percent conversion of cooperatives in the Crimea instead of the initially proposed 30 percent.[58] In August 1943, Kleist appealed to *Wi-Stab-Ost* for an improvement of the Crimean population's rations through the annual import of 10,000 tons of barley, a reform proposal unique in both nature and scale.[59]

But Kleist's efforts could not redress the loss of civilian living standards imposed by the needs of 3 million occupying soldiers. Though deaths by starvation never equaled the famine levels of winter and spring 1942, they remained a constant feature of occupation: during the early winter of 1942–43, ten civilians were dying daily in Rzhev.[60] The newborn were particularly vulnerable. One of the officers attending the reform conference of December 18, 1942 noted that infant mortality in Estonia had increased eightfold since the pre-war period, and in one town under Army Group North's jurisdiction 10 of 13 babies died shortly after birth in early 1943.[61] Among adults, weakness from malnutrition led to significant increases in infectious diseases while women's bartering of sex for food rations contributed to a rise in venereal disease.[62] In other cities, inhabitants fought a daily battle against hunger by scrounging, improvising from foodscraps, and selling their possessions to buy food at ever-rising prices.[63]

A hungry people under occupation can little appreciate concessions that do not put food into their stomachs; neither can an army fighting for its life on enemy soil undertake major programs to win over the occupied population. Even within these limits, *Ostpolitik* reformers in the German Army found they were never masters in their own house: the *Wi-Stab-Ost* and the Eastern Ministry blocked or impeded proposals that clashed with their own interests, and many army commanders endorsed only that which they considered safe or expedient. The reformers probably accompanied as much as was feasible, and kept alive the reform issues for the Vlasov movement to utilize. The internal contradictions and ambiguities that had emerged, however, assumed greater prominence in antipartisan warfare and the treatment of *Osttruppen*.

NOTES

1. See "Abschlussbericht," T–501/34/868ff., and Toppe, "Military Government," FMS Ms. No. P–033, pp. 21–28.

2. Pozdnyakov, "National Instinct," FMS Ms. No. P–23, pp. 4–5.

3. "Abschlussbericht," T–501/34/937, and Anisimov, *German Occupation*, pp. 10–11.

4. Anisimov, *German Occupation*, pp. 3, 16–18.

5. See, for example, "Auszug aus einem Bericht des VAA beim AOK 16 vom 21.12.41 über Bevölkerungspropaganda," T–120/289/444/221885–886.

6. Erich Kern, *Der Grosse Rausch* (Oldendorf: Verlag K.W. Schütz KG, 1974) provides several examples. Hitler and Himmler estimated the number of illegitimate children fathered by German soldiers at roughly 1 million in the first year of occupation alone ("Rede des Reichsführers-SS am 16 September 1942 in der Feldkommandostelle vor den Teilnehmern an der SS-und Polizeiführer-Tagung," T–175/103/2624970–971).

7. See "Notizen über die Besprechung betr. Zwangs-Bewirtschaftung von Lebensmitteln am 12.6.43," T–311/166/7217820–822.

8. See, for example, the reports collected in: Chef Allgemeinen Wehrmachtamts an SS-Obergruppenführer Wolff, August 2, 1943, T–175/122/2647328–336.

9. Dallin, *German Rule*, p. 73n.

10. Obkdo. der H.Gr. Mitte/Ic, directive of May 31, 1943, T–315/654/541–42; Der Chef der Militärverwaltung beim Obkdo. der H.Gr. Mitte, "Erfahrungsbericht für die Zeit vom 22.6. 1941 bis August 1944," T–311/233/448.

11. See the exchange of OKW/WPr-Heeresgruppe Nord correspondence, June 11–22, 1943, T–311/102/7135036–041, 7135044–048.

12. AOK 4/Ic, "Der deutsche Soldat und seine politischen Aufgaben im Osten," May 1943, T–501/243/807–830.

13. 12. Panzer-Division, Abt. Ic/Betr. Offz., "Wehrgeistige Führungsarbeit," June 9, 1943, T–314/1091/70.

14. Obkdo. der H. Gr. Nord/Stabsoffizier für Propagandaeinsatz, "Protokoll," June 30, 1943, T–311/102/7134912–914.

15. Wi In Nord, *Zwei Jahre Kriegswirtschaft*, pp. 134–35.

16. Anisimov, *German Occupation*, pp. 1–6, 17–18, 22–25, and Armeeoberkommando 18/Ic. "Propaganda in die russ. Zivilbevölkerung," April 30, 1943, T–311/115/7154836–850.

17. Sdf. (Z) Klein, "Kurzer Bericht über die Fahrt des General Wlassow nach Pleskau, Strugi und Luga (30.4.–3.5.1943)," 7 May 1943, T–311/115/7154888.

18. See "Bericht Dr. Weissauer vom 25.4.1943: Stellungnahme der Abteilung VII (Entwurf)," April 30, 1943, and Weissauer, "Stellungnahme von Abt. VII zu meinem Berichtsentwurf," May 5, 1943, T–311/115/7154879–883.

19. SD *Meldungen* Nr. 39, T–175/236/2725455.

20. Zimmermann, "Protokoll," Document NO–1481, RG 238, NA.

21. Anisimov, *German Occupation*, p. 30.

22. AOK 18/OQu/Qu 2, "Sammelheft für Befehle über Aufbau und Aufgaben der landeseigenen Verwaltung," October 1, 1942, T–312/848/9014724.

23. Demographic data taken from Dr. Boening to Sauckel, February 7, 1943, Doc. BB–1020, RG 238, NA; on the forest "republics," see Alexander Dallin, *The Kaminsky Brigade: 1941–1944, A Case Study of German Exploitation of Soviet Disaffection* (Cambridge, MA: Russian Research Center, Harvard University, 1956), V. Volzhanin, "Zuyev's Republic," FMS Mss. No. P–124 (Historical Division, U.S. Army, Europe, 1951), and Pozdnyakov, "National Instinct," FMS Mss. No. P–123, pp. 23–31.

24. Hoffmann, *German Resistance*, pp. 264–71; Strik-Strikfeldt, *Against*, pp. 42, 48–49, 67; Thorwald, *Illusion*, pp. 96–98; and Scheurig, *Tresckow*, pp. 135–43, 154–56.

25. Hoffmann, *German Resistance*, pp. 276–83.

26. "Erfahrungen in der Verwaltung des Landes und politische Zielsetzung," December 25, 1942, T–501/27/000008–11. Though Dallin (*German Rule*, pp. 548–49) attributes this memorandum to Tresckow, it is more likely Lieutenant-Colonel von Kraewel.

27. Panzer-Armeeoberkommando 3, Abt. OQu, "Erfassung des russischen Volkes," February 27, 1943, Document WB–3104, RG 238, NA.

28. Armee-Oberkommando 2/Ia, "Ausnutzung des russischen und ukrainischen Menschen," May 11, 1943, Document NOKW–2484, RG 238, NA.

29. Kommandierender General der Sicherungstruppen und Befehlshaber im Heeresgebiet Mitte/Ia, "Besprechungspunkte für die Dienstbesprechung am 27.d.Mts.," (November 1942), T–501/27/170–71; Chef der Militärverwaltung, "Erfahrungsbericht," T–311/233/462–67.

30. Oberkommando der Heeresgruppe Mitte/OQu, an OKH/GenStdH/GenQu, "Krankenversorgung für einheimische Arbeitskräfte," February 22, 1943, T–454/94/000023–28.

31. Heeresgruppe Mitte, "Erfahrungsbericht," August 10, 1944, T–311/233/467; information on the school system is located in *SD Meldungen* Nr. 41, T–175/236/2725540–546.

32. Abt. VII beim Befehlshaber H.Geb. B, "Lagebericht," October 10, 1942, T–501/25/1049.

33. See Dallin, *German Rule*, pp. 226–49; Aleksandr M. Nekrich, *The Punished Peoples*, trans. by George Saunders (New York: W.W. Norton, 1978), pp. 36ff.; and Mühlen, *Hakenkreuz*, pp. 44ff.

34. Himmler to Schellenberg, July 14, 1942, T–175/55/2569345.

35. Bräutigam, *So hat es*, pp. 506–13; Herwarth, *Two Evils*, pp. 221–24; Dallin, *German Rule*, pp. 244–48. An excellent documentary source is file EAP 99/37, T–454/16/927ff.

36. Joachim Hoffmann, *Deutsche und Kalmyken 1942 bis 1945* (Freiburg: Rombach Verlag, 1974), esp. pp. 13–30, 54–82, 90–98, for the Soviet view, see Nekrich, *Punished Peoples*, pp. 66–85.

37. Compare OKH/GenQu/Abt. Kriegsverwaltung, ''Kosaken-Selbstverwaltung,'' September 21, 1942, T–454/23/718–21, and Befehlshaber H. Geb. A, Abt. VII/Ia, ''Einrichtung eines Versuchsgebiets,'' September 27, 1942, T–501/26/626–30. *Sonderführer* Siefers, ''Bericht über das ''Versuchsgebiet'' im Kuban-Kosaken-Raum,'' January 10, 1943, T–454/93/279–315.

38. Kommandierender General der Sicherungstruppen und Befehlshaber im Heeresgebiet A/Ia, ''Erweiterung des Kosaken-Versuchsgebietes,'' November 28, 1942, T–454/17/532–35; Bräutigam, ''Aufzeichnung,'' October 14, 1942, T–454/16/1000.

39. See Bräutigam's letter to the Eastern Ministry, December 26, 1942, and Gerhard von Mende's teletype reply, December 31, 1942, T–454/37/794–98.

40. Hoffmann, *Deutsche und Kalmyken*, p. 57.

41. OKH/GenQu/Abt. Kriegsverwaltung, ''Kosaken-Selbstverwaltung,'' September 21, 1942, T–454/23/716–21.

42. Reitlinger, *House*, pp. 300–01.

43. Comment by Hans Seraphim in the manuscript he co-authored with Ralph von Heygendorff and Ernst Köstring, ''Eastern Nationals as Volunteers in the German Army,'' FMS Mss. No. C–043 (Historical Division, U.S. Army, Europe, 1948), p. 22.

44. See Mühlen, *Hakenkreuz*, pp. 189–95, and Nekrich, *Punished Peoples*, pp. 36–85, who exaggerates popular discontent with the occupation.

45. Obkdo. d. H.Gr. A/Ia, ''Behandlung der Zivilbevölkerung im Operationsgebiet,'' February 17, 1943, T–311/165/7217474–478.

46. Obkdo. d. H.Gr. Süd/OQu, ''Behandlung der Zivilbevölkerung im Operationsgebiet,'' February 26, 1943, T–77/1105/178–81.

47. Riecke to Kleist, March 11, 1943, T–311/165/7217468–469.

48. OKVR Hufnagel (?), ''Vermerk für Herrn Generalfeldmarschall,'' March 18, 1943, T–311/165/7217470–473.

49. See Michael Luther, ''Die Krim unter deutscher Besatzung im Zweiten Weltkrieg,'' *Forschungen zur osteuropäischen Geschichte*, Band III (Berlin: Osteuropa Institut/Freie Universität Berlin, 1956), pp. 38–41; and Rich, *War Aims*, Vol. II, pp. 383–85.

50. Hoffmann, *Ostlegionen*, pp. 39–50.

51. Luther, ''Die Krim,'' pp. 60–83.

52. See Oberkommando des H.Gr. A/OQu/Abt. VII, ''Krim-Tatarischen Frage,'' March 21, 1944, T–311/166/7217600–604; and Mühlen, *Hakenkreuz*, pp. 184–85.

53. Luther, ''Die Krim,'' p. 84; RSHA, *Ereignismeldungen UdSSR* Nr. 178, T–175/235/2723976.

54. Heeresgruppe A, ''Krim-Tatarischen Frage,'' T–311/166/217600–604; Mühlen, *Hakenkreuz*, pp. 119–28, 184–87; and Luther, ''Die Krim,'' pp. 84–85.

55. Manstein to Eugen Dürksen, May 9, 1943, quoted in Nekrich, *Punished Peoples*, p. 24.

56. Kommandierender General der Sicherungstruppen und Befehlshaber im Heeresgebiet A, "Sonderbefehl zur Bergung der Ernte," August 27, 1942, T–501/20/154–55.

57. Buchbender, *Tönende Erz*, p. 278.

58. See Schiller, "Vermerk betrifft: Agrarreform in Taurien," July 7, 1943, T–454/98/100.

59. Heeresgruppe A/OQu/VII/Qu 2, "Ernährung der einheimischen Zivilbevölkerung," draft dated August 11, 1943, T–311/166/7217781–784.

60. SD *Meldungen* Nr. 42, T–175/236/2725571.

61. Zimmermann, "Protokoll," Document NO–1481, RG 238, NA; SD *Meldungen* Nr. 43, T–175/236/2725599.

62. SD *Meldungen* Nr. 35, and Nr. 41, T–175/236/2725306–307, 2725536–539.

63. In addition to the SD *Meldungen* cited above, see A. Anatoli (Kuznetsov), *Babi Yar*, trans. by David Floyd, Pocket Books (New York: Farrar, Strauss and Giroux, 1971), esp. pp. 128–32, 169–76. Food prices in Orel from October 1, 1942 to February 28, 1943 are provided in SD *Meldungen* Nr. 49, T–175/236/2725799–800.

10

POLITICAL REFORM VS. BODY COUNTS: THE CRISIS OF THE GERMAN ANTIPARTISAN EFFORT

Germany's mistakes in occupation policy were magnified by the growth of a well-organized Soviet partisan movement. In autumn 1941, Soviet guerrillas signified little more than a nuisance and a pretext for the slaughters committed by the *Einsatzgruppen*: By early 1943 they posed a major threat to German rule in Russia.[1] During the period under study, German authorities acknowledged the failure of previous measures but disagreed whether to retain terror as the basis of antipartisan warfare, or incorporate the strugle within a political framework that engaged the support of the occupied population.

As they gained in strength, Soviet ''bandits'' (the official German designation after July 1942) struck back against the occupation at several levels. Militarily, they provided the Red Army with valuable intelligence on German dispositions and movements and continually harassed supply lines and communications: in the single month of June 1943, partisans destroyed 298 locomotives, 1222 train cars and 44 bridges in the area of Army Group Center alone.[2] In economic terms, partisan activities severely disrupted grain production in central Russia and the northern Ukraine.[3] Above all, however, the partisans preserved Soviet political authority in the occupied areas. In scattered localities the partisans actually exercised governing power, extending to perhaps 1 million inhabitants. More significantly, Russians serving in the occupation administration, the auxiliary police, or as beneficiaries of the agrarian reform found themselves the special targets of the partisans. Stalin in May 1943 granted broad powers to guerrilla units to execute any civilians contributing to the German war effort, including relatives. This policy of terror, which resulted in the deaths of several thousand Russian civilians from 1941 to 1943, was effectively combined with propaganda appeals to collaborators to encourage redefection to the Soviet side. The vulnerability of collaborationists to retribution and intimidation undermined the most generous German concession.[4]

German antipartisan policy was characterized by its inconsistency as well as its brutality. Even in 1941, when indiscriminate reprisals substituted for adequate training and doctrine, German field commanders operated largely at their own discretion.[5] In September 1941 an OKW directive established a reprisal ratio of 50 to one hundred Communists to be executed for each German soldier killed; yet a subsequent order issued by the Fourth Army *Korück* reduced this ratio to two to one.[6] The chaotic structure of administration allowed military government officers to exaggerate the partisan threat in their own areas or even strike their own bargains with guerrilla bands in their sectors.[7]

By August 1942 the situation had so deteriorated that even Hitler accepted the need to overhaul the antipartisan effort. Führer Directive No. 46, issued by the OKW Operations Staff on August eighteenth, reversed previous policies but reaffirmed the foundation on which they had been built. The new approach emphasized the importance of offensive action, provided for substantial reinforcement of the rear areas, and authorized the expansion of native Russian units engaged in antipartisan fighting. Organizationally, the directive clarified matters by dividing operational responsibility between Himmler in the *Reichskommissariate* and the OKH for the area under military government. Himmler was also designated the "central authority for the collection and evaluation of all information concerning . . . bandits." Above all, the political importance of popular support at last received recognition:

The confidence of the local population in German authority must be gained by handling them strictly but justly. . . . In this struggle against the bandits the cooperation of the local population is indispensable.

Yet the new directive contradicted its own provisions by lapsing into Nazi rhetoric. The above quotation was followed by the exhortation that "reprisals for action in support of the bandits must be all the more severe" and the warning, "Misplaced confidence in the native population . . . must be strictly guarded against."[8] In short, the directive conceded that the partisans could not be defeated without the help of the Russian population, but the population could not be trusted.

The futility of the policy of terror became evident even to SS officials by the late summer. In September the *Reichssicherheitshauptamt* issued a brief handbook on antipartisan operations which strongly discouraged the use of collective reprisals against the local population, where the latter had not voluntarily cooperated with partisans; in contrast to previous practices, the handbook held that reprisals were not justified against villages that merely provided food to partisans.[9] But if German authorities recognized that the ruthless, indiscriminate use of terror to break the partisan movement had failed, the question remained: What was to replace it?

For the reformers, the answer was both obvious and a key rationale for the general liberalization of occupation policy. In his memorandum of November 1942, FHO chief Colonel Reinhard Gehlen stressed the need of popular support against the partisans: "[I]f the population rejects the partisans and lends its full support to the struggle against them, no partisan problem will exist."[10] *Wi-Stab-Ost* officials in the guerrilla-infested areas of Army Group Center made the same point even more strongly in May 1943: "It must be clear that the complete destruction of the partisans is only possible through the Russians themselves. If we succeed in capturing the enthusiasm of the entire Russian population . . . we can master the partisans within the foreseeable future."[11]

An alternative view of the partisan war, however, prevailed in quarters much closer to the führer. This concept began where the reformers ended, with the destruction of the guerrilla bands as the foundation for an intensified economic exploitation and a further preparation for the racial-colonial settlement of the future. Hitler himself set the tone in a directive of October 18, 1942, commonly known as the "Commando Order" but which included the following comments on the partisan conflict in Russia:

Only where the struggle against the partisan nuisance was begun and carried out with ruthless brutality have successes been achieved. . . . Throughout the eastern territories the war against the partisans is therefore a struggle of total annihilation of one side or the other.[12]

Eight days later *Reichsmarschall* Hermann Goering, acting as director of the Four Year Plan, issued a directive concerning the economic aspects of antipartisan operations. This order, consonant with Goering's policy of "immediate and maximum exploitation" from the beginning, applied the following formula for "partisan-infested areas:" all livestock and foodstuffs to be confiscated, all able-bodied men and women to be evacuated for use as labor and children to be sent to special camps, the whole of which would receive precedence over considerations of agricultural production.[13] Himmler implemented this policy with an order to his subordinates on October thirtieth.[14]

Thus, the rival concepts for dealing with the partisan menace began to assume concrete form in the autumn of 1942. Caught squarely between them was the OKW Operational Staff, composed of military men who perceived the need for a change in policy but who were too close to Hitler to oppose his views. Yet it fell to this staff to compose a general handbook for the German Armed Forces on the combatting of partisans.

The product, the "Combat Directive for Anti-Partisan Warfare in the East" issued on November 11, 1942, illustrates the ambiguity and uncertainty of the revised principles of the German anti-partisan effort. The manual provided advice on the use of certain battle tactics and organization, but the directive's drafters later admitted they were not drawing upon an extensive amount of actual experience.[15] Most confusing were the measures prescribed for dealing with guerrillas and the local population. Partisan deserters were now granted prisoner-of-war status "according to circumstances," but captured partisans and their civilian supporters were to be "shot or better, hanged." The burning of villages as reprisal measures was forbidden, but collective measures against propartisan communities could still extend to the complete destruction of villages, at the discretion of the commanding officer. "Unjust punishment shakes the confidence of the population and creates new partisans," warned the manual; but "the severity of our measures and the fear of expected punishment must restrain the population from aid or support of the partisans." The manual thus provided justification for political reformer and fanatic Nazi alike.[16]

Hitler's own reaction to the handbook further illustrates the confusion of ideas that characterized the antipartisan effort. *Generaloberst* Alfred Jodl, chief of the OKW Operations Staff, issued the handbook without Hitler's formal approval due to the latter's misgivings over the lenient provisions. During a conference on December 1, 1942, when Hitler voiced his concern that the new policy might handcuff the troops in dealing with partisans, Jodl reassured him: "[The soldiers] can do whatever they want to in combat; they may hang them, hang them upside down or quarter them; there is nothing about that [in the directive]. The only limitation concerns reprisals after the battle. . . . ''[17]

But even this did not assuage Hitler. On December sixteenth he issued through OKW an order for the combatting of partisans "with the most brutal (*allerbrutalsten*) means . . . against women and children as well." The order moreover exempted German soldiers from accountability under military law for actions against the guerrillas. A subsequent directive of April 27, 1943 reiterated these themes and elevated the conduct of antipartisan operations to the same status as frontline combat.[18]

The complete inconsistency of the new course of German antipartisan policy quickly became evident to those charged with the task of implementing it. Not surprisingly, German field commanders interpreted these directives as they saw fit. Some pursued humanitarian policies to undermine partisan morale. The commander of Fourth Army, for example, conducted an effective propaganda campaign against the guerrillas and treated prisoners well, so that by the spring of 1943 his area was virtually clear of partisans.[19] General Rudolf Schmidt, commanding Second Panzer Army, countered the December 16th directive by limiting its applicability to acts committed in the heat of battle; it was not, Schmidt stressed, an endorsement for indiscriminate slaughter.[20] Others recognized that a further step was necessary to win the "hearts and minds" of the people: the commanders of the Second Panzer Army Rear Area and the 203rd Security Division both urged the immediate establishment of clear political goals to secure popular support against the partisans.[21] Still others, however, fell back upon the policy of counter-terror to meet the partisan menace. On April 1, 1943 the commander of Third Panzer Army authorized the use of "every means" against the guerrillas, and ordered: "Captured bandits—if necessary after a brief interrogation—are to be shot."[22]

The tentative and provisional nature of the November directive is best illustrated by the changes recommended by German commands to modify its provisions. Army Group Center objected to the considerations regarding prisoners and suggested that captured partisans be executed after interrogation, except for those who furnished valuable intelligence or who volunteered for antipartisan service; partisan deserters could be treated as prisoners-of-war or deserters. The Second Army's recommended changes included the authorization of "any and all means" to obtain information during interrogations, and a restatement of the Goering directive for the mass evacuation and labor utilization of the populace from "infested" areas. The agricultural section of *Wi-Stab-Ost* remonstrated strongly against unnecessary destruction of life and livestock beyond that incidental to actual combat, and proposed a direct involvement of the local *La-führer* in antipartisan operations.[23]

To eliminate this ambiguity and demonstrate the value of a positive program, Gehlen initiated a major campaign in the spring and early summer of 1943 to improve the treatment accorded deserters and prisoners from partisan bands. From April through June Gehlen waged a propaganda war on two fronts, preparing convincing leaflets for the partisans (including appeals by former guerrillas) and convincing memoranda for OKH to accord humane treatment of partisan deserters and prisoners.[24] Gehlen's efforts won OKH's approval on July first of "Basic Order No. 13a," an extension of a directive issued in April 1943 to grant favorable treatment to Red Army deserters. By this order Soviet partisans who fell into German hands received the same treatment as regular Soviet forces: Those who surrendered outside of combat situations were to be given preferential treatment as deserters, all partisans captured in battle would be treated as prisoners-of-war. Only those captured in German uniform, caught in an act of sabotage, or of whom a "malicious act" could be proven, were to be shot.[25]

The earliest results of the new policy were hardly conclusive. During May and June 1943 Army Group Center took advantage of the lull along the front to mount five antipartisan operations in its rear areas, using regular combat troops with *Luftwaffe* support in addition to Gehlen's new propaganda campaign. The most successful operation, code-named ZIGEUNERBARON ("Gypsy Baron"), succeeded in breaking up the guerrilla bands in one sector with losses of 1584 killed, 1568 captured, and the impressive total of 869 deserters, thus demonstrating the significance of disorganization and disrupted command for increased partisan desertion. But the other operations could not match this accomplishment. The partisan *otrady* (units) evaded the German sweeps, the two largest of which netted a total of only 30 partisan deserters.[26]

Moreover, Gehlen did not enjoy a consensus of support for his policy among German field commands. Both the Second Army and Second Panzer Army command staffs considered Gehlen's directive too lenient, and believed the population would misinterpret the new policy as a "wavering attitude" by the

Germans. In transmitting these objections Field Marshal von Kluge, commanding Army Group Center, added his own reservations, particularly the application of "deserter" status to any partisans while operations were in progress.[27] As late as December 1943, the Xth Army Corps cited the necessity of "Draconian punishment" to deal with partisans and urged a return to the practice of executing captured guerrillas.[28]

Precisely such measures remained standard procedure in the areas under civil administration, where they were integrated with the genocide of Soviet Jews. Under Himmler's authority, SS, police, and *Wehrmacht* units carried out bloody sweeps of the Reich commissariats with such tallies of "body counts" as the following for the southern regions from September through November 1942 alone:[29]

Bandits killed in battle:	1337
Prisoners immediately executed:	737
Prisoners executed after interrogation:	7828
Bandit suspects and auxiliaries shot:	14,257
Jews executed:	363,211

In early February 1943, *Ostminister* Rosenberg complained to Himmler of the excessive destruction wrought in these operations, pointing to the increased partisan activity in the areas as evidence of the ineffectiveness of such measures.[30] Later that month Himmler's "Plenipotentiary for Bandit Warfare," SS-*Obergruppenführer* Erich von dem Bach-Zelewski, obliged with a directive to SS and police commanders reminding them that the destruction of partisans was not synonymous with the destruction of all human life in the guerrilla areas, and that even captured bandits could be utilized as labor in Germany.[31]

Such positive signs, however, carried little meaning against established SS practices, and the worst of these was yet to come. In June 1943, SS-*Obergruppenführer* Curt von Gottberg conducted Operation KOTTBUS against a "partisan republic" on the eastern border of *Generalkommissariat* White Russia. The Germans encountered stiff partisan resistance (nearly seven hundred German casualties), but when the guerrillas slipped away the operation degenerated into a slaughter of the local population. Gottberg claimed 6042 partisans killed in combat, 3709 others "liquidated," and 599 prisoners—but only a thousand rifles and machine guns were recovered. In addition, Gottberg noted that "approximately two to three thousand local people were blown up in the clearing of the [partisan] minefields."[32]

KOTTBUS provoked a storm of protest from the German civil administrators responsible for that region. Propaganda Director Lauch, who accompanied the expedition as the representative of *Generalkommissar* Wilhelm Kube, was horrified by the indiscriminate slaughter of inhabitants, the burning of villages, and the wholesale destruction of property and livestock. "The whole is a sorry picture of senseless destruction . . . all those events prove irrevocably the uselessness of pushing a successful propaganda campaign, as we have no good points what-soever in our favor to impart to the population.'' Kube drew the necessary conclusions as to the ultimate results of such practices: ''If the treatment of the native population in the occupied eastern areas is continued in the same manner . . . then in the coming winter we may expect not partisans, but the revolt of the entire country.''[33]

Even SS officers began to question the cost of these operations. In a letter written in July 1943, SS-*Brigadeführer* Eberhard Herf, commander of native police units in the Ukraine, assessed Operation KOTTBUS as follows:

Yesterday a *Gauleiter* . . . broadcast certain secret reports [intended for the führer] showing that some 480 rifles were found on 6,000 dead ''partisans.'' Put bluntly, *all these men had been shot* to swell the figure of enemy losses and highlight our own ''heroic deeds.'' I am under no illusions that, this being the system, the winter 1943–44 will see the beginning of the end in the rear areas and probably at the front as well. The increase in guerrilla warfare is simply and solely due to the way the Russians have been treated.[34]

These complaints, however, accomplished nothing. Gottlob Berger fended off Kube's attacks as ''unchecked'' and irrelevant as the *Ostministerium* lacked ''exact insight into the situation'' in the field. When Herf approached Himmler directly on the discrepancy between body counts and weapons recovered, the *Reichsführer* retorted: ''You appear not to know that these bandits destroy their weapons to play the innocent and so avoid death.''[35]

Ironically, on at least one occasion SS and army authorities did attempt to punish a German atrocity. Following a partisan ambush, a *Wehrmacht* sergeant and some of his men carried out their own reprisal upon a nearby village, brutally murdering four or five Russian citizens. SS-*Obergruppenführer* von dem Bach-Zelewski and General von Schenckendorff jointly arraigned the accused before a court martial. The offenders were convicted and sentenced to death, but the sentence was overturned by OKW, faithful to Hitler's directive of December 16, 1942.[36]

The resolution of the conflict between the alternative policies finally came in the summer of 1943, through the direct intervention of the führer. Hitler rejected the political approach on May nineteenth in his mediation of the dispute between Rosenberg and Koch: ''The fight with the partisans does not depend on political circumstances. . . . It has been established that just in places where generals with particular 'political savvy' are in command, the population is most harassed by partisans.''[37]

On July tenth Hitler ordered the mass evacuation of the guerrilla strongholds in the northern Ukraine and central Russia, with the great bulk of the able-bodied population to be utilized as forced labor in the rear areas of the Reich.[38] The *Ostministerium* objected strongly to the potentially disastrous consequences of this directive, but to no avail.[39] As with so many other aspects of *Ostpolitik*, the Soviet advance of summer 1943 rendered the full execution of these plans academic.

Fittingly, an OKW directive of August 18, 1943 reaffirmed the same inconsistency and ambiguity of German antipartisan policy that had stimulated attempts
to change it. The Armed Forces High Command, in coordination with *Reichsführer* Himmler, nominally endorsed Gehlen's liberal provisions for the treatment
of captured partisans, with one difference: in the event of "particularly malicious
acts" of the partisans, local German commanders were permitted the discretion
of shooting their prisoners and the populations of implicated areas.[40] In short,
nothing had changed.

In any case, the Armed Forces High Command had essentially conceded defeat
in its pacification program one month earlier. In an assessment of the partisan
situation on July eighth, the OKW Operations Staff concluded "that our own
anti-partisan measures, despite the employment of strong forces . . . have not
attained the desired success . . . [W]e must recognize that a pacification of the
Eastern territories by our continued measures is not to be expected."[41]

In summer 1943 German antipartisan policy thus stood as a compromise
between two irreconcilable viewpoints while the partisan movement remained
stronger than ever. Gehlen's endeavors had not proved fruitless, as they directly
contributed to the sparing of thousands of captured guerrillas and "suspects"
during the large-scale operations of spring 1944.[42] But the effort to incorporate
antipartisan warfare within a positive political framework failed. Given the very
nature of guerrilla warfare, and the lack of a general redirection of *Ostpolitik*,
this was hardly surprising. Yet if German policy understandably stumbled in
appealing to those who resisted occupation, could it improve in rewarding those
who took up arms on its behalf?

NOTES

1. Most notable among the many works on this subject are: *Sovetskie partizany. Iz
istorii partizanskogo dvizheniia v gody Velikoi Otechestvennoi voiny* (Moscow: Gosu-
darstvennoe izdatel'stvo politicheskoi literatury, 1963), and *Vsenarodnoe partizanskoe
dvizhenie v belorussii v gody Velikoi Otechstvennoi voiny iynn 1941–iyul 1944: Dokumenty
i materialy v trekh tomakh*, comp. Institut Istorii Akademii nauk BSSR (3 vols. in 4
parts) (Minsk: Belarus, 1967–1982).

2. Hermann Teske, "Railroad Transportation, Operation ZITADELLE," FMS Ms.
No. D–369 (Historical Division, United States Army Europe, 1948), p. 10.

3. See above Chapter 7.

4. Armstrong, *Partisans*, pp. 249–76, 328–32; Leo Heiman, "Organized Looting:
The Basis of Partisan Warfare," *Military Review*, Vol XLV, No. 2 (February 1965),
p. 67; and Tim Mulligan, "Reckoning the Cost of People's War: The German Experience
in the Central USSR," *Russian History IX*, Pt. 1 (1982), pp. 32–34, 37–41.

5. See MGFA, *Das deutsche Reich*, Bd. 4, pp. 1030–61.

6. Howell, *Partisan Movement*, pp. 59–60, 70.

7. Vladimir Pozdnyakov, "German Counterintelligence Activities in Occupied Russia
1941–45" (Historical Division, U.S. Army Europe, 1951), FMS Mss. No. P–122,
pp. 85–86, 116–18.

8. Walter Hubatsch, Ed., *Hitlers Weisungen für die Kriegführung* (Munich: Deutscher Taschenbuch Verlag, 1965), pp. 232–37.

9. RSHA, "Bandenbekämpfung," September 1942, T–175/222/2759971–988.

10. Gehlen, "Dringende Fragen," T–78/556/538.

11. Wi-Stab-Ost, Abt.I/Id, "Monatsbericht Wi Stab Ost (1.5–31.5.1943)," June 16, 1943, T–77/1090/345.

12. See Hubatsch, *Weisungen*, pp. 239–42.

13. Directive of *Reichsmarschall* Goering, October 26, 1942, Document 1742-PS, *TMWC*, XXVIII, 1–2.

14. Reichsführer-SS Himmler, "SS-Befehl," October 30, 1942, T–175/81/2601765.

15. Affidavit of General Horst von Buttlar-Brandenfels, December 12, 1946, Document NOKW–577, RG 238, NA.

16. OKW/Wehrmachtführungsstab, "Kampfanweisung für die Bandenbekämpfung in Osten," November 11, 1942, T–501/32/0039–77.

17. See Helmut Heiber, ed., *Hitlers Lagebesprechungen: Die Protokollfragmente seiner militärischen Konferenzen 1942–1945* (Stuttgart: Deutsche Verlags-Anstalt, 1962), pp. 65–69, and Jodl's testimony in *TMWC*, XV, 545, 557–58.

18. See Müller, *Besatzungspolitik*, pp. 139–40, 146–48.

19. Affidavit of General Röttiger, December 8, 1945, Document 3713-PS, *TMWC*, XXXII, 477–79.

20. Ziemke, *Stalingrad to Berlin*, p. 115.

21. Korück 532 to PzAOK 2, July 9, 1943, T–311/219/1084–86; 203. Sich.Div./Ia, "Erfahrungsbericht über 'Maikäfer I–V' in der Zeit vom 3.–17.5.1943," May 29, 1943, T–315/1586/941–51.

22. PzAOK 3/Ic, "Ic-Nachrichten," April 1, 1943, Document NOKW–765, RG 238, NA.

23. Obkdo. d. H.Gr.Mitte/Ia, "Ergänzungs- und Änderungsvorschläge zu dem Merkblatt," April 14, 1943, Document NOKW–473, RG 238, NA; and Wi-Stab-Ost/Chefgruppe La, "Kampfanweisung für die Bandenbekämpfung," January 15, 1943, Document OCC–930, RG 238, NA.

24. See the material in OKH file H 3/746, T–78/489/6475099ff.

25. OKH, "Grundlegender Befehl Nr. 13a über die Behandlung von Partisanen," July 1, 1943, T–78/489/6475158–159.

26. Armstrong, *Partisans*, pp. 505–13.

27. Kluge to Gehlen, "Behandlung von Bandenüberläufern und Bandenüberläufer-Propaganda," June 23, 1943, T–78/489/6475103–105.

28. Generalkommando X. A.K./Ic, "Behandlung von Banditen," December 3, 1943, Document WB–4025, RG 238, NA.

29. Reichsführer-SS, "Meldungen an den Führer über Bandenbekämpfung: Meldung Nr. 51, Russland-Süd, Ukraine, Bialystok: Bandenbekämpfungserfolge vom 1.9. bis 1.12.1942," December 28, 1942, Document NO–3392, RG 238, NA.

30. Rosenberg to Himmler, February 4, 1943, EAP 99/154, MR 280, RG 242, NA.

31. Der Bevollmächtigte des Reichsführers-SS für Bandenbekämpfung, "Richtlinien für die Massnahmen zur Bandenbekämpfung," February 26, 1943, T–311/219/851.

32. Chief of Anti-partisan Units, "Special Report concerning the major operation 'Kottbus'," June 23, 1943, Document NO–2608, ND–2608, *NMI*, XII, 305–9.

33. Extracts from Lauch's report, June 2, 1943, and Kube to Rosenberg, June 3, 1943, Document NO–3028, *NMT*, XIII, 518–20.

34. SS-Brigadeführer Eberhard Herf to SS-Obergruppenführer Maximilien von Herff, July 19, 1943, published in Krausnick, *Anatomy*, pp. 346–47.

35. Ibid., and Berger to Bräutigam, July 13, 1943, *NMT*, XIII, 521–22.

36. Interrogation of Erich von dem Bach-Zelewski, January 17, 1947, RG 238, NA.

37. Otto Hewel, "Auszug aus Notiz für RAM v. 24.5," Document NG–3288, RG 238, NA.

38. Der Reichsführer-SS an dem Chef Bandenkampf-Verbände, July 10, 1943, Document NO–022, RG 238, NA.

39. Labs to Allwörden, "Evakuierung bandenverseuchter Gebiete," July 20, 1943, Document 1548-PS, RG 238, NA.

40. OKW/WFST directive, August 18, 1943, Document 747-PS, RG 238, NA.

41. *KTB/OKW*, III (2), p. 775.

42. See the data in Mulligan, "Reckoning," pp. 43–44.

11

THE *OSTTRUPPEN*: ASKARIS OR ALLIES?

In the euphoria of July 1941 Hitler specifically excluded any participation of the eastern peoples in the war against Stalin: *"We must never permit anybody but the German to carry arms!"*[1] As already noted, within a year Hitler had been forced to renounce this policy. The establishment of such troops, however, did not signify a change in *Ostpolitik* any more than Imperial Germany's reliance on native *askaris* in German East Africa had implied a surrender of colonial authority.[2] As Germany increased its use of Eastern troops during the 1942–43 period, the related questions of their military status, organization, compensation, decorations, and combat employment also grew in significance, particularly as all of the questions ultimately touched upon the contradictions within German policy—and among *Ostpolitik* reformers.

Within the Army High Command, two reformers occupied advantageous positions affecting the treatment of eastern nationals. Stauffenberg, as a section chief in the *Organisationsabteilung*, and Altenstadt, head of a section of OKH's military government department (*Abteilung Kriegsverwaltung*) under Quarter-master-General Wagner, shared the goal of a *levée en masse* of the Russian population against the Soviet regime. According to Heinz Herre, like-minded colleague in Gehlen's *Fremde Heere Ost*, the reformers promoted their views continually in discussions with other General Staff officers and won from Wagner a virtual free hand in dealing with the eastern troops. From his small headquarters barracks Stauffenberg was in constant telephone contact with other officers and officials on questions of *Ostpolitik* totally unrelated to his nominal duties. Though the Reich's political leadership did not yet accept the need for a change in policy, so these men believed, the foundation could be laid by increasing the reliance on eastern nationals to the point of gradual dependence.[3]

These efforts achieved a significant success with the most numerous category of Soviet nationals in German service, the *Hilfswillige* ("auxiliary volunteers," usually abbreviated as *Hiwis*). Since autumn 1941 Soviet prisoners-of-war and volunteers had been serving with the German Army as interpreters, cooks, drivers, mechanics and other noncombatant roles, comprising as much as one-half of the personnel in some rear area German units. An official estimate in March 1943 reckoned their total at 310,000.[4] These figures reflect in part Stauffenberg's work the previous October when the *Organisationsabteilung* finally legalized the *Hiwis*' status and established guidelines for their incorporation within army units.[5] In April 1943 OKH distributed a handbook on their treatment that provided for eligibility for family annuities in addition to pay, land grants, and distinctive uniforms and decorations.[6]

Because the *Hilfswillige* were integrated into German units, however, their improvement required less of OKH's reformers than for their compatriots serving in combat units, known collectively as *Osttruppen* ("eastern troops"). Though less numerous than the auxiliaries, the eastern troops presented a much more complex problem for German policy. In addition to the differentiation of treatment necessitated by the multinational character of the *Osttruppen*, the central questions of their existence—the size of the units, employment in combat, legal status, officer composition—ultimately hinged on the question of political reliability. The motivations among eastern troops ranged from ethnic or national antagonism, ideology, and opportunism to the simple escape from German captivity.[7]

In the absence of a consistent policy, German field commands improvised their own organization and employment of eastern nationals. In the southern sector, the preferential treatment accorded minority nationalities resulted in the establishment of six national "legions" (Turkestani, Azerbaidzani, North Caucasian, Georgian, Armenian, Volgatatar) whose field units totalled 15 battalions by autumn 1942 and another 21 battalions by spring 1943; each of these included 30 to 50 German officers and men as cadres with 300–700 legionnaires. In the Caucasus many of these battalions were committed to frontline combat duty even though inadequately armed and equipped, with consequent heavy losses in killed and wounded.[8] By contrast, the "Sonderverband Bergmann," under the command of *Ostpolitik* reformer Theodor Oberländer, distinguished itself in several engagements with a mixed force of Germans and Caucasians.[9] Similar results were obtained with the Kalmyk Cavalry Corps, numbering 3000 Kalmyks and a German cadre of only 71.[10]

Considerable differentiation of policy existed even among the ethnic Russians in German armed service, as illustrated in Army Group Center's sector. At the local level was the *Ordnungsdienst*, auxiliary policy recruited voluntarily by native authorities, whose duties and numbers (from 11,500 in February 1942 to 45,000 by August 1943) expanded to an important role in combatting partisans.[11]

In the autonomous Lokot' district, Bronislav Kaminsky expanded his militia to a private army of 10,000 men with some heavy weapons (including tanks) by spring 1943, designated by its leader the "Russian Popular Army of Liberation" (*Russkaia Osvoboditelnaia Narodnaia Armiia*, or RONA).[12]

Distributed among Army Group Center's combat units were several dozen "Ost-" battalions and independent companies, recruited mostly from Russian prisoners-of-war and usually engaged in security duties.[13] Two exceptions, however, offered a foundation for an expanded and more permanent role for eastern troops. One, the "East Replacement Regiment Center," developed into a replacement training center and depot under Russian command for all the army group's eastern units.[14] The other was the "Experimental Unit Center," originally organized by the *Abwehr* from Russian emigrés for commando operations but later enlarged to include released prisoners-of-war in regular combat duties. Actively supported by Tresckow and Gersdorff of the army group's headquarters staff, the formation numbered 7000 men by December 1942. With Russian commanders, Russian uniforms, and the Imperial Czarist cockade the unit considered itself the "Russian National People's Army" (*Russkaia Natsionalnaia Narodnaia Armiia*, abbreviated RNNA).[15]

Significantly, the largest and most independent Russian formation in German service at this time never set foot on Russian soil. In September 1941 the emigré community in Yugoslavia formed the "Russian Guard Corps Serbia" to fight against the Serbian communists. In January 1943 the 7500-strong formation was incorporated within the *Wehrmacht*, but retained its own command structure and Czarist insignia. The inter-relationship of the "Guard Corps" with other *Osttruppen* became evident during January–March 1943 when German authorities debated their eligibility for land grants in Russia and dispatched three hundred former Red Army soldiers to the "Guard Corps" as reinforcements.[16]

The expanded use of eastern troops during the 1942–43 period is vividly illustrated by the ration-strength of Army Group North. Through the end of 1942 only the German 18th Army kept separate returns for this category: These indicated a total of 6718 *Osttruppen* (over 70 percent of them Estonian) as of November 20, 1942, a figure that declined in the early winter fighting to 5765 by December thirty-first.[17] The data for the entire army group from February to July 1943, however, reveal a major growth in eastern troop strength (see Table 5). This 240 percent increase over five months is even greater when allowance is made for the replacement of casualties. In heavy fighting on March 20, 1943, for example, a single Estonian battalion of the 18th Army lost two hundred killed and wounded.[18]

The existing profusion of *Osttruppen* categories and formations in an active theater of operations precluded any unified policy on their behalf by Stauffenberg, Altenstadt and their associates. They adapted to the situation, however, with a strategy for a centralized administration of eastern troops but which allowed considerable flexibility in the field. Stauffenberg's department launched the plan on November 7, 1942 with the proposed creation of the office of *General der*

Table 5
Osttruppen Ration Strength, Army Group North, February–July 1943

	Feb.	Mar.	Apr.	May	June	July
18th Army	10,155	16,179	18,949	23,061	25,795	29,412
16th Army	10,590	12,644	14,728	21,957	23,666	27,158
Army Group Rear Area	7923	7772	10,324	12,119	14,281	12,102
Total	28,668	36,595	44,001	57,137	63,742	68,672

Source: Oberkommando der Heeresgruppe Nord/IVa,"Verpflegungs-stärken nach dem Stände von den 1.2.43, 1.3.43, 1.4.43, 1.5.43, 1.6.43, 1.7.43," T-311/115/7155291, 7155258, 7155391, 7155317, 7155598-599. Data do not include Hilfswillige.

Osttruppen (general of eastern troops) as a central inspectorate within OKH.[19] The office's proposed authority, however, was apparently considerably diluted before OKW approved the draft.[20] The post became operational on December fifteenth with administrative responsibility for the treatment, organization, training and equipment for all eastern nationals serving with the German Army, including *Hilfswillige* and the *Ordnungsdienst*; it was also responsible for determinations of appropriate German cadres and for the management of personnel matters.[21] Though lacking in executive authority, the new post nevertheless represented both a gain and an opportunity for the reformers, depending on the office's occupant.

Lieutenant General Heinz Hellmich, recalled from reserve duty, became the first *General der Osttruppen* on the recommendation of his former subordinate Colonel Alexis von Roenne, operations officer in Gehlen's FHO. Having spent more than two years as a prisoner of the Russians during World War I, Hellmich understood some Russian but could not speak the language. He possessed no particular qualifications for his assignment beyond those of a decent man with good intentions. He cooperated with the army reformers but displayed little initiative or drive, traits that may have been lost with the deaths of his two sons in the early years of the war. Though his position resulted directly from attempted political change, Hellmich himself shied away from political questions, as when he expressed sympathy with Vlasov's goals during his first meeting with the Russian defector but carefully avoided any commitment of support.[22]

Far worse was Hellmich's choice of staff officers, drawn largely from his former field command. Only two of this group could speak Russian, and except for the chief medical officer and the *OMi* liaison officer they approached their tasks as routine staff assignments. The intelligence officer on the staff actively worked against the reformers' goals, in the opinion of the latter. The one exception, Hellmich's chief of staff Lieutenant Colonel Wessel von Freytag-

Loringhoven (who had earlier organized the cossack units with Army Group South) was understood to be only temporarily assigned.[23]

To a large degree this problem resulted from the reformers' own decision to concentrate their efforts in Army Group A's sector in the Caucasus. The region's relatively privileged status provided the opportunity to expand the role of native formations to complement Kleist's experiment in military government.[24] The officers assembled for this task in the summer and autumn of 1942 represented a collection of Germans uniquely qualified for command of eastern nationals. Most senior of these was General Ernst Köstring, born in Moscow to German parents and former military attache to the USSR with 30 of his 66 years spent in Russia. In August 1942 Stauffenberg and Herwarth von Bittenfeld persuaded Köstring to accept the post of "commissioner-general of Caucasian Affairs," with Herwarth (a former diplomatic official in Moscow from 1931 until 1938) as his aide.[25]

Another Russian expert, Oskar Ritter von Niedermayer, provided a direct link between the Rapallo era of cooperation between Weimar Germany and Soviet Russia and the *Ostpolitik* reformers of 1942–43. After spending most of World War I in Iran and Turkey, Niedermayer played an important role in Moscow in 1931–32, negotiating armaments and goods agreements between Germany and Russia. In late May 1942 he received command of the yet-to-be formed 162nd (Turkic) Infantry Division, drawn from the national legions of the Caucasus. Niedermayer spent the autumn of 1942 among the recruiting and training camps in Poland and the Ukraine, as well as several trips to East Prussia to discuss the division's establishment with Stauffenberg.[26]

Colonel Hellmuth von Pannwitz lacked the Soviet expertise of others but as a boy he socialized with the Cossack cavalry who patrolled the Russian frontier near his Silesian home. He also enjoyed the advantage of impressive National Socialist credentials. A *Freikorps* veteran, Pannwitz commanded an SA cavalry squadron in 1934; during the Röhm Purge that year, Pannwitz's cooperation with the Gestapo in Silesia earned him party membership and the recognition of party and SS officials. During September and October 1942 he was engaged in organizing and upgrading Army Group A's cossack formations, over which he was given command on November 8, 1942.[27]

In terms of military organization, the reformers initially adhered to the limitation of eastern units to battalion-sized formations; the 162nd Infantry Division was conceived by Stauffenberg as an administrative umbrella under which military training and political indoctrination could be implemented.[28] But after Stalingrad and the huge losses in German manpower, plans were revised to create mixed German eastern divisions. In March 1943 the *Organisationsabteilung* (now without Stauffenberg, who had transferred to a field command in North Africa) approved a proposal by the 162nd's staff for its conversion to a regular combat division, composed of approximately 40 percent German and 60 percent Turkic personnel. By April nineteenth OKH had secured Hitler's approval for the project and prepared plans for two additional German-Turkic divisions, though these would be restricted to defensive actions in quiet sectors.[29] The establishment of the cossack cavalry division finally received OKH approval on April twenty-third. After five months' training in Mielau (Mlawa), East Prussia, the division fielded six cavalry regiments averaging 2000 Cossacks and 150 Germans each, with technical units composed entirely of Germans.[30]

The 162nd Division's proposal probably reflected the impracticability of the reformers' original plans. The intended activation of 25 Turkic infantry battalions by October 1, 1942, each to consist of about 37 German cadre personnel and 950 native troops, foundered on the shortcomings of both the Turkic recruits and their German organizers.[31] It became evident that the majority of the recruits volunteered simply to escape the miserable conditions of captivity. They moreover suffered from education handicaps that greatly impaired their training: one training camp reported that one-fourth of its Turkic recruits were illiterate and 35 percent could converse and write only in their native dialect.[32] Moreover, the overburdened German logistics system could not cope with the requirements of these units. The volunteers lacked sufficient clothing, weapons, and equipment; the units suffered from shortages in heavy weapons, spare parts, vehicles, and particularly horses for transportation. Less than half of the battalions were ready for combat by mid-December.[33] At the front, these shortcomings were revealed and the use of such units questioned: one German division broke up its battalion and distributed its companies among regular German infantry, while another division disarmed its battalion altogether and restricted the legionnaires to noncombat duties.[34]

More significant than equipment shortages, the attitudes of German cadre personnel posed a major problem to the development of eastern units. In Oberländer's "Sonderverband Bergmann" and Pannwitz's cossack division German officers and noncommissioned personnel were rather carefully selected, with knowledge of Slavic languages less essential than an understanding of the nature of the eastern nationals with whom they worked.[35] But even with the assignment of commanders like Köstring and Niedermayer, the training cadres for the Turkic battalions drew upon the staffs of prisoner-of-war camps, men who were used to treating their trainees as captives. Through the end of 1942 an insufficient number of translators were available; and even well-meaning German officers serving with these troops erred in projecting their own nationalist motives on the legionnaires or otherwise neglecting the latter's cultural traits.[36]

Yet conditions among the legionnaires were much more favorable than those among the *Osttruppen* in general. Shortages in weapons, clothing, and equipment were even more pronounced. Köstring later described the majority of German cadre personnel as "utterly incompetent," whose officers considered duty with these units a penalty.[37] Such attributes were scarcely concealed from the troops and merely facilitated the work of the Soviet agents who easily infiltrated these units to encourage redefection to the Red Army.[38] With the Soviet successes in summer 1943, it is not surprising that the desertion rate among *Osttruppen* was estimated at 8 to 10 percent.[39] A particularly high desertion rate for a unit occasionally resulted in the relief of the German commander,[40] but more typically provoked a terrible retribution: one mass desertion led to the execution of 137 other members of the battalion by the SS within 48 hours.[41]

In spring 1943, German authorities attempted to improve the lot of the eastern troops. In late May, Hellmich's staff gained the services of Heinz Herre from FHO as chief of staff to the *General der Osttruppen*, and in the next weeks he replaced most of Hellmich's appointees with better-qualified staff officers.[42] By this time all military commands down to the army level had been assigned "commanders of eastern troops f(or) s(special) d(uty)" (*Kommandeure der Ost-truppen z.b.V.*) to represent Hellmich's headquarters in the field. The standardization of treatment and pay for the *Hilfswillige* in April has already been noted. Through the spring of 1943 Hellmich's office distributed recommendations on the treatment and utilization of eastern nationals, sponsored training sessions in specialized combat for eastern units, and prepared translations of training manuals into Russian. Most significantly, an officers' training school for indigenous officers was established in June 1943 at Mariampol, Lithuania, under the direction of a former Soviet colonel.[43] Hellmich also interceded with other Reich authorities on behalf of the *Osttruppen* and their family members for increased food rations and legal- and medical disability–assistance.[44]

But these measures ultimately depended on German field commands to implement them, and the latter often challenged Hellmich, even on matters where all were agreed on reformist goals. In March 1943, for example, Hellmich proposed the formation of a Crimean Tatar Legion in the same manner of the other minority nationalities; Field Marshal von Kleist, whose liberal policies in the Caucasus exemplified *Ostpolitik* reform, opposed the move and instead recommended that Tatar volunteers be withdrawn from their units and concentrated in the Crimea as a self-defense force.[45] The question of training Russian officers of the eastern units appears to have touched a particularly sensitive nerve among German commands. The Mariampol school may well have resulted from Hellmich's decision to withdraw former Soviet officers from the *Osttruppen* ranks as "security risks" until more units were organized.[46] Army Group Center refused to accept any of the first graduates of the program, effectively limiting the training school's purpose from graduating native officers to producing mere certifications of officers qualified to command.[47]

Despite the presence of reformers like Tresckow and Gersdorff, Army Group Center's command staff had already bungled the handling of its largest Russian unit. During the first week of November 1942 Kluge's headquarters decided to reorganize the "Experimental Unit Center" as a regiment along the same lines as all other eastern units; to the unit's members, this was a betrayal of their purpose as the "Russian National People's Army." The strong protests of Russian officers accomplished only the retention of Russian uniforms and officers. With their battalions scheduled for a scattered commitment along the front, RNNA commanders General Georgi Zhilenkov and Colonel Vladimir Boyarsky continued to resist the changes in discussions with German officials on December twenty-ninth and with Kluge himself on December thirty-first; as a result, Army Group Center lost confidence in a front-line commitment of the unit, relieved Zhilenkov and Boyarsky of command, and broke up the formation for piecemeal deployment in rear-area security. Three hundred men reportedly deserted to the partisans when the decision was announced.[48]

Moreover, Hellmich's avoidance of controversial issues could not conceal the ultimate policy implications of even material rewards for eastern troops. This occurred in 1943 on the question of land grants to eastern nationals who had distinguished themselves in military service, even though Hitler himself had agreed to their preferential treatment in this regard the previous summer.[49] On February 9, 1943 OKH issued a directive that increased rewards in land grants, property additions, livestock, and farm machinery to deserving *Osttruppen*, as well as longer furloughs to work the land.[50] This appears to have brought about results: during the period April 21–May 20, 1943 the Second Panzer Army alone awarded a total of 250 hectares of land (roughly 617.5 acres) to 172 Russians serving in police or military units or with the civil administration, the most common grant being one hectare but extending to as many as seven.[51] But when Army Group North drafted a plan to reward *Osttruppen* with five hectares, *Wi-Stab-Ost* agricultural chief Riecke's objections forced the plan's revision to smaller grants.[52]

More significantly, the land grant issue aroused the concern of Himmler. The *Reichsführer* attacked the OKH proposal as "fundamentally erroneous," offering his own view that native soldiers be granted just enough land to guarantee their continued service throughout the war.[53] In the ensuing discussions to resolve the issue, OKH found itself removed from the picture while OKW and Himmler agreed on the priority of reserved lands for German soldiers as future colonists and restricted land grants to *Osttruppen*. By the end of July 1943 Himmler had won his point with OKW's ruling that not more than 2 percent of all eastern nationals in German service (about 24,000 total) would become eligible for land in any year, and the actual granting of land would be largely postponed until war's end.[54]

It is therefore ironic that the man who so strongly opposed rewarding collaborators with their own land should also arm, equip and organize eastern nationals on a scale the *Wehrmacht* never dared. In part this followed from the *Reichsführer*'s designated security responsibilities in the Reich commissariats, but principally it represented the rapid growth of the *Waffen*-SS in the period after Stalingrad. Despite heavy losses in Russia and a drop-off in volunteers, the *Waffen*-SS doubled in size between summer 1942 and summer 1943 by recruiting ethnic Germans from southeastern Europe and foreign volunteers from across Europe.[55] Himmler himself had misgivings over the quality of some of these formations, and none more so than those of the eastern nationalities.

Himmler's reluctant but eventual acceptance of the Baltic SS formations in 1942–43 has already been noted.[56] As with the Turkic nationalities, the generic term *legion* described only the administrative framework for the establishment of field units; unlike the Caucasian legions, this structure allowed native officers to hold senior rank and exercise some command in the field, though operational command remained firmly in German hands. As SS formations, they enjoyed weapons, uniforms, and equipment much superior to those of their *Wehrmacht* counterparts. In late February the 15th Latvian SS Volunteer Division came into being under the formal command of former Latvian Minister of War Rudolf Bangerskis, now with the full rank of *SS-Gruppenführer und Generalleutnant der Waffen-SS*. In fact, however, the division did not become fully operational until summer and was actually commanded by *SS-Brigadeführer und General-major der Waffen-SS* Peter Hansen (succeeded in May 1943 by Carl Graf von Pückler-Burghaus). Meanwhile three Latvian auxiliary police battalions already serving in the front lines combined with German support units to form the "Latvian SS Volunteer Brigade" in May 1943, the same month that the "Estonian SS Volunteer Brigade" was established, with the national hero Johannes Soodla carrying out the same titular functions as Bangerskis.[57]

It is important to recognize the initial appeal of the SS at a time when the German Army acknowledged the outstanding quality of their own Estonian battalions, yet had to beg for permission to award them the Iron Cross.[58] Lured by promises of equal treatment, at least 33 of 45 identified deserters from these units as of May 1943 had joined the Estonian SS Brigade. At that time one of those who had remained wrote Dr. Mäe, head of the Estonian "self-administration," whether the battalions could not be transferred directly to the Estonian Legion.[59] The SS, however, quickly dissipated this goodwill. In early April 1943 Latvian recruits were rushed into the front lines in violation of an understanding of a minimum six months' basic training before combat, while a battalion of the Estonian Brigade was shipped off to the Ukraine as reinforcements for the SS "Wiking" division.[60] A former Estonian reserve officer who served with both the German Army and the SS rated relations between the nationalities better in the *Wehrmacht*, noting that inexperienced junior SS officers angered many of his countrymen through their arrogance.[61] This man joined several hundred Estonians who fled to Finland to offer their services in the Finnish Army, a development to which, in a final ironic touch, German Army authorities in Helsinki turned a blind eye.[62]

Himmler was even more uneasy regarding a Ukrainian SS, a project whose initial proposal by Gottlob Berger in April 1941 he had categorically rejected.[63] But at the beginning of March 1943 SS-*Gruppenführer* Dr. Otto Wächter, governor of Galicia in the *Generalgouvernement*, resurrected the proposal in discussions with Himmler. Undoubtedly influenced by SS losses and the Stalingrad defeat, Himmler this time concurred and secured Hitler's permission for an SS Volunteer Division "Galicia," relying upon the local population to supply the necessary horses, wagons, and winter clothing as well as recruits. Wächter's subsequent appeal for volunteers met with some 80,000 applications by the beginning of June. Unprepared for such numbers, the SS recruiting offices had processed only 26,436 applications by June twenty-first, of whom only 13,562 qualified for military service and only 3,281 met *Waffen*-SS standards.[64]

The influence of Ukrainian nationalism that lay behind this response was unsettling to Himmler. SS recruiting staffs were instructed to avoid references to any "brotherhood" or "alliance" between Germans and Ukrainians, as well as any mention of political independence.[65] The *Reichsführer* rationalized the division as a continuation of Habsburg military tradition, and accorded priority to former Austro-Hungarian officers in filling officer posts. When Himmler officially forbade any reference to Ukrainian nationality on July 14, 1943, even Wächter protested against the fiction of a "Galician" identity and warned of the possible consequences of any attempt to strip the recruits of their national consciousness.[66] Wächter's pragmatism matched that of Ukrainian nationalist and religious leaders, who believed German victory impossible but gambled on the opportunity to establish a military force for future independent action.[67] The "SS Volunteer Division 'Galicia' " (later the "14th Waffen-Grenadier-Division der SS (Galizische Nr. 1)") became combat-ready only in time to be shattered at Brody in July 1944. Not until five months later would the SS replace the designation "Galician" with "Ukrainian" in the division's title, by which time the unit would never again set foot on its native soil.[68]

Of more immediate significance to Himmler were the auxiliary police and antipartisan formations employed in the Reich commissariats, numbering over 238,000 by the beginning of 1943.[69] As he utilized these auxiliaries not only for antipartisan activities but the extermination of the occupied Jewish population, Himmler attached considerable importance to the ideological training of these troops. In mid-March 1943 he concluded an agreement with the *Ostministerium* that awarded him this responsibility (possibly in the context of the abortive Rosenberg-Himmler alliance). The agreement stressed the need to develop "the strong instinctive anti-Semitism of the eastern nations" as the foundation of the future New Order.[70] To reinforce ideology, Himmler also provided cash incentives. In early June 1943, even as he fought against land grants to *Osttruppen*, the *Reichsführer* significantly increased the settlement pay awarded Ukrainian auxiliaries on completion of service, over the objections of OKH and the economic authorities (who could not match these increases for their own eastern troops).[71]

Himmler's agreement with the *Ostministerium* in part merely recognized existing conditions, but it also allowed him to plan for the future. Himmler established, for example, a special training camp for selected eastern recruits at Trawniki, near Lublin, Poland. A battalion of these auxiliaries—openly referred to by their SS commander as "askaris"—participated in the crushing of the Warsaw Ghetto in April–May 1943, but their conduct there was later described by their superiors as "a real disappointment."[72]

But Himmler's indoctrination program was to suffer a greater blow. One of the SS-sponsored units, known as the Brigade *Druzhina* (a medieval Russian term for an elite bodyguard), consisted of Russians and Ukrainians recruited from a pool of potential intelligence agents and saboteurs for use behind Soviet lines. Under the command of former Red Army Lieutenant Colonel Vladimir Rodionov (who assumed the name ''Gil''), the 2000-strong brigade acquired a reputation for ruthlessness in antipartisan operations, including the notorious Operation ''Kottbus'' in Belorussia in June 1943. Only two months later, however, Rodionov and most of the *Druzhina* redefected to the Soviets after killing its German contingent, thereafter operating as partisans. One can only imagine the outcry in National Socialist circles had this involved an army rather than an SS unit.[73]

The *Druzhina*'s redefection provided a fitting epitaph to the story of the East European SS in 1943. Just as the *Waffen*-SS represented a military force outside of the German Army, so Himmler had mobilized eastern nationals into SS service to rival that of the *Wehrmacht*. In so doing he expanded his military arm, strengthened his war against the Jews and broadened his political power in the East. Yet none of his objectives and justifications proved valid. The selection of ''racially suitable'' Estonians and Latvians for frontline duty had not sacrificed their nationalism to Germanization; the appeal to Habsburg military tradition had not disguised the reliance on Ukrainian nationalism to produce recruits; and ideological training had failed to prevent the largest mass redefection of an eastern unit during the war. The *Reichsführer*'s subsequent rhetoric reaffirmed National Socialist dogma regarding eastern nationalities,[74] but his actions had already compromised those principles in an irreversible manner.

No final statistics of the total participation of eastern nationals in German military service are available. An estimate prepared by Hellmich's staff on February 2, 1943 reckoned the total number of former Soviet nationals in military service at 750,000, including 400,000 *Hilfswillige*.[75] An authoritative post-war study of the German Army estimates the combatant eastern troops at 130,000–150,000 by the beginning of 1943 and between 220,000–320,000 *Hiwis* as of June 1943.[76] These figures cover only the army, however, omitting eastern nationals serving in SS units and those employed in areas under OKW authority (for example, the Reich Commissariats). The most comprehensive calculation therefore appears to be that of the OKW's *Allgemeine Wehrmachtamt*, the coordinating office in the awarding of land grants to *Osttruppen*: in July 1943 that office concluded that some 1.2 million eastern military and police auxiliaries qualified for awards.[77] Even this total omits at least 30,000 permanent casualties suffered by eastern units through June 1943.[78]

Though the fighting value of these troops varied considerably, they contributed enormously to the German war effort in the performance of noncombatant and auxiliary duties.[79] The expanded and more systematic utilization of eastern manpower in 1943 freed many more Germans for frontline service: It is worth noting that the German Army's field strength on July 1, 1943 numbered 4,484,000 (nearly 700,000 more than at the beginning of BARBAROSSA), of whom roughly 1 million had been added from January–June 1943.[80] By any standards, and particularly under the unique conditions of the Russo-German war, the achievement was significant.

But tapping this reservoir of manpower raised weighty questions, many of which were voiced openly by the *Osttruppen* in summer 1943 regarding their second-class treatment and especially their political future. A German officer who served in an eastern unit commented that June that the volunteers, originally concerned only with material considerations, had now developed a political consciousness and a growing distrust of German intentions.[81] Without the clear political goal of a non-Stalinist but independent Russia, the increased reliance on Russian troops might well backfire on Germany. The issue involved nothing less than a basic reexamination of *Ostpolitik*, of the kind raised but deferred in December 1942. In spring 1943 the various threads of occupation policy, propaganda, and the *Osttruppen* came together in the person of a single Soviet defector, who represented both the ultimate threat and the last opportunity for German eastern policy.

NOTES

1. "Aktenvermerk," *TMWC*, XXXVIII, 88.

2. See L.H. Gann and Peter Duignan, *The Rulers of German Africa 1884–1914* (Stanford, CA: Stanford University Press, 1977), pp. 115–30, 158–61, 219–22.

3. Heinz Danko Herre, "Stauffenberg und Altenstadt werden aktiv, Herbst 1942," ZS 406/III, pp. 49–58, IfZ.

4. Herre, "Deutsche Erfahrungen in der Verwendung von Kriegsgefangenen gegen die Sowjetunion," ZS 406/II, 10–14, IfZ.

5. KTB OKH/Organisationsabteilung, 11.–20.10.1942, 22.10 and 29.10.1942, T–78/417/6386595, 6386598, 6386603.

6. OKH/GenStdH/Gen.d.Osttr., "Landeseigene Hilfskräfte im Osten—Hilfswillige," April 29, 1943, ML 310, RG 242, NA.

7. See David Littlejohn, *The Patriotic Traitors: The Story of Collaboration in German–Occupied Europe 1940–45* (Garden City, NY: Doubleday & Company, Inc., 1972), pp. 292–334; and Joachim Urban, "Die ostvölkischen Freiwilligenverbände des deutschen Heeres in der Zeit von 1943 bis 1945," ZS 422, IfZ.

8. See Hoffmann, *Die Ostlegionen*, pp. 30–39, and the data on T–311/150/7196862–868, 7196877–880, 7197599–601.

9. Sonderverband "Bergmann," "Bericht über den Einsatz des Sonderverbandes "Bergmann" vom 1. Dezember 1942–15 Februar 1943," February 16, 1943, T–311/151/7198701–703.

10. Hoffmann, *Deutsche und Kalmyken*, pp. 112–19, 187–88.

11. Eric Waldman, "German Use of Indigenous Auxiliary Police in the Occupied USSR," Operations Research Office Technical Memorandum T–320 of Johns Hopkins University, May 1955. Emphasis in original.

12. Dallin, *Kaminsky Brigade*, pp. 32–55.

13. Walther Hansen, "Im Bereich des Kommandierenden Generals der Sicherungstruppen und Befehlshabers im Heeresgebiet Mitte," ZS 405/II, pp. 42–48, IfZ.

14. Walther Hansen, "Das Ost-Ersatz-Regiment Mitte, spater Ost-Ausbildungs-Regiment," ZS 405/II, pp. 28–41, IfZ.

15. Steenberg, *Vlasov*, pp. 56–62, and Thorwald, *Illusion*, pp. 96–100.

16. See Dirk-Gerd Erpenbeck, *Serbien 1941. Deutsche Militärverwaltung und serbischer Widerstand* (Osnabrück: Biblio Verlag, 1976), pp. 92–93, and the exchange of correspondence between Himmler and his subordinates on T–175/73/2590542–570.

17. Compare Armeeintandant 18 to Heeresgruppe Nord/OQu, November 23, 1942 and January 3, 1943, T–311/115/7155173–174, 7155132–133.

18. "Anruf Gen. Maj. Speth an Chef des Generalstabes, Oberkommando der Heeresgruppe Nord, 21.3.1943, 22,30 Uhr," T–78/352/631220.

19. KTB OKH/Org. Abt., November 7, 1942, T–78/417/6386609.

20. The original OKH draft was lost. Herre notes the forwarding of the draft to OKW on November fifteenth after OKH had weakened it (Herre diary of November 13–15, 1942, IfZ).

21. OKH/Org. Abt. (II), "General der Osttruppen," T–78/121/6047659; Der Kom.Gen.d.Sich.Trp. und Befh.i.H.Geb.Mitte, "General der Osttruppen," December 28, 1942, T–501/27/286.

22. See Hellmich's personnel file, RG 242, NA; Thorwald, *Illusion*, p. 75; Michel, *Ost und West*, pp. 63ff.; and Strik-Strikfeldt, *Against*, pp. 118–20.

23. Herre, "Persönlichkeiten bei Dienststellen General der Osttruppen bzw. Freiwilligenverbände," and diary notes, ZS 406/III, pp. 39–43 and 406/IV, pp. 9–14, IfZ.

24. See above, Chapter 9.

25. Interrogation of Ernst Köstring (SAIC/FIR/42), 11 September 1945, RG 165, NA; Herwarth, *Two Evils*, pp. 221ff.

26. Franz W. Seidler, "Oskar Ritter von Niedermayer im Zweiten Weltkrieg: Ein Beitrag zur Geschichte der Ostlegionen," *Wehrwissenschaftliche Rundschau* (hereafter WWR), XX, 3 (March 1970): 168–74, and XX, 4 (April 1970): 193–208; Hoffmann, *Die Ostlegionen*, pp. 60–76; and the KTB of 162. (Turk) I.D./Ia, T–315/1455/736, 742–45, 752–57.

27. Pannwitz's NSDAP personnel file, Berlin Document Center; Samuel J. Newland, "Cossacks in Field Grey: A History of the Recruitment of the Cossacks into the German Army 1941–1945" (unpublished Ph.D. dissertation, University of Kansas, 1982), pp. 168–77.

28. Hoffmann, *Die Ostlegionen*, pp. 60–65; Seidler, "Niedermayer," pp. 194–96.

29. KTB of 162. (Turk) Inf.-Div./Ia, March 12, April 16 and 19, 1943, T–315/1455/775–76.

30. Newland, "Cossacks," pp. 187–92, 203–06.

31. Seidler, "Niedermayer," pp. 194–95; Hans Seraphim et al., "Eastern Nationals," FMS Mss. No. C–043, pp. 18–20.

32. Seraphim, "Volunteers," pp. 10–11; Oberstleutnant Wendt, "Erfahrungsbericht," February 12, 1943, T–311/150/7197029–032.

33. Hoffmann, *Die Ostlegionen*, pp. 70–76, and Seidler, "Niedermayer," pp. 194–96.

34. 101. Jäger-Division/1. Gen.st.ofz. to OKH, December 6, 1942, T–78/539/912–16; 1. Gebirgs-Division/Ia to Gen.Kdo. XLIX (Geb.) A.K., "Überlaufen von Georgiern," December 19, 1942, T–311/151/7198831–833.

35. Newland, "Cossacks," pp. 246–48; author's correspondence with Theodor Oberländer, August 10, and November 9, 1984.

36. Hoffmann, *Die Ostlegionen*, pp. 64–70; Seraphim, "Volunteers," pp. 22–29, 53–54.

37. Köstring interrogation (SAIC/FIR/42), RG 165, NA.

38. See F.L. Carsten, "A Bolshevik Conspiracy in the Wehrmacht," *The Slavonic and East European Review*, Vol. XLVII, no. 109 (July 1969): 483–509, and Pozdnyakov, "German Counterintelligence," FMS Mss. No. P–122, pp. 168–87.

39. Köstring, "Commentary," FMS Mss. No. C–043, p. 96.

40. Kommandant, *Korück 584* to Chef d. Gen.st. der 16. Armee, "Ost (Freijäger) Batl. 668," May 3, 1943, Document NOKW–2397, RG 238, NAA.

41. Kommandierender General der Sicherungstruppen und Befehlshaber im Heeresgebiet Süd, "Hiwi und landeseigene Verbände," August 1, 1943, T–311/266/1010–14.

42. Herre, "Chef des Stabes beim G.d.O.," ZS 406/III, p. 16, 39–43, IfZ.

43. General der Osttruppen beim Ob.d.H., "Mitteilungen Nr. 2." June 24, 1943, T–501/30/627–29; Thorwald, *Wen Sie*, pp. 246–48.

44. See the correspondence of Hellmich with the *Ostministerium*, April 23 and 28, 1943, T–454/37/703–06.

45. Hoffmann, *Die Ostlegionen*, p. 49.

46. See *Kommandeur der Osttruppen z.b.V.* 720 to Hellmich, "Ehemalige russische Offiziere in den landeseigenen Verbänden," May 13, 1943, T–312/1233/000046.

47. Rudolf Baumeister, "Erfahrungen mit Ostfreiwilligen im II. Weltkrieg," *Wehrkunde*, Bd. IV, Heft 4 (April 1955), p. 156.

48. See the KTB of Kommandierender General der Sicherungstruppen und Befehlshaber im Heeresgebiet Mitte/Ia for November 5, 7, 21, and December 29–31, 1942, T–501/26/919, 921, 936, and 993–95; Anlage 201 zum KTB, "Aktennotiz," November 21, 1942, T–5501/27/141–42; and the impressionistic account in Steenberg, *Vlasov*, pp. 56–62.

49. Hubatsch, *Weisungen*, p. 236.

50. OKH/GenStdH/GenQu Abt. Kr. Verw., "Landeseigene Hilfskräfte," February 9, 1943, T–311/165/7217479–480.

51. Panzerarmeeoberkommando 2/OQu, "Landeseigene Hilfskräfte," May 31, 1943, T–313/174/7431332.

52. Chef Wi Stab Ost/Ord. Offz., "Bericht über die Dienstreise," June 30, 1943, T–77/1090/379–80.

53. SS-*Obersturmbannführer* Brandt to SS-*Oberführer* Creuz, March 11, 1943, T–175/19/2524168.

54. See the letters of General Hermann Reinecke (*Chef des Allgemeinen Wehrmachtamts*, OKW) to Himmler, June 29, 1943, and to Keitel, July 29, 1943, T–175/19/2524101–103, 2524121–122.

55. Höhne, *Order*, pp. 471–77; Stein, *Waffen-SS*, pp. 168ff.

56. See above, Chapter 6.

57. See Bender and Taylor, *Uniforms*, Vol. 4, pp. 67–94, and Vol. 5, pp. 60–68, 146–58.

58. Telephone conversations among Generals Speth, Schmundt and the chief of staff of Army Group North, 21–22 March 1943, T–78/352/6312200–2202.

59. AOK 18/Ic, "Estnische Bataillone," May 7, 1943, and letter of Viktor Last to Dr. Mäe, April 8, 1943, T–312/1599/858–861, 870.

60. Bender and Taylor, *Uniforms*, Vol. 5, pp. 64–65, 151–52.

61. Statement of Lieutenant Herbert-Erich Valdsoo, December 23, 1943, in OSS R & A report 60315, RG 226, NA.

62. See Evald Uustalu, *For Freedom Only: The Story of Estonian Volunteers in the Finnish Wars of 1940–1944* (Toronto: Northern Publications, 1977), pp. 20–25.

63. Stein, *Waffen-SS*, p. 151.

64. See the exchange of correspondence among Himmler, Wächter and Berger, March 4–June 21, 1943, T–175/74/2592443–491; and the general account in Basil Dmytryshyn, "The Nazis and the SS Volunteer Division 'Galicia,' " *The American Slavic and East European Review*, Vol. XV, no. 1 (February 1956), pp. 1–6.

65. Wächter, "Leitsätze für Redner der Werbekomissionen," April 28, 1943, T–580/89/Ordner No. 440.

66. Himmler directive to all *Hauptamtchefs*, July 14, 1943, and Wächter to Himmler, "SS-Schützen-Division Galizien," July 30, 1943, T–175/74/2592406–411, 2592415.

67. See Armstrong, *Nationalism*, pp. 170–74.

68. Himmler to Wächter, August 11, 1943, and Wächter to Himmler, September 4, 1943, T–175/74/2592399–400, 2592404–05. On the subsequent history of the division, see Wolf-Dietrich Heike, *Sie wollten die Freiheit: Die Geschichte der Ukrainischen Division 1943–45* (Dorheim/H.: Podzun-Verlag, 1974).

69. Hilberg, *Destruction*, pp. 243–44.

70. Leibbrandt and Berger, "Agreement between the Reich Leader SS and Chief of the German Police and the Reich Minister for the Occupied Eastern Territories," March 15, 1943, Document NO–1818, *NMT*, XIII, 389–90.

71. Wi-Stab-Ost/Chefgruppe Arbeit, "Beitrag zum KTB, 4.6.43: Erhöhung der Abfindung für ukrainische Schutzmannschaften," June 11, 1943, T–77/1089/1335–36.

72. See Kazimierz Moczarski, *Conversations with an Executioner* (ed. by Mariana Fitzpatrick), (Englewood Cliffs, NJ: Prentice-Hall, Inc., 1981), pp. 117–18, 136.

73. See Alexander Dallin and Ralph S. Mavrogordato, "Rodionov: A Case-Study in Wartime Redefection," *American Slavic and East European Review*, Vol. XVIII, no. 1 (February 1959), pp. 25–33; and Schellenberg, *Hitler's Secret Service*, pp. 272–73.

74. See "Rede des Reichsführers-SS bei der SS-Gruppenführertagung in Posen am 4. Oktober 1943," Document 1919–PS, *TMWC*, XXIX, 123.

75. Hauptmann Dosch, "Vortrags-Notiz," February 2, 1943, T–78/501/6489700–707.

76. Mueller-Hillebrand, *Zweifrontenkreig*, p. 114.

77. Chef des allgemeinen Wehrmachtamts im Oberkommando der Wehrmacht an den Chef OKW, July 29, 1943, T–175/19/2524101–103.

78. See the sources cited in Mulligan, "Politics," p. 347n.

79. One assessment in July 1943 rated them as 33 percent good, 53 percent average, and 14 percent poor: von Etzdorf, "Die landeseigenen Hilfskräfte im Osten," July 2, 1943, T–120/275/364/205898–900.

80. Mueller-Hillebrand, *Zweifrontenkrieg*, p. 109.

81. Sdf. Treugut, "Stimmung in den russischen Freiwilligen Bataillonen," June 24, 1943, T–503/232/565–67.

12

THE GENERAL WHO SPOKE RUSSIAN

For those desiring a change in *Ostpolitik*, the waging of "political warfare" appeared to offer the means to reopen the issue without an overt challenge to Hitler and the adherents of colonialist war aims. Political warfare could be justified on military grounds, and might be waged behind the front lines as well as across them; where the reasoned memorandum had failed, the fait accompli disguised as a propaganda measure might succeed. From autumn 1942 to summer 1943, political warfare became identified with one Russian general who offered his name and services to the Germans in common cause against Stalin. During this period, the Vlasov movement shook *Ostpolitik* to its foundations and compelled Hitler's intervention to restore order.[1]

The risks of political warfare had been recognized. Hitler, with his perception of Imperial Germany's misguided experiments in political warfare in Poland and the Ukraine during World War I, forbade at the beginning of BARBAROSSA any mention of post-war political settlements.[2] Yet by autumn 1941 reformers began proposing the establishment of an anti-Stalinist regime under German sponsorship.[3] An early candidate for the key post in this scheme, captured Soviet general Mikhail Lukin, refused further collaboration after becoming thoroughly disillusioned with German policy and practices.[4] By August 1942 the head of OKW/WPr's Foreign Branch, Colonel Hans-Leo Martin, concluded that the creation of a Russian pseudo-government might benefit Germany during the first weeks of its existence, "but then must inevitably lead to a dangerous setback" when its lack of real political power became evident.[5]

Ironically, one month later two of his subordinates would interview a Russian general who would make Martin change his mind.[6] The general was Andrei A.

Vlasov, a veteran of 24 years in the Red Army and a member of the Communist Party since 1930. In the winter of 1941 he had played a major role in the successful defense of Moscow, exhibiting qualities of leadership and personal charisma that set him apart as a commander. Doubts about the regime hardened into opposition with the sacrifice of his army on the Volkhov River in July 1942. In discussions with Captain Wilfried Strik-Strikfeldt, a Baltic German and former Czarist officer serving with Gehlen's FHO, and Captain Nikolaus von Grote and Lieutenant Eugen Dürksen of Martin's OKW/WPr section, Vlasov offered his services in a nationalist opposition to the Soviet regime. Thus was born the "Vlasov Movement."[7]

In September Vlasov was brought to a special compound for anti-Stalinist officers in Berlin run by the OKW/WPr, where he met those who would become his staff: Mileti A. Zykov and Georgi N. Zhilenkov, former Red Army commissars fortunate enough to have escaped the execution of the *Kommissarbefehl*, and Vasili F. Malyshkin, a former army chief of staff. Two months later OKW/WPr established the "Eastern Propaganda Section for special duty" for 1200 disaffected Soviet officers at Dabendorf, south of Berlin. By exploiting the differences and duplications of four separate military authorities (FHO, OKW/WPr, *General der Osttruppen* and the regional army military district) that shared jurisdiction over their activities, Strik-Strikfeldt, Grote and Dürksen staffed and equipped a political warfare center unrivaled in the European theater.[8]

But by this time Vlasov and his supporters had encountered their first setbacks. In his first memorandum to his captors in August 1942 Vlasov had urged the formation of a Russian Army as the military arm of the anti-Stalinist political movement he envisaged.[9] Vlasov consequently signed his name to propaganda leaflets distributed across the lines in September, but he soon began to petition the Germans to make good their propaganda promises.[10] Through October 1942 the OKW/WPr forwarded all of Vlasov's proposals to Keitel, who rejected them as political concerns outside the competence of military propaganda.[11]

The strong Russian nationalism behind Vlasov's proposals is evident in the surviving fragment of an undated memorandum signed by Vlasov, Malyshkin and Zhilenkov. The extract described at length their position on two key issues. The first concerned the creation of a "Russian Liberation Army" (*Russkaia Osvoboditelnaia Armiia*, abbreviated ROA), with regular divisions, Russian officers and Russian uniforms, as well as a central ROA headquarters—that is, the same status accorded the allied Rumanian, Hungarian, and Italian armies. Secondly, the memorandum guaranteed the right of self-determination to the minority nationalities after the war, but criticized the promotion of separatist movements as too divisive. The distribution of this memorandum among German circles is unknown, but its contents could only have aroused concern among the German military and the *Ostministerium*.[12]

Small wonder that Vlasov's sponsors recognized the need to conceal these differences and show some immediate results. In late November Grote and Strik-Strikfeldt hit upon the idea of using the "Russian liberation committee" as a propaganda premise whose success would make it a fact. The result was the "Smolensk Manifesto," drafted by Grote and signed only reluctantly by Vlasov. The proclamation issued by Vlasov's "Russian Committee" appealed to the Russian people to join the anti-Stalinist movement and specifically urged Soviet soldiers to join the "ROA." A 13-point program outlined a future Russia with guaranteed "freedom of religion, conscience, speech, assembly and the press," social justice and a minimum living wage to disabled veterans and their families; the *kolkhozy*, compulsory labor and the "reign of terror and violence" would be abolished. The manifesto specifically disavowed any German claims "on the *Lebensraum* of the Russian people or on their political and national freedom."[13]

But to issue the manifesto required the approval of *Ostminister* Rosenberg, whose commitment to a separatist policy has already been described. Vlasov's proclamation prompted Rosenberg to reiterate his views in letters to Hitler, OKW and OKH, demanding equal representation for the minority nationalities in any political movement.[14] He delayed approval of the manifesto's distribution until January twelfth, and stipulated that dissemination be strictly limited to the Soviet side of the lines.[15] But with Rosenberg's signature secured, Vlasov's sponsors took matters into their own hands. With millions of copies already printed, Strik-Strikfeldt and Grote began distribution of the Manifesto within hours of approval. Friendly contacts in the *Luftwaffe* assured the "mistaken" dropping of many leaflets behind German lines, while occupation newspapers in Smolensk published copies of the text.[16]

By this *fait accompli*, the "Russian National Committee" assumed reality as a propaganda measure. Yet the Smolensk Manifesto's impact in encouraging desertion from Soviet forces failed to match expectations. Reports of large-scale desertions are contradicted by the statistics maintained by Gehlen's FHO, a Vlasov ally: for the full month of January 1943 the total number of Red Army deserters amounted to only 1266, a considerable decline from the previous month.[17] An outraged Rosenberg meanwhile demanded an inquiry into the violation of his restrictions, and stopped the further distribution of leaflets behind German lines.[18]

Yet Rosenberg proposed to incorporate Vlasov within his own program. In return for his support of the "Russian National Committee" in the area of Army Group Center, Rosenberg looked for military backing for the establishment of a Ukrainian counterpart. As Koch's hostility precluded such a development within the RKU, Rosenberg proposed to seat the "Ukrainian National Central Committee" in the area of the Ukraine under German military government, where it would carry out its limited tasks under joint *Ostministerium*-army supervision.[19] In mid-February the *OMi* liaison officer to the *Abwehr* outlined Rosenberg's political warfare program as follows: a Russian National Committee in Smolensk; a Ukrainian Committee somewhere in the army's zone; a Caucasian Committee composed of four subsections representing the minority nationalities; and a cossack liaison office in Germany, in addition to the accelerated agrarian reform. The national committees would be supported by their respective "liberation armies,'' though this critical relationship between political and military collaboration received no elaboration.[20]

The *Ostminister* further believed that his program provided him effective control over Vlasov. To keep a close watch on the Soviet defector, Rosenberg planned to assign a plenipotentiary to Army Group Center to coordinate political activities. While the future role of the Russian Committee remained to be determined, it would be made clear that the ''Russians thus no longer stand above the other nationalities of the Soviet Union, but beside them.''[21] There were even proposals to include ethnic Russians as members of the Ukrainian committee, so as to deny Vlasov representation of the Russian minority in the Ukraine.[22] Draft plans in early March 1943 limited the Russian National Committee's ''powers'' to propaganda activities, charity and welfare work, recruitment and material considerations for the *Osttruppen*, and the political organization of anti-Soviet elements.[23]

But as the Vlasov movement took stock of its situation in the late winter of 1943, the compact with Rosenberg remained only a step on a long road. Another was taken on March first when the Dabendorf camp became operational, with a 28-course propaganda school and publishing offices for two Russian-language newspapers, *Zaria* (''Dawn'') and *Dobrovolets* (''The Volunteer'') for distribution among the *Ostruppen* and prisoners-of-war. Dabendorf trainees also began to wear on their left sleeves the newly approved symbol of the ''ROA,'' a blue St. Andrew's cross on a white field.[24] At the highest levels of the German military, however, Vlasov found few friends. Keitel's opposition has already been noted; Hellmich's attitude was alternately characterized as a sympathetic helplessness and outright hostility;[25] and by mid-March Chief of the General Staff Kurt Zeitzler had ''completely given up the fight for Vlasov,'' according to Gehlen.[26] To dispel the notion that he might be no more than a propaganda trick, Vlasov's supporters had to publicize his existence and gain more allies from within the German political structure.

Fittingly, the Vlasov movement's earliest attempts at winning recognition involved the German diplomatic service. Shortly after Vlasov's capture Colonel Alexis Freiherr von Roenne arranged an interview with Gustav Hilger, Russian expert of the Foreign Ministry.[27] Impressed by Vlasov's ''strong and upright personality,'' Hilger endorsed his offer of collaboration to the Foreign Ministry in August 1942.[28] In early April 1943 Hilger submitted two memoranda to Ribbentrop, urging formal recognition of the ''Russian Committee'' and the Smolensk Manifesto.[29] Ernst Woermann, a diplomatic official who had previously assisted Subhas Chandra Bose in the drafting of a declaration of independence for India, also circulated a memorandum of support for Vlasov within the Foreign Ministry before the end of March.[30] Hilger apparently drafted a declaration along these lines on April 6, 1943. This established the ''Russian Committee'' under Vlasov as a provisional government for the Russian-populated areas under military administration, with its seat in Smolensk or Pskov. The ultimate objective envisioned a Russian state based upon capitalism, and thus so fundamentally antagonistic to the Soviet system that "a union with Soviet rump-Russia (that unconquered by Germany) would be excluded for all time." Vlasov was also to be given a role in the training, leadership and propaganda work among the eastern troops.[31]

These were liberal terms, conceding more to Vlasov than Rosenberg was willing to offer the Ukrainians.[32] But when Ribbentrop raised the issue to Hitler on April thirteenth, the führer rejected the proposal as "unnecessary . . . valueless . . . a sign of weakness," which could only lead to undesirable fraternization.[33] The Foreign Ministry continued its support of Vlasov through the summer of 1943,[34] but the problem of the Foreign Ministry's essential irrelevance remained. Hilger's and Ribbentrop's last efforts were made in ignorance that the issue had already been decided.

Several factors favored an alliance between the Vlasov Movement and a more powerful figure in the Nazi hierarchy, Joseph Goebbels. The propaganda minister's long-standing animosity toward Rosenberg and ambitions in the East have already been noted. A close working relationship moreover already existed between the ministry and OKW/WPr, with Colonel Martin doubling his duties as head of the Foreign Propaganda Branch and liaison officer to Goebbels.[35] Most important, the Propaganda Minister in early 1943 had begun to appreciate the need for a change in *Ostpolitik*. In a directive of 15 February to Party officials he stressed the need to win the cooperation of the Eastern peoples; disparaging remarks and discussions of postwar German colonization were therefore to be avoided.[36] He enjoyed little success in his effort in March-April to force the withdrawal of the racist SS pamphlet *Der Untermensch* ("The Subhuman")[37] but did bring about some improvement in the treatment of the *Ostarbeiter*.[38]

Goebbels was also well aware of the climate for change of *Ostpolitik*. His deputy for Eastern propaganda, Dr. Eberhard Taubert, endorsed *Ostpolitik* reform and favorably reported on the effect of the Smolensk Manifesto.[39] Colonel Martin meanwhile kept up a gradual pressure on Goebbels along similar lines.[40] That these efforts yielded results is evident from Goebbels' diary comments of April 4, 1943, that Vlasov presented Germany "a great propaganda opportunity," and again on April fifteenth: "From a number of statements by Bolshevik prisoners I gather that General Vlasov's appeal caused some discussion after all in the Soviet Army. The appeal will be even more effective if we get behind it more energetically."[41] It was, in fact, a Propaganda Ministry official who approached Strik-Strikfeldt with a veiled offer of support for Vlasov and a radical change in policy.[42]

But Goebbels would not risk a confrontation with Hitler to bring this about. The propaganda minister refused to meet with Vlasov for fear of Hitler's wrath.[43] "Of course [Vlasov's appeal] depends upon the issuance of a proclamation for the East," Goebbels wrote,[44] and when his own effort in this area fell through in February-March 1943[45] he was left without a justification for involvement. The expanded power base in the East he sought would be granted him by Hitler in August 1943, but by then it would be too late.

To broaden its influence within Germany, the Vlasov movement also cultivated relations with several journalists and writers. Most favorable among these was Edwin Dwinger, the correspondent whose criticism of *Ostpolitik* has already been noted. During spring 1943 Dwinger wrote Himmler and the Foreign Ministry on Vlasov's behalf.[46] Another was Günter Kaufmann, editor of the Hitler Youth magazine *Wille and Macht*, who devoted the June 1943 issue to the Vlasov movement.[47] In May 1943 Melitta Wiedemann, editor of the Anti-Komintern magazine *Aktion*, also contacted Himmler in support of Vlasov and a fundamental change in policy, repeating Dwinger's argument that a German colonization of Russia was already precluded by Germany's losses in the war. Later Wiedemann entertained Vlasov in her Berlin home, where she arranged interviews for Vlasov with such SS officers as *Gruppenführer* Otto Wächter, governor of Galicia.[48]

But lacking any political authority for support, these individual efforts remained isolated and vulnerable gestures. One of Himmler's staff officers put off Wiedemann with reference to the "clear directives" issued by Hitler regarding Vlasov.[49] The distribution of the offending issue of *Wille und Macht* was halted and further publication banned.[50] Dwinger received an official reprimand from Gottlob Berger and found himself effectively retired.[51]

Vlasov meanwhile assumed greater reality for his primary audience. With the Russian language newspapers operating out of Dabendorf, Vlasov had a means of communicating with the men of the "ROA"—and with some freedom, as German military censors made no effort to control these publications until well after their establishment.[52] To evade Rosenberg's restrictions on the Smolensk Manifesto Vlasov drafted an open letter, "Why I Took up Arms against Bolshevism," acceptable to the *Ostministerium* as a personal rather than a political appeal for use on both sides of the front. Published on March 3, 1943, the letter contained no references to "Jewish Bolshevism" but spoke openly of the abuses of Stalin's regime; neither did it mention Hitler, but advocated "alliance and cooperation with the German people and the great German nation." Such unusual candor undoubtedly contributed to the letter's considerable impact, extending even to the "Russian Guard Corps" in Serbia.[53]

To fully utilize his charismatic personality, Vlasov's sponsors decided to send him on a speaking tour of the areas under military government. From February twenty-fifth to mid-March Vlasov toured the rear area of Army Group Center, speaking for the first time to Russian audiences as well as to senior German field commanders. Received by Field Marshal von Kluge and General von Schenckendorff (commander of the army group *Heeresgebiet*), the former Soviet general expressed his views to several *Osttruppen* units, Russian mayors, public gatherings and groups of German officers in Smolensk, Mogilev, Berezino, Bobruisk, Veretsy, and Orsha. The trip was considered a major success,[54] though some of Rosenberg's representatives who attended Vlasov's talk in Mogilev found the audience unreceptive and apathetic, and Vlasov himself "obviously nervous."[55]

Both impressions were valid. The tour established Vlasov's existence, but left open the question of his significance. The *Wehrmacht* propaganda staffs in the field brought home this point in their summary reports for March 1943. "The appeal of General Vlasov meets with the greatest interest," reported Army Group A, "the population awaits further announcements and measures in this area." The staff for Army Group North coupled their summary with a warning: "Here too the General Vlasov project stands in the forefront of interest. *It should be considered absolutely essential to make the most of the committee's activity, if our propaganda is not to lose all credit with the population.*"[56]

Vlasov, more than anyone else, understood that his speeches could not substitute for a change in German policy. He stressed this point in his discussions with German officers during the tour,[57] and in his own summary prepared on his return to Berlin: "The population wants to know what . . . it is being asked to fight and shed its blood for . . . It is essential to completely alter the policy toward the Russian people."[58] It was, of course, precisely the gamble of the Vlasov movement that the response among the occupied population and the Russians in eastern units would compel a redirection of *Ostpolitik*.

Spring's arrival increased the tempo of activity. On March twenty-second Dabendorf graduated its first class, many of whom dispersed to ROA recruiting offices among the *Osttruppen* and in prisoner-of-war camps; others remained at Dabendorf to staff the Russian language newspapers, now with a readership of over 120,000.[59] To sustain the center, orders were issued to the army groups in the field to supply a regular quota of Russian recruits to Dabendorf for future training.[60] On April 12, 1943 about two hundred former Soviet officers and men attended a speech by Vlasov's associate Malyshkin in Brest-Litovsk on the nature of the envisaged future Russian state, and closed with a resolution of support for Vlasov and the liberation movement.[61]

Vlasov meanwhile embarked on another speaking tour of the Army Group North rear areas. From approximately mid-April to early May[62] Vlasov visited Riga, Pskov, Luga, Pliskov, Gatchina and Dno, addressing Russian audiences, newspaper staffs, *Osttruppen* and German officers on the need for an independent Russian army and the guarantee of an independent Russian state for a mass movement against Stalin.[63] The army's own political ineptitude was also evident when, in Pskov, Vlasov was taken to a furrier where 12- to 14-year old children were hard at work, a scene he later admitted "did not leave him a favorable impression." At a subsequent visit to a felt manufacturer, Vlasov was not recognized by most of the Russian staff, one of whom remarked, "This German general speaks Russian very well."[64]

Of more immediate significance, a growing number of German officers were now being exposed to Vlasov, with decidedly mixed reactions. In their summaries of this tour military government officials lauded Vlasov's performance and urged concrete political concessions to follow up the opportunity created.[65] The Army Field Police on the other hand rated the steady deterioration in popular morale unaffected by Vlasov's visit, that "his words met with little response."[66] Others agreed that Vlasov's personality and ideas might well have a major, possibly even decisive impact, but warned of the attendant serious risks: The Russian defector could become ''a most dangerous opponent . . . as dishonorable and devious as any Bolshevik.''[67] Most significantly, Field Marshal von Küchler drew a sharp distinction between Vlasov's political value and the questionable premise of an independent Russian army:

For the Russian area, the Vlasov Movement has special significance. Vlasov has as an objective the leadership of a 'Russian Liberation Army.' This appears dangerous. What is necessary is to confirm him as the political leader of a new, free national Russia. . . .[68]

In publicizing their champion Vlasov's sponsors succeeded too well. His public activities necessitated consideration of his authority, an issue that involved the Reich leadership. On March fourth, *Reichsführer* Himmler, undoubtedly advised of Vlasov's initial tour, wrote Bormann about Vlasov's activities and requested Hitler's decision regarding the establishment of a Russian committee and army of liberation.[69] Immediately after rejecting Ribbentrop's pro-Vlasov proposal in mid-April, the führer prohibited Vlasov from further statements or political activities.[70] With this, the Vlasov movement effectively (though temporarily) lost Vlasov, and with him its only direct link to the occupied Russian population.

Keitel's directive, however, came too late, or lacked sufficient urgency, to cancel Vlasov's trip to Army Group North, nor did it affect the initial planning for a demonstration of Vlasov's military value. On April fifteenth Hitler issued the operational order for ''Unternehmen ZITADELLE'' (Operation ''Citadel''), an offensive conceived in March to eliminate the Soviet salient in the German lines around Kursk; the earliest date for the attack was set for May third.[71] The next day, Lieutenant Colonel Herre secured approval from OKW/WPr for linking the attack with a distinct propaganda campaign encourage Red Army desertion. Herre's proposal was built around ''Basic Order No. 13,'' issued by OKH on April twenty-first: deserters from the Red Army were to be accorded preferential treatment, with the option of serving in one of the ''national liberation armies'' or labor duty and the guarantee of rapid repatriation at war's end.[72] The campaign, codenamed SILBERSTREIF (''Silver Lining''), was timed to coincide with ''Citadel'' but would occur along the entire length of the Eastern Front, with teams of 20 to 25 Dabendorf-trained Russian propagandists distributed to each German frontline division to make loudspeaker appeals and process deserters as they came across.[73]

Problems began for SILBERSTREIF with the postponement of Operation ''Citadel'' to the beginning of June.[74] Herre, caught up in the hectic preparations of coordinating the operation, learned only on the evening of May third that the action would proceed on May sixth, unaccompanied by an offensive. SILBER-STREIF began on schedule with 18 million leaflets dropped or fired behind Soviet lines the first day alone, accompanied by broadcasts over huge loud-speakers audible up to 3.5 kilometers in the Soviet rear. But by May ninth even

Herre acknowledged disappointment over the meager results: For the entire month of May only 2424 Soviet deserters crossed the lines, an increase of less than five hundred over the previous month. June brought virtually no improvement (2555 deserters). Only with the long-delayed launching of ZITADELLE in July did the total rise to nearly 6600, but even this remained well below the totals associated with the German summer offensives of 1942.[75]

Lacking any real authority within the National Socialist power structure, the Vlasov movement in spring 1943 needed nothing less than a miracle to salvage its goals. Stripped of accompanying military action, SILBERSTREIF failed to provide that miracle. The massive propaganda effort, including the use of 1 billion propaganda leaflets, proved insufficient against Soviet security measures and counterpropaganda.[76] The latter included the disarming of entire platoons caught reading the leaflets, increased political instruction among the troops, the dismissal of Vlasov's name and photograph as forgeries, and the doubling of watches that left no soldier alone at his post.[77] Significantly, the number of deserters rose when "Citadel" was finally launched as the confusion of combat loosened Soviet controls, while the sector of the greatest German advances (Army Group South) also produced the largest number of deserters.[78] Another factor contributing to "Silver Lining's" miscarriage was the lack of cooperation exhibited by many German Army field units. ROA propagandist teams participated in the operation with 130 German field divisions, but nearly one in five reported their presence to have been of little or no value due to inadequate support by divisional staffs.[79] In one recorded incident, a German regimental commander returned a deserter to Soviet custody because the Russian admitted to killing and robbing his commanding officer before deserting.[80]

These incidents reflected the same uneasiness over an independent Russian army earlier expressed by Field Marshal von Küchler. In part this resulted from justified concerns for military security and pragmatism. Aware of the successful Soviet attacks against the Rumanian, Hungarian, and Italian allied armies during the winter of 1942–43, even Dabendorf graduates agreed that a consolidated "Russian Liberation Army" in the field would offer the Red Army a vulnerable target.[81] In May the commander of *Osttruppen* in the Second Army wrote that former Soviet officers serving in the eastern units were "security risks" and proposed their segregation from other Russian personnel until more appropriate positions became available for them.[82] German commanders moreover dreaded the loss of *Hiwis* from their understrength units as volunteers for combat service, and actively sought to reduce or impede that which German propaganda had promised.[83]

With its military hopes blunted, the Vlasov movement turned its efforts toward the establishment of a political foothold in occupied Russia. For this even Keitel had issued a mild endorsement on April eighteenth, recognizing the value of "national committees" as sounding boards for popular opinion, with limited economic and propaganda responsibilities.[84] The directive apparently prompted Altenstadt to force a decision from Rosenberg in support of Vlasov. On May sixteenth Altenstadt informed *Ostministerium* representatives that if they did not participate in the establishment of a Russian "constituent assembly" by May twenty-fifth, the army would act on its own.[85]

Altenstadt was not bluffing. Whatever their misgivings about Vlasov's military aspirations, army commanders accepted the need for political concessions. In late February 1943, the Third Panzer Army urged the establishment of individual "liberation councils" in the *raions* under the direction of the Russian committee, which in turn would represent the population in official negotiations with the Reich government.[86] The staffs of the 16th and the 2nd Armies followed with proposals for an expansion of local government, simplified taxes, and enlarged roles for the native judiciary, educational, and health services.[87] The most significant endorsement came from Field Marshal von Kluge of Army Group Center, who informed OKH on May twenty-second that he intended to install, on his own authority if necessary, a national committee in his area. Praising Vlasov's propaganda operation, Kluge stressed the need for clear concessions; "the overall situation," he emphasized, "demands a political solution." Without awaiting a reply, Kluge forwarded copies to his subordinate commands with orders to prepare recommendations for the committee's installation.[88]

Kluge's preparations indicated the army's utter exasperation with Rosenberg. Believing his proximity to the führer as commensurate with his influence, the military overestimated his significance and misjudged his interests. Even OKW Operations Staff chief Jodl, possibly at the suggestion of some of his colleagues, wrote the Eastern minister on May tenth on Vlasov's behalf, urging Rosenberg's intercession with Hitler.[89] But Rosenberg was then preoccupied with his battle with Koch over Ukrainian policy, for which he had staked all—and lost—on an alliance with Himmler. Altenstadt's ultimatum came at the moment of Rosenberg's defeat before Hitler, and he had little stomach for a new fight, let alone one in which he only half-heartedly believed. Two "subdued" subordinates of his did meet briefly with Hellmich and Herre on May twenty-fifth, but only to reschedule the main conference on the national committees for the next day.[90]

The meeting convened in Wagner's headquarters in Mauerwald, East Prussia. Neither Rosenberg, Vlasov, nor any of the latter's intimate associates attended; Otto Bräutigam and two other *Ostministerium* officials confronted perhaps 20 *Wehrmacht* officers including Gehlen, Kluge, Hellmich, and Herre. The various accounts of the meeting disagree on several points, including the question of Wagner's attendance at all.[91] All versions confirm, however, the basic theme of the meeting. The army considered a favorable military decision no longer possible, and that a political solution had to be sought; the Eastern Ministry maintained that political arguments could be effective only after military necessity had been brought home to the führer. The establishment of the Russian and Ukrainian committees was discussed but nothing concrete decided. In his report to Rosenberg, Bräutigam repeated the arguments of the attending officers that Germany's future depended on the decision at hand.[92]

Rosenberg, probably sensing an opportunity to recoup his losses against Koch, threw himself into a last effort to reverse the course of *Ostpolitik*. On May twenty-eighth he wrote Hitler via Bormann in favor of the establishment of national committees, accompanied by a declaration purportedly signed by Vlasov renouncing any claim to the Ukraine and the Caucasus.[93] In a despatch to OKW the next day Rosenberg responded to Keitel's endorsement of the committees with an offer of political and economic support for the national legions and "liberation armies."[94] The Eastern minister also proposed to meet with Jodl, Keitel, and Hitler to discuss the Vlasov question in late June.[95]

Meanwhile Army Group Center proceeded with provisional plans for the Russian National Committee. Chaired by Vlasov, the committee would include Kaminsky of the Lokot' district, the mayor of Gomel, one or two representatives of *Generalkommissariat* White Russia, and such others as deemed reliable. The committee would be seated in Mogilev with regional offices in Smolensk, Orel, and Gomel. Under the direction of an army plenipotentiary, the committee's initial advisory powers would be gradually expanded to include responsibilities in the administrative, welfare, cultural, and legal spheres; eventually the committee would become the basis for the government of an autonomous Russia under German supervision. Of course, to maintain security the *Abwehr* would have to plant some spies within the committee and its organizations.[96]

While the army and Rosenberg launched these initiatives, Vlasov attained his greatest international notoriety. In the Rumanian-occupied city of Odessa, the Italian consul-general reported the "real sensation" among the population caused by Vlasov's appeal, "the first political gesture the Germans have made since the beginning of the campaign."[97] In April and May the publication of Vlasov's open letter in the major newspapers of Bulgaria and Serbia generated considerable interest among the emigré Russian communities in those countries; the Croatian and Rumanian press also provided substantial coverage of the topic.[98] Finnish and Swedish newspapers picked up the story in early June, while Swedish King Gustav V displayed "much interest and pleasure" in news of General Vlasov during an audience with the German ambassador.[99]

But it was too late. Even as he gained international recognition Vlasov ceased to exist as a political force. In a conference with Keitel and Zeitzler at the Berghof near Berchtesgaden on June 8, 1943, Hitler buried any notion of a commitment to Vlasov. "We will never build up a Russian army, that's a phantom of the first order," Hitler declared. "One day we would get a sort of strike slogan [t]hat will run along the entire front." As for Vlasov's political activities in the rear areas, the führer asserted: "That must be stopped. I need him only at the front . . . I don't need General Vlasov at all in the occupied areas . . . He will function only across, to the other side."

For Hitler, the crucial issue raised by Vlasov concerned not propaganda tactics but basic war aims. Vlasov himself represented far less a threat than those Germans who embraced his program. When Keitel fretted over the wording of a propaganda leaflet, Hitler dismissed his argument: "That's not so tragic . . . I see only one thing today, and it is the deciding thing for me: we must avoid creating a false conception on our own side.'' Hitler feared that the winter defeats had panicked many Germans into the support of a compromise solution: ''In the gradual spread among us of something like this—in that alone I see a danger.'' As he had three weeks earlier during the debate between Rosenberg and Koch over the Ukraine, Hitler fell back upon the lessons taught by German policy in the First World War. Throughout the conference he returned to Imperial Germany's cardinal error of granting political concessions to the Poles:

In this field we already received a tragic lesson in the World War with Poland. . . . When the great crises occurred in 1916 . . . everyone unquestionably lost his head, unfortunately even the soldiers. . . . Every thinking person would have said immediately: You will not get 500,000 men for the fight against Russia, but rather an army established by the Poles to proceed against Germany and to liberate Poland.[100]

Hitler's verdict actually had little immediate impact. The material improvements and regularized treatment of the *Osttruppen* remained intact, Vlasov's propaganda use across the lines received authorization, and Vlasov himself continued to entertain influential visitors and travel within Germany, conditions which led one historian to characterize Hitler's decision of June eighth as ''a pitiful recording of what a dictator should not be.''[101] Yet Hitler had clearly discerned the issue at the hear of the Vlasov affair, German war aims in the East, and rejected their revision. Moreover, he fixed the political limits of the Vlasov movement until the issue was no longer significant.

Over the next few weeks these boundaries of reform were sharply defined. Shortly after the Berghof conference Keitel issued a directive to Rosenberg that forbade the national committees' participation in the recruiting of volunteers, banned Vlasov's appearance in the occupied areas, and prohibited any implementation of the Smolensk Manifesto program without Hitler's express consent, as ''no German agency may take seriously the bait offered in these 13 points.''[102] On June twenty-third, Führer Directive No. 46 was modified by cancellation of the provision for the expansion of native eastern units.[103] Effective July 1, 1943, new eastern units were no longer to be established, though those already in existence finally received recognition in standardized tables of organization and equipment from OKH.[104] Later that month responsibility for Vlasov shifted entirely to OKW/WPr, with Keitel himself exercising direct authority over Vlasov's movements.[105]

On the evening of July first Hitler drove home to his field commanders what he had deliberately concealed from the Army High Command prior to BARBAROSSA. With the long-delayed ZITADELLE offensive about to begin, Hitler discussed Germany's strategic situation before an audience of Eastern Front army group, army, and some corps commanders at OKH headquarters. In the course of his presentation Hitler dispelled the rumors of the establishment of a Russian government in the occupied areas and returned to the lessons of the Great War, when Germany mistakenly subsidized the creation of a Polish state. This would not happen again, Hitler asserted, as the morale of the common soldier required the retention of conquered lands as "positive war aims." After two years, BARBAROSSA's goal stood firm: "We need *Lebensraum*. This must be made clear: the fight, gentlemen, is a fight for *Lebensraum*. Without this *Lebensraum* the German Reich and the German nation cannot endure."[106]

Ironically, this complete defeat for Vlasov still fell short for the keeper of the flame, *Reichskommissar* Koch. In a conference at the *Ostministerium* on July thirteenth, Koch demanded the disbanding of the "so-called Liberation Army Vlasov" and the mass employment of *Osttruppen* and *Hilfswillige* entirely as labor.[107] Even Hitler acknowledged some concessions to military necessity and the *Reichskommissar*'s proposal was ignored; that autumn, when increased desertions among the eastern units became a problem, Hitler still would not disband them but transferred them *en masse* to occupation duties in the western theater.[108]

Hitler's role in shelving the Vlasov movement in 1943 thus proved decisive. That this intervention was required pays tribute to Vlasov and his sponsors, lacking any power base within the National Socialist political structure. A final assessment of this first, and decisive, stage of the Vlasov movement requires a review of the roles played by key individuals and institutions within that structure.

Among Vlasov's purported enemies, *Reichsführer*-SS Himmler occupies a prominent place. Historians attribute many of Vlasov's setbacks during this period to his actions or influence.[109] Himmler unquestionably rejected Vlasov's views, as when he wrote von dem Bach-Zelewski in January 1943, "[W]e may never agree to the ideas of this Russian general, for then we create a new Russian nation . . . for myself, the more important thing at any rate (is) the establishment of a free Siberian peasant state, so that Siberia will become the home of the Russian nation and Russian freedom."[110] In speeches in October 1943 Himmler assailed Vlasov as a "butcher's boy" and "a swine" while reaffirming Germany's expansion to the Urals.[111] But invective does not constitute action, and Himmler appears to have preferred a wait-and-see attitude over intervention. Possibly he sensed a change in the political wind and intended leaving open his options. In January 1943, as he considered an alliance with Rosenberg against Koch, Himmler sounded out Hitler on the possible use of a captured Soviet general named Privalov, who had also offered his services against Stalin.[112] With Vlasov, the conflict between ideologue and pragmatist within Himmler could not be compromised or rationalized, as he had done with the Baltic and Ukrainian SS formations. The issues at stake required a commitment that the *Reichsführer* was not prepared to make. The eventual outcome, however, was consistent with his earlier decisions: in January 1944, five months after he forbade SS-*Sturmbannführer* Gunter d'Alquen (commander of SS war correspondent detachment "Kurt Eggers" and editor of the SS newspaper *Das Schwarze Korps*) further propagandizing for Vlasov, Himmler approached d'Alquen on Vlasov's possible use with SS support.[113]

If Himmler posed less of a threat to Vlasov, the army and the Eastern Ministry provided more than dubious allies. Rosenberg, never more than lukewarm in his support, was in any case preoccupied with the Ukraine. Zeitzler did not even attempt to defend Vlasov before Hitler at the June eighth conference, after which Hellmich's hostility toward Vlasov noticeably increased.[114] The field commanders supported the movement's political program but balked at its military aspirations. The planned authority of the Russian National Committee envisaged by both agencies moreover fell well below that of the Foreign Ministry, not to mention the full independence demanded by Vlasov.

But even with the committed support of the German military, Vlasov would still have confronted the daunting task of unifying the anti-Stalinist opposition. The political leaders of the Ukrainians and the Caucasus peoples were strongly nationalist and distrusted Vlasov.[115] Among Russian collaborationists, Vlasov aroused jealousy and fear of displacement. Bronislav Kaminsky of the Lokot' district and Mikhail Oktan, editor of a newspaper in Orel, overcame their mutual enmity only in their common animosity toward Vlasov; both were slated for prominent positions within the Vlasov committee as proposed by Field Marshal von Kluge.[116] Hitler's verdict thus obviated many difficulties and potential conflicts for German administrators and anti-Stalinist collaborationists alike.

The question remains: could Vlasov have turned the tide against Stalin in spring 1943? Moscow certainly reckoned him a serious enough threat to mount a major counter-propaganda campaign against him, and even attempted to assassinate him.[117] Two conditions, however, undermined any realistic chance for the movement's success. First, control of the means and proclaimed aims of the movement rested not with Vlasov but with his German sponsors. So long as this relationship existed, the broader but ultimately unavoidable issues of the genocide of Russian Jews and control of the post-war Russian economy could not even be raised, much less reconciled. Without greater independence, Vlasov could never have attained the status of a full ally. Perhaps even more to the point, Hitler's consent to the project—improbable as that was—would not have been enough. The confused and fragmented structure of *Ostpolitik*, so skillfully exploited by Vlasov's sponsors in establishing their candidate, could as easily have sabotaged Vlasov's efforts through the opportunities afforded a recalcitrant *Reichskommissar* or independent economic authorities. The attainment of Vlasov's program required not only the radical reversal of occupation policy but a complete overhaul of occupation structure as well.

NOTES

1. The literature on the Vlasov Movement is too extensive for review here. To the already-cited works by Strik-Strikfeldt, Steenberg, Fischer, and Thorwald should be added the recent studies by Joachim Hoffmann, *Die Geschichte der Wlassow-Armee* (Freiburg: Rombach Verlag, 1984), and Catherine Andreyev, *Vlasov and the Russian Liberation Movement: Soviet Reality and Emigré theories* (New York: Cambridge University Press, 1987).

2. See John H. Buchsbaum, "German Psychological Warfare against the Soviet

Union, 1941–1945'' (Dept. of the Army: Office of the Chief of Military History, 1953), Chap. IV, pp. 22–23, Chap. V, pp. 38–43.

3. Strik-Strikfeldt, *Against*, pp. 45–56.

4. Alexander Dallin, "From the Gallery of Wartime Disaffection," *The Russian Review*, Vol. XXI, no. 1 (January 1962), pp. 75–80; Strik-Strikfeldt, *Against*, pp. 34–36, 93–94.

5. OKW/Wpr (Martin), "Die Scheinregierung," August 6, 1942, T–311/101/7133815–821.

6. See Hans-Leo Martin, *Unser Mann bei Goebbels: Verbindungsoffizier des Oberkommandos der Wehrmacht beim Reichspropagandaminister 1940–1944* (Neckargemünd: Vowinckel, 1973), pp. 127–28.

7. See Andreyev, *Vlasov*, pp. 19–29, 37–42.

8. Steenberg, *Vlasov*, pp. 44–48, 53–55; Strik-Strikfeldt, *Against*, pp. 85–92; and Eugen Dürksen, "Das Laboratorium in der Viktoriastrasse," ZS 402/I, IfZ, Munich.

9. A German translation of Vlasov's and Colonel Boyarski's letter of August 3, 1942 appears on T–175/66/2582777–778.

10. See Buchbender, *Tönende Erz*, pp. 221–24.

11. Steenberg, *Vlasov*, pp. 49–50, Thorwald, *Illusion*, pp. 92–94.

12. Untitled fragment of memorandum signed by Vlasov, Malyshkin, and Zhilenkov, Document NOKW–3569, RG 238, NA, and discussed in Dallin, *German Rule*, p. 567n.

13. Strik-Strikfeldt, *Against*, pp. 45–46, 104–06; Andreyev, *Vlasov*, pp. 45, 97–100, 206–209.

14. See Dallin, *German Rule*, pp. 561–62, and Volkmann, "Vlasov-Unternehmen," pp. 139–42.

15. Thorwald, *Wen Sie*, pp. 188–89.

16. Strik-Strikfeldt, *Against*, pp. 106–08, Thorwald, *Wen Sie*, p. 190; and Eugen Dürksen, "Smolensker Kommittee," ZS 402/II, IfZ.

17. Compare Thorwald, *The Illusion*, p. 111, and Buchbender, *Tönende Erz*, p. 225.

18. Dallin, *German Rule*, pp. 562–63; Strik-Strikfeldt, *Against*, p. 108.

19. OMi memoranda, February 10–24, 1943, on T–454/89/461, T–454/91/682, and T–454/21/915–16.

20. Abwehrabteilung II, "Vortragsvermerk zur Amtschef," February 15, 1943, T–77/1505/861.

21. Leibbrandt, "Russisches Nationalkomitee," February 15, 1943, T–454/21/915–16.

22. Kinkelin, "Vermerk über Bildung von Komitees," n.d., T–454/89/417–18.

23. Hauptabteilung Politik draft, "Vorschläge," March 8, 1943, T–454/17/687–91.

24. Fischer, *Soviet Opposition*, pp. 63–70, 188–93; Steenberg, *Vlasov*, pp. 84–85.

25. Compare Strik-Strikfeldt, *Against*, pp. 118–20; and Michel, *Ost und West*, pp. 137–38, 162–65.

26. Gehlen to von Roenne, March 16, 1943, T–73/539/523.

27. Strik-Strikfeldt, *Against*, p. 78.

28. See Gustav Hilger, "Aufzeichnung über Vernehmungen," August 8, 1942, in *KTB/OKW*, Bd. II (1942), pp. 1287–90.

29. Hilger, "Notiz: Aktion Wlassow," April 1, 1943, and "Notiz: Rundfunkansprache Wlassows," April 2, 1943, T–120/748/1247/337917–925.

30. "Runderlass des Unterstaatssekretärs Woermann," March 24, 1943, in *ADAP*, E: V, 451–52.

31. (Hilger), "Aktion Wlassow," April 6, 1943, T–120/748/1247/337912–916.

32. Compare Chapter 5, above.

33. Unsigned note in von Etzdorf's papers, "Zu 13.IV.43: Ostpolitik," T–120/738/1457/366524, and Ribbentrop's notes on T–120/738/1457/366525–527.

34. See Volkmann, "Vlasov-Unternehmen," pp. 127n., 143–46, and Hilger's interrogations of Soviet officers on T–120/395/997/305035–055.

35. See Buchbender, *Tönende Erz*, pp. 201–03, and Martin, *Unser Mann*, passim.

36. Goebbels directive, "Behandlung der europäischen Völker," February 15, 1943, T–454/80/478–82.

37. Baird, *Mythical World*, pp. 162–65.

38. See above, Chapter 8.

39. See Taubert to Goebbels, "Deutsche Politik im Ostraum," December 28, 1942, and Taubert to Goebbels, January 27, 1943, both on T–580/647/Ordner 406–07; and Taubert to Goebbels, "Propaganda im Ostraum," February 3, 1943, R55/1292, BA Koblenz.

40. Martin, *Unser Mann*, pp. 129–31.

41. See Goebbels' (unpublished) diary entry on April 5, 1943, T–84/272/000039, and the published entry of April 15, in *Diaries*, p. 330.

42. Strik-Strikfeldt, *Against*, pp. 109–10.

43. Martin, *Unser Mann*, pp. 132–33.

44. Goebbels, *Diaries*, p. 330 (entry for April 16, 1943).

45. See above, Chapter 4.

46. Dwinger, "Das russische Grossreich und die Neuordnung Europas" (Spring 1943), T–175/103/2625524–528; and "Was muss im Augenblick geschehen, um Stalins System zu stürzen?" (n.d.), T–120/363/876/288633–648.

47. Thorwald, *The Illusion*, pp. 148–50; Strik-Strikfeldt, *Against*, p. 123.

48. Melitta Wiedemann to Himmler, May 26, 1943, T–175/38/2548176–184; Thorwald, *The Illusion*, pp. 152–53.

49. SS-*Obersturmbannführer* Brandt to Wiedemann, June 30, 1943, T–175/38/2548175.

50. Thorwald, *The Illusion*, p. 150.

51. Berger to Himmler, "Hauptsturmführer Dwinger," T–175/48/2560341; Dwinger, *General Wlassow, ein Tragödie unserer Zeit* (Frankfurt um Main: O. Dikreiter Verlag, 1951), p. 248.

52. Hoffmann, *Wlassow-Armee*, pp. 18–19.

53. See Andreyev, *Vlasov*, pp. 51, 102–07, 210–15; Fischer, *Soviet Opposition*, pp. 33–36; and Benzler to the Foreign Ministry, March 19, 1943, T–120/39/50/33635.

54. See Strik-Strikfeldt, *Against*, pp. 126–27; Steenberg, *Vlasov*, pp. 69–73, 80–82; and Thorwald, *The Illusion*, pp. 112–16, 119–20. See also Oberstlt. Schubuth, "Reise mit General Wlassow zum H.-Geb. Mitte 1943," ZS 417, pp. 8–18, IfZ.

55. Einsatzstab Reichsleiter Rosenberg (ERR), "Bericht: General Wlassow in Mogilev," March 24, 1943, Document NG–2726, RG 238, NA.

56. OKH/Gen.Qu., "Bericht aus dem Operationsgebiet," T–77/1035/6507732, 6507735. Emphasis in the original.

57. For example, the ERR's "Bericht," Document NG–2726, RG 238, NA.

58. See Thorwald, *Wen Sie*, pp. 206–09.

59. Steenberg, *Vlasov*, p. 86; Fischer, *Soviet Opposition*, pp. 65–70.

60. See, for example, Heeresgruppe A/Ia to Befehlshaber Heeresgebiet A, March 21, 1943, T–311/150/7197902.

61. See Andreyev, *Vlasov*, pp. 114–20, and Fischer, *Soviet Opposition*, pp. 61–62, 206.

62. The dates of this tour are disputed among the memoirs of participants; the best appears to be Steenberg (*Vlasov*, pp. 87–93) with the period April 19–May 10.

63. Reports of Vlasov's remarks are located on T–311/115/7154861–899, T–315/1607/497–99, and OSS R & A report no. 43714, RG 226, NA.

64. Sdf. (Z) Klein, "Kurzer Bericht," T–311/115/7154885–886.

65. See the reports reproduced on T–77/1035/6507940–94.

66. Gruppe Geh. Feldpolizei 713, "Lage und Stimmung der Bevölkerung," May 25, 1943, T–315/1607/492–93.

67. Prop. Abt. Ostland/Staffel Pleskau, "Die Lage," and Korück 583, "Besuch General Wlassow," T–311/115/7154899, 7154889–891.

68. Oberkommando der Heeresgruppe Nord/Ia, "Stichworte für den Führervortrag," May 7, 1943, T–78/38/6293892.

69. Himmler to Bormann, March 4, 1943, quoted in Dallin, *German Rule*, p. 572.

70. Compare Strik-Strikfeldt, *Against*, pp. 137–38, and Thorwald, *The Illusion*, pp. 125–27. For discussion of the directive's origin and significance, see Mulligan, "Politics," p. 376n.

71. Ernst Klink, *Das Gesetz des Handelns: Die Operation "Zitadelle" 1943* (Stuttgart: Deutsche Verlags-Anstalt, 1966), pp. 277–79, 292–99.

72. Herre diary, April 16–22, 1943, ZS 406/IV, pp. 13–14, and essay "Die Aktion Silberstreif," ZS 406/II, IfZ; Klink, *Gesetz*, pp. 300–01.

73. Buchbender, *Tönende Erz*, pp. 232–42.

74. Klink, *Gesetz*, pp. 105ff.

75. See Buchbender, *Tönende Erz*, pp. 240–46; Klink, *Gesetz*, pp. 137–39; Herre's diary, April 27–May 9, 1943 and his "Die Aktion Silberstreif," ZS 406/II (pp. 15–18) and 406/IV (pp. 15–17); and OKH/FHO, "Überläuferzahlen ab 1. Jan. 1943," T–78/489/474678.

76. Buchbender, *Tönende Erz*, pp. 244, 246.

77. See Buchbender, *Tönende Erz*, p. 243, the KTB of Panzerarmeeoberkommando 4/Ia, May 23, 1943, T–313/365/8650513, and Alexander Dallin and Ralph S. Mavrogordato, "The Soviet Reaction to Vlasov," *World Politics*, Vol. VIII, no. 3 (April 1956): 307–22 (esp. pp. 316–20).

78. Buchbender, *Tönende Erz*, p. 244, and Klink, *Gesetz*, pp. 208ff.

79. Strik-Strikfeldt, *Against*, p. 142.

80. Pozdnyakov, "Counterintelligence," FMS Mss. No. P–122, p. 178.

81. OKW/Chef H. Rüst. und B.d.E. to OKW/WPr, "Bericht von 2 Kosaken-Offizieren über die russische Befreiungsarmee," May 12, 1943, T–77/1035/6507819–824.

82. Kommandeur der Osttruppen z.b.V. 720, "Ehemalige russische Offiziere," May 13, 1943, T–312/1233/000046.

83. See, for example, the reports of 18th Panzergrenadier Division, on T–315/701/975–79, 1067–68.

84. Keitel, "Nationale Komitees im Osten," April 18, 1943, T–77/1499/655.

85. See the Herre diary extracts of April 26, May 7, and 16, 1943, ZS 406/IV, pp. 14–17, IfZ.

86. Panzerarmeeoberkommando 3/Abt. OQu, "Erfassung des russischen Volkes," February 27, 1943, Document WB–3104, RG 238, NA.

87. Armeeoberkommando (AOK) 16/Ic, "Propaganda," April 30, 1943, T–311/115/7154803–812; AOK 2/Ia, "Ausnutzung des russischen und ukrainischen Menschen," May 11, 1943, Document NOKW–2484, RG 238, NA.

88. See Klink, *Gesetz*, pp. 124–26. A copy, with accompanying instructions to the Ninth Army, is located on T–312/320/7888689ff.

89. See Otto Bräutigam, "Vortragsnotiz," May 27, 1943, ML 474, RG 242, NA, and ibid., *So hat es*, p. 480.

90. Herre diary, May 25, 1943, ZS 406/IV, p. 19, IfZ.

91. The primary source accounts of this meeting are Herre's diary, May 26, 1943, ZS 406/IV, pp. 19–20, IfZ; and Bräutigam, "Vortragsnotiz," May 27, 1943, ML 474, RG 242, NA. Compare also Thorwald, *Wen Sie*, pp. 226–33 and *The Illusion*, pp. 132–34, with Dallin, *German Rule*, p. 572n.

92. Bräutigam, "Vortragsnotiz," ML 474, and *So hat es*, pp. 480–81.

93. See Rosenberg to Hitler, October 12, 1944, Document Rosenberg–14, TMWC, XLI, 187, and Dallin, *German Rule*, pp. 608–09.

94. Rosenberg to OKW/WFSt, May 29, 1943, T–77/1499/654.

95. Bräutigam, *So hat es*, p. 481.

96. See Oberbefehlshaber der Gruppe Weiss/Ia an den Chef des Generalstabes der Heeresgruppe Mitte, "Einführung russischer Komitees," June 3, 1943, and accompanying enclosure, T–312/320/7888685–688, 7888692–693.

97. Ministero degli Affari Esteri, "Pro-Memoria per l'Eccellenza il Gen. Ambrosio," May 10, 1943, T–821/128/875–890.

98. The press comments are quoted or summarized in OSS R&A report nos. 34,835, 35,520, 37,403, 39,058 and 34,649, RG 226, NA.

99. Deutsche Gesandtschaft Helsinki an das Auswärtige Amt, June 10, 1943, and Deutsche Gesandtschaft Stockholm an das Auswärtige Amt, "Schwedische Presse," June 2, 1943, T–120/2733/5820H/E424075–077; Thomsen an das Auswärtige Amt, June 17, 1943, *ADAP*, E: VI, 182–83.

100. "Besprechung des Führers mit Generalfeldmarschall Keitel und General Zeitzler am 8.6.1943 auf dem Berghof," in Heiber, *Hitlers Lagebesprechungen*, pp. 252–68.

101. Reitlinger, *House*, pp. 338–39.

102. "Brief Keitel an Rosenberg, Juni 1943," T–120/395/997/305022.

103. Hubatsch, *Weisungen*, p. 237.

104. OKH/GenStdH/Org.Abt., "Gliederung und Stärken der landeseigenen Verbände," August 15, 1943, T–78/414/6382710–713.

105. Abt. Fremde Heere Ost (Chef), "Vortragsnotiz zum Brief des RmfdbO an Chef OKW," July 24, 1943, T–81/219/0369477.

106. "Auszug aus der Ansprache des Führers an die Herresgruppenführer pp. am 1.7.43 abends (S. 55–61)," Document 739-PS, in Helmut Krausnick, "Zu Hitlers Ostpolitik im Sommer 1943," *VfZ*, II, 3 (July 1954): 305–12. For a discussion of other sources, see Mulligan, "Politics," p. 392n.

107. Conference memorandum of July 13, 1943, "Problems concerning the employment of labor," August 20, 1943, Document NO–1831, *NMT*, XIII, 1016–22.

108. See Thorwald, *The Illusion*, pp. 162–70, and Fischer, *Soviet Opposition*, pp. 50–57.

109. For example, Dallin, *German Rule*, pp. 572, 592ff.; Fischer, *Soviet Opposition*, pp. 72ff.; Thorwald, *The Illusion*, pp. 125, 150, 170–72; and Andreyev, *Vlasov*, p. 50.

110. Himmler to von dem Bach-Zelewski, January 1943, T–175/128/2624189–192.

111. See Himmler's speeches to SS officers in Posen, October 4, 1943, Document 1919-PS, *TMWC*, XXIX, 117–19, and in Bad Schachen, October 14, 1943, Document 070-L, *TMWC*, XXXVIII, 514–15.

112. Himmler to Hitler, January 1943, T–175/66/2582899–901.

113. Himmler to d'Alquen, July 1943, T–175/267/2762207, and interview with Gunter d'Alquen, September 30, 1983.

114. Strik-Strikfeldt, *Against*, p. 169.

115. See Armstrong, *Nationalism*, pp. 180–86, and von zur Mühlen, *Hakenkreuz*, pp. 130–38, 158–65.

116. See Dallin, *Kaminsky Brigade*, pp. 93–95, 109–11, and the same author's "Portrait of a Collaborator: Oktan," *Soviet Survey*, no. 35 (January–March 1961), pp. 116–17.

117. See Dallin and Mavrogordato, "Soviet Reaction," passim; and Hoffmann, *Wlassow-Armee*, pp. 331–52.

CONCLUSION

In July 1943, a disgruntled Russian propagandist returning from a speaking tour of *Osttruppen* units compared his efforts to a morphine injection given a seriously ill patient; the morphine might temporarily ease his pain, but without medication the effect would be lost.[1] The analogy could be extended to the whole of *Ostpolitik* reform of 1942–43.

It may be argued that it was already too late to effect major changes. Popular willingness to cooperate with German authority had by then evaporated through the mistreatment of prisoners-of-war; mass shootings of Jews, hostages, and "undesirables"; famine conditions in Ukrainian cities; and the daily reminders that the best public facilities were reserved "For Germans Only." Yet paradoxically the Stalingrad debacle, by its very magnitude, established credibility for a policy change to indigenous anti-Soviet elites. If German military victory in 1943 was no longer possible—and this was precisely the premise of many *Wehrmacht* officers who endorsed reform—the potential gains of *Ostpolitik* reform remained substantial: an increase of as many as 200,000 recruits from the Baltic states, strengthened ties within the Axis coalition and with Finland especially, greater productivity and political cooperation from the Ukrainian peasantry, and the enhanced support of the Russian population and the *Osttruppen*. The benefits derived by granting the occupied populace a stake in collaboration, combined with a defensive military strategy and the increased industrial output of the Donetz basin, might have made possible von Manstein's strategic objective of playing for a draw in the East.

Yet it cannot be overlooked that the 1942–43 reform efforts originated almost entirely within the German occupation administration, a "reform from above" that lacked binding ties with the people who were the objects of reform. Ideas and proposals offered by emigrés, active collaborationists and defectors were diluted or ignored altogether. For the great bulk of the occupied population, the 1942–43 debate over *Ostpolitik* passed as muffled voices behind locked doors. As one Russian who served in the civil administration observed,

Many people condemned the attitude of the Germans toward the Russian anti-Bolshevik movement on the grounds that if the Germans had immediately taken steps to create a free Russia, they could have acquired a loyal and powerful ally for themselves in the east and the outcome of the war would have been quite different. I did not agree with them: the Germans and a free Russia, liberated by them, were two irreconcilable things. In order to do that they would have had to stop being Germans.[2]

Yet the German reformers themselves were greatly divided in their policies. While most agreed on the need for changes in policy, no consensus existed as to the nature or scope of the measures to be implemented. The alliance between Rosenberg and the army foundered on the status of the minority nationalities. Sharp divisions existed within the army over the granting of self-government, the treatment of partisans, and the use of eastern troops. Economic authorities demonstrated the greatest consistency, but they were concerned only with material rewards and incentives that simultaneously reinforced German domination of the economy. Hitler's veto of reform obviated the need to resolve these contradictions and excused reformers from the responsibility to compromise and coordinate their efforts.

Hitler's role in blocking reform, however, remains paramount. This had not been a foregone conclusion, at least not to contemporaries who had seen the führer accommodate the policy reforms of the first half of 1942. Reformers counted on the deteriorating strategic situation to compel a return to *Realpolitik* in the East, but did not reckon on Hitler's ideological commitment to extremist war aims. Sensing the crisis of faith among his subordinates, Hitler reaffirmed his goal of *Lebensraum* on the eve of his last offensive in Russia, divulging to his field commanders that which he had concealed from his supreme command two years earlier.

In comparing Imperial Germany's policy of 1916–18 with the reform efforts of 1942–43, Hitler correctly perceived the reemergence of the antagonism between *Weltpolitik* and *Lebensraum* concepts of imperialism that had characterized eastern policy in the First World War. Recognizing this incompatibility, he had maintained the appearance of an integrated strategy before BARBAROSSA only by misleading Rosenberg and lying to the military. His concessions in the winter and spring of 1942 were granted primarily for economic reasons, as the Blitzkrieg's failure in Russia and the United States' entry into the war imposed new demands on the German war economy. But the clamor for policy changes after Stalingrad compelled Hitler to assert the priority of *Lebensraum* as Germany's principal war aim. In this, and especially in the related campaign of genocide against Soviet Jews, Hitler demonstrated that the basis of his *Ostpolitik* was racial rather than political. He thereby severed the line of continuity with his predecessors, whose policies were shaped by political concerns and who acknowledged some limitations to German power, even in the aftermath of military victory.[3]

Another distinction between the two eras concerned the nature of National Socialist power politics, which largely molded the character of the reform efforts through the chaotic administrative structure that embodied its contradictions and rivalries. The structural flaws of the occupation apparatus provided numerous opportunities for individual initiative and therefore reduced the significance of cooperative action. Divided by conceptual differences but with considerable freedom of action within the limits of their own jurisdictions, reformers had little inclination to work together. After Hitler rejected a general reform of policy in December 1942, the centrifugal force that powered National Socialist politics splintered the reform movement according to its specialized interests. As a result, reformist elements achieved some gains, but lacked cohesion and were left exposed to external conditions—as in the Caucasus, where the military's experiment in liberal government fell victim to the Soviet advance at Stalingrad— or to Hitler's ultimate authority, as Rosenberg learned in May 1943 and the Vlasov movement discovered in June.

The dynamics of National Socialist politics influenced *Ostpolitik* reform in other ways. The relative independence of party officials benefited reform in Litzmann's defiance of Lohse in Estonia, but Koch's disobedience of Rosenberg frustrated all efforts in the Ukraine. The reform period also coincided with a significant expansion of power of the SS, a process to which reform contributed. Occupying the most powerful position in the configuration of Nazi political power, Himmler expanded his combat arm, consolidated his police powers in the Reich commissariats and broadened them in the military areas, and began to infiltrate key positions within the *Ostministerium*.

These gains however reflected less a calculated scheme or even ruthless opportunism than a dilution of the ideological foundation of the SS, as wartime necessity compelled a greater concern for the pragmatic. Like Nazi Germany itself, the SS developed contradictions and ambiguities that were papered over with rationalizations or ignored altogether. Ukrainian, Latvian and Estonian nationalism were exploited for the *Waffen*-SS with the justification of an enhanced Germanization of suitable elements; a former *Einsatzgruppe* commander like Ohlendorf opposed Koch's brutality without ever questioning the validity of the "Final Solution"; and for all his invective against Vlasov in 1943, Himmler became Vlasov's patron in 1944. That this could occasionally prove embarrassing was demonstrated at a führer conference on March 23, 1945, when a briefing officer's reference to the Ukrainian (formerly "Galician") SS division prompted a perplexed Hitler to observe: "I just heard for the first time, to my amazement, that a Ukrainian SS division has suddenly appeared. I don't know a thing about this Ukrainian SS division."[4]

Yet, as has been seen, Hitler remained the key determinant of policy. The chaotic structure of power helped maintain Hitler's preeminence by draining off potential opposition into basins of restricted independence. Not only did reformers have little reason to cooperate, but the ability to shape policy even in a very limited manner provided a safety valve for opposition to the führer's prerogatives. Ironically, the major breakdown in this system, the July 20, 1944 conspiracy, traced its roots in part to the *Ostpolitik* reform period. For the future conspirators Stauffenberg and Tresckow, though they did not meet until August 1943, their experiences in eastern policy provided common ground for cooperation.[5]

The greatest significance of the reform efforts remains in the context of the Soviet-German war—not for what "might have been," but in the political and military dimensions of that conflict. Some lives were spared by Gehlen's changes in antipartisan policy, and some material improvements eased conditions in some areas, but these may have only made the *Osttruppen*, the *Ostarbeiter* and peasants all the more conscious of the lack of fundamental changes in German policy. Hopes aroused by Vlasov's statements and by rumors of restored sovereignty for the Baltic states proved false and morale plummeted even further. For Vlasov, the 1942–43 effort constituted the first act in a tragedy that would end on a Soviet gallows; for thousands of Russians in German service, dissatisfaction led them to brave Soviet retribution and redefect to the Red Army in the wake of the German defeat at Kursk in the summer of 1943.

But it is in their relationship to that military defeat that the reform efforts most directly affected the course of events. Incompatible as reform's multiple goals and interests were in the long run, the short-term benefits were undeniable: the German war effort secured the maximum use of all options during its severest test on the Eastern Front. For a nine-month period (October 1942–June 1943), Hitler simultaneously obtained higher production in Russian agriculture and raw materials while procuring additional slave labor for German factories. Militarily, reformers contributed to the growth and consolidation of a heterogenous force of Ukrainian, Latvian, and Estonian nationalists, Caucasian separatists, anti-Stalinist Russians and Czarist emigrés, an army of 1 million men during a period of critical manpower shortages. The combat risks of such a force were minimized by confining them to rear area and noncombat roles, releasing more German personnel for frontline duties. By summer 1943, the *Wehrmacht* had made good its losses from the winter and rebuilt its strategic reserve, while the German war economy at last approached a "total war" footing. *Ostpolitik* reform thus provided Hitler an invaluable flexibility in surmounting the military crisis of winter 1942–43, in exchange for minor economic and military rewards and not one political concession.

Yet even as the reform efforts facilitated German military recovery, so too they strengthened Hitler's resolve to risk his rebuilt forces in pursuit of a military solution in the East. Rejecting his generals' advice to adopt a defensive strategy, Hitler continued to seek the military victory necessary to achieve his war aims in Russia. The decision to attack at Kursk derived from ideological as well as military considerations, in response to the pressures upon him to consider political solutions to German's strategic dilemma. That Italy and Japan counseled the conclusion of a separate peace with Stalin probably did not surprise him, but when his own generals and ministers urged a reversal of *Ostpolitik* Hitler grasped the need for action. "The victory at Kursk must act as a beacon for the world," inscribed Hitler on his operational order for ZITADELLE; and in a subsequent directive to his commanders, he spoke openly of the need to restore faith among Germany's allies and the neutral states, "but above all to infuse the German soldier himself with new confidence."[6]

Thus Operation ZITADELLE, originally recognized by Vlasov's supporters as an opportunity to exhibit the value of political warfare, became instead a demonstration of Hitler's unyielding commitment to victory on his own terms. This but reflected the greater ironies underlying the entire *Ostpolitik* reform episode. The reformers, though they correctly perceived the widespread dissatisfaction with the Soviet regime, could not understand that the basis for a lasting cooperation between the Russian population and Nazi Germany did not exist. This misjudgment derived from the much more deeply rooted illusion among German officials that National Socialism, whatever its unique character, remained a fundamentally rational system based on *Realpolitik*. Behind the reformers' memoranda and contrived faits accompli lay a faith in National Socialism's ultimate capacity to confront reality and revise its policies accordingly. The power of this illusion spurred on the reformers to notable material contributions to the German war effort, only to have them thrown away by Hitler in pursuit of his own chimera of *Lebensraum* and the decisive military victory required to impose that solution. With the defeat at Kursk, Hitler's pursuit of limitless goals with limited means finally collapsed, and the outcome of the Soviet-German war was sealed.

NOTES

1. Oberleutnant Boschenko, "Bericht über eine Rednerreise," T-454/21/989–98.

2. Petrov, *It Happens in Russia*, p. 428.

3. Though his *Lebensraum* ideology attained supremacy in 1918, Ludendorff's proposals for a restoration of the Russian monarchy to combat Bolshevism were rejected: See Baumgart, *Ostpolitik 1918*, pp. 60–92, 247–57. See also Chapter 1, above.

4. Heiber, *Hitlers Lagebesprechungen*, p. 940.

5. See Hoffmann, *German Resistance*, pp. 264–89, 309; Herwarth, *Against Two Evils*, p. 242; and Scheurig, *Tresckow*, pp. 154–58.

6. See Klink, *Gesetz*, pp. 292, 329–30.

SELECTED BIBLIOGRAPHY

PRIMARY SOURCES: UNPUBLISHED

National Archives, Washington, D.C.

Record Group 242, National Archives Collection of Seized Enemy Records 1941–
    Microcopy T-77: Armed Forces High Command (OKW)
    Microcopy T-78: Army High Command (OKH)
    Microcopy T-81: NSDAP/Deutsches Ausland-Institut
    Microcopy T-84: Miscellaneous German Records
    Microcopy T-120: German Foreign Ministry
    Microcopy T-175: Reichsführer-SS and Chief of the German Police
    Microcopy T-311: Field Commands, Army Groups
    Microcopy T-312: Field Commands, Armies
    Microcopy T-313: Field Commands, Panzer Armies
    Microcopy T-314: Field Commands, Corps
    Microcopy T-315: Field Commands, Divisions
    Microcopy T-454: Reich Ministry for the Occupied Eastern Territories
    Microcopy T-501: Field Commands, Rear Areas, Occupied Territories, and Others
    Microcopy T-580: Captured Records Filmed at Berlin (American Historical Association)
    Microcopy T-1022: German Navy
Record Group 226, Records of the Office of Strategic Services
Record Group 165, Records of War Department General and Special Staffs
Record Group 59, General Records of the Department of State
Record Group 457, Records of the National Security Agency

Bundesarchiv, Koblenz

Akten des Reichsministeriums für die besetzten Ostgebiete
Akten des Reichsministeriums für Volksaufklärung und Propaganda
Akten des Reichssicherheitshauptamtes

YIVO Institute for Jewish Research, New York

Berlin Collection, Files Occ E 3a–16, 3b 7–8, 6, 8, 18–19, 41.

Institut für Zeitgeschichte, Munich

Sammlung Thorwald

Document Center, Berlin

NSDAP personnel files

PRIMARY SOURCES: PUBLISHED

Baranauskas, B., and Ruksenas, K., Eds. *Documents Accuse*. Vilnius: "Gintaras," 1970.
Boelcke, Willi A., Ed. *Deutschlands Rüstung im Zweiten Weltkrieg: Hitlers Konferenzen mit Albert Speer 1942–1945*. Frankfurt am Main: Akademische Verlagsgesellschaft Athenaion, 1969.
———, Ed. *The Secret Conferences of Dr. Goebbels: The Nazi Propaganda War 1939–43*. Translated by Ewald Osers. New York: E.P. Dutton, 1970.
Germany. Auswärtiges Amt. *Documents on German Foreign Policy 1918–1945*, Series D, Vol. XII: *The War Years, 1941*. Washington, DC: U.S. Department of State, 1962.
———. *Akten zur deutschen Auswärtigen Politik 1918–1945*, Serie E: 1941–1945, Bände III–VI. 8 vols. Göttingen: Vandenhoeck & Ruprecht, 1974–1979.
Germany. Wehrmacht. Wirtschaftsinspektion Nord. *Zwei Jahre Kriegswirtschaft im russischen Nordraum. Ein Tätigkeits-und Leistungs-Bericht der Wirtschaftsinspektion Nord*. Pleskau (Pskov): Wi In Nord, September 1943.
Goebbels, Joseph. *The Goebbels Diaries 1942–1943*. Translated, edited and with an introduction by Louis P. Lochner. New York: Doubleday, 1948.
Halder, Franz. *Generaloberst Halder Kriegstagebuch*. 3 vols. Stuttgart: W. Kohlhammer Verlag, 1962–1964.
Heiber, Helmut, Ed. *Hitlers Lagebesprechungen: Die Protokollfragmente seiner militärischen Konferenzen 1942–1945*. Stuttgart: Deutsche Verlags-Anstalt, 1962.
Hitler, Adolf. *Mein Kampf*. Translated by Ralph Manheim. Boston: Houghton Mifflin, 1943.
———. *Hitler's Secret Book*. Introduction by Telford Taylor. Translated by Salvator Attanasio. New York: Grove Press, 1961.
———. *Hitler's Secret Conversations 1941–1944*. Introduction by H.R. Trevor-Roper and translated by Norman Cameron and R.H. Stevens. New York: Farrar, Strauss and Young, 1976 (reprint).

Hubatsch, Walter, Ed. *Hitler's Weisungen für die Kriegführung 1939–1945.* Munich: Deutscher Taschenbuch Verlag, 1965.

Müller, Norbert, Ed. *Deutsche Besatzungspolitik in der UdSSR.* Berlin and Cologne: Pahl-Rugenstein Verlag, 1980.

Oberländer, Theodor. *6 Denkschriften aus dem Zweiten Weltkrieg über die Behandlung der Sowjetvölker.* Ingolstadt: Zeitgeschichtliche Forschungsstelle Ingolstadt, 1984.

Office of the Chief Counsel for the Prosecution of Axis Criminality. *Nazi Conspiracy and Aggression.* 8 Vols. and Supplements A and B. Washington, D.C.: Government Printing Office, 1946–1947.

Prestupnye Tseli-Prestupnye Sredstva: Dokumenty. Comp. by the Institut Marksizma-Leninizma Pri Tsk KPSS. Moscow: Izdatel'stvo politicheskoi literatury, 1968.

Schiller, Otto. *Ziele und Ergebnisse der Agrarordnung in den besetzten Ostgebieten.* Berlin: Reichsministerium für die besetzten Ostbebiete, November 1943.

Schramm, Percy E., and Greiner, Helmuth, Eds. *Kriegstagebuch des Oberkommandos der Wehrmacht (Wehrmachtführungsstab), 1940–1945,* Band III. 4 vols. in 7 parts. Frankfurt am Main: Bernard & Graefe Verlag für Wehrwesen, 1961–1965.

Trevor-Roper, Hugh R., Ed. *Blitzkrieg to Defeat: Hitler's War Directives 1939–1945.* New York: Holt, Rinehart & Winston, 1964.

Trials of the Major War Criminals before the International Military Tribunal Nuremberg, 14 November 1945–1 October 1946. 42 vols. Nürnberg: The International Military Tribunal, 1947–1949.

Trials of the Major War Criminals Before the Nuremberg Military Tribunals Under Control Council Law No. 10. 15 vols. Washington, DC: Government Printing Office, 1949–1954.

INTERVIEWS AND CORRESPONDENCE

d'Alquen, Gunter, interviews and correspondence, 1981–1984.

Oberländer, Dr. Theodor, interview and correspondence, 1983–1984.

Stammler, Dr. Heinrich A., correspondence with the author, 1981–1984.

T——— (name withheld on request), interview and correspondence, 1979–1980.

MEMOIRS

von Blücher, Wipert. *Gesandter zwischen Diktatur und Demokratie: Erinnerungen aus dem Jahren 1935–1944.* Wiesbaden: Limes Verlag, 1951.

Bräutigam, Otto. *So hat es sich zugetragen.* Würzburg: Holzer Verlag, 1968.

Dwinger, Edwin E. *General Wlassow, ein Trägodie unserer Zeit.* Frankfurt am Main: O. Dikreiter Verlag, 1951.

Gehlen, Reinhard. *The Service: The Memoirs of General Reinhard Gehlen.* Introduction by George Bailey and translated by David Irving. New York: The World Publishing Company, 1972.

Herwarth von Bittenfeld, Hans-Heinrich. *Against Two Evils.* With S. Frederick Starr. Introduction by Fitzroy McLean. New York: Rawson, Wade, 1981.

Kleist, Peter. *Zwischen Hitler und Stalin.* Bonn: Athenäum-Verlag, 1950.

Martin, Hans-Leo. *Unser Mann bei Goebbels. Verbindungsoffizier des Oberkommandos der Wehrmacht beim Reichspropagandaminister 1940–1944.* Neckargemünd: Vowinckel Verlag, 1973.

Michel, Karl. *Ost und West: Der Ruf Stauffenbergs.* Zürich: Thomas Verlag, 1947.

Petrov, Vladimir. *It Happens in Russia.* London: Byre & Stottiswoods, 1951.

Rosenberg, Alfred. *Letzte Aufzeichnungen. Ideale und Idole der nationalsozialistischen Revolution.* Göttingen: Plesse Verlag, 1955.

————. *Memoirs of Alfred Rosenberg.* Edited by Serge Lang and Ernst von Schenck and translated by Erich Posselt. Chicago: Ziff-Davis, 1949.

Schellenberg, Walter. *The Labyrinth: The Memoirs of Walter Schellenberg.* Introduction by Alan Bullock and translated by Louis Hagen. New York: Harper and Bros., 1956.

Speer, Albert. *Inside the Third Reich.* Introduction by Eugene Davidson and translated by Richard and Clara Winston. Avon Books. New York: Macmillan, 1970.

————. *Spandau: The Secret Diaries.* Translated by Richard and Clara Winston. New York: Simon and Schuster, 1977.

Strik-Strikfeldt, Winfried. *Against Stalin and Hitler 1941–1945.* Translated by David Footman. New York: John Day, 1973.

OFFICIAL STUDIES

U.S. Army Foreign Military Studies Manuscripts

von Bosse, Alexander. "The Cossack Corps." Historical Division, U.S. Army, Europe, 1950. Ms. No. P-064.

von Heygendorff, Ralph, Seraphim, Hans, and Köstring, Ernst. "Eastern Nationals as Volunteers in the German Army." Historical Division, U.S. Army, Europe, 1949. Ms. No. C-043.

Pozdnyakov, Vladimir. "German Counterintelligence Activities in Occupied Russia 1941–1945." Historical Division, U.S. Army Europe, 1953. Ms. No. P-122.

————. "National Instinct and Governmental Institutions under German Occupation in Western Russia." Historical Division, U.S. Army Europe, 1951. Ms. No. P-123.

Toppe, Alfred, et al. "German Military Government." Historical Division, U.S. Army Europe, 1948. Ms. No. P-033.

————. "Personnel and Administration Project No. 2a: Part IV." Historical Division, U.S. Army Europe, 1949.

Volzhanin, V. "Zuyev's Republic." Historical Division, U.S. Army, Europe, 1951. Ms. No. P-124.

Other Studies

Buchsbaum, John H. "German Psychological Warfare on the Russian Front 1941–1945." Washington, DC: Office of the Chief of Military History, Department of the Army, 1953 (Mimeographed).

Howell, Edgar M. *The Soviet Partisan Movement 1941–1944.* Washington, DC: Dept. of the Army pamphlet no. 20-244, 1956.

Waldman, Eric. "German Occupation Administration and Experience in the USSR."

Technical Memorandum ORO-T-301. Operations Research Office, Johns Hopkins University, May 1955.

———. "German Use of Indigenous Auxiliary Policy in the Occupied USSR." Technical Memorandum ORO-T-320. Operations Research Office, Johns Hopkins University, May 1955.

SECONDARY SOURCES: BOOKS

Alexeev, Wassilij, and Stavrou, Theofanis G. *The Great Revival: The Russian Church Under German Occupation*. Minneapolis, MN: Burgess Publishing Company, 1976.

Anatoli, A. (Kuznetsov). *Babi Yar*. Translated by David Floyd. Pocket Books. New York: Simon and Schuster, 1971.

Andreyev, Catherine. *Vlasov and the Russian Liberation Movement: Soviet Reality and Emigré Theories*. New York: Cambridge University Press, 1987.

Anisimov, Oleg. *The German Occupation in Northern Russia During World War II. Political and Administrative Aspects*. New York: Research Program on the U.S.S.R., Study No. 56, 1954.

Armstrong, John A., Ed. *Soviet Partisans in World War II*. Madison, WI: University of Wisconsin Press, 1964.

Baird, Jay W. *The Mythical World of Nazi War Propaganda, 1939–1945*. Minneapolis, MN: University of Minnesota Press, 1974.

Bender, Roger James, and Taylor, Hugh Page. *Uniforms, Organization and History of the Waffen-SS*, Vols. 4 and 5. 5 vols. San Jose, CA: R. James Bender Publishing, 1975–1982.

Bilmanis, Alfred. *Latvia Under German Occupation*. Washington, DC: Department of State, 1943.

Binion, Rudolph. *Hitler Among the Germans*. New York: Elsevier Scientific, 1976.

Brandt, Karl, Schiller, Otto, and Ahlgrimm, Franz. *Management of Agriculture and Food in the German-Occupied and Other Areas of Fortress Europe: A Study in Military Government*. Stanford, CA: Stanford University Press, 1954.

Bräutigam, Otto. *Überblick über die besetzten Ostgebiete während des 2. Weltkrieges*. Tübingen: Institut für Besatzungsfragen, 1954.

Brissaud, André. *Canaris: Le "petit amiral" prince de l'espionage allemand (1887–1945)*. Paris: Librairie Academique Perrin, 1970.

Buchbender, Ortwin. *Das tönende Erz: Deutsche Propaganda gegen die Rote Armee im Zweiten Weltkrieg*. Stuttgart: Seewald Verlag, 1978.

Cherednichenko, V. *Collaborationists*. Kiev: Politvidav Ukraine, 1975.

Czollek, Roswitha. *Faschismus und Okkupation: Wirtschaftspolitische Zielsetzung und Praxis des faschistischen deutschen Besatzungsregimes in den baltischen Sowjetrepubliken während des zweiten Weltkrieges*. Berlin: Akademie-Verlag, 1974.

Dallin, Alexander. *German Rule in Russia 1941–1945: A Study of Occupation Policies*. New York: St. Martin's Press, 1957.

———. *The Kaminsky Brigade: 1941–1944. A Case Study of German Exploitation of Soviet Disaffection*. Cambridge, MA: Russian Research Center, Harvard University, 1956.

Deakin, F.W. *The Brutal Friendship: Mussolini, Hitler and the Fall of Italian Fascism*. New York: Harper & Row, 1962.

Drozdzynski, Aleksander, and Zaborowski, Jan. *Oberländer: A Study in German East Policies*. Poznan/Warsaw: Wydawnictwo Zachodnie, 1960.

Fest, Joachim. *The Face of the Third Reich*. Translated by Michael Bullock. New York: Pantheon Books, 1970.

Fireside, Harvey. *Icon and Swastika: The Russian Orthodox Church under Nazi and Soviet Control*. Cambridge, MA: Harvard University Press, 1971.

Fischer, Fritz. *Germany's Aims in the First World War*. New York: W.W. Norton, 1967.

Fischer, George. *Soviet Opposition to Stalin: A Case Study in World War II*. Cambridge, MA: Harvard University Press, 1952.

Fleischhauer, Ingeborg. *Das Dritte Reich und die Deutschen in der Sowjetunion*. Stuttgart: Deutsche Verlags-Anstalt, 1983.

———. *Die Chance des Sonderfriedens: Deutsch-sowjetische Geheimgespräche 1941– 1945*. Berlin: Siedler Verlag, 1986.

Gerber, Berthold. *Staatliche Wirtschaftslenkung in den besetzten und annektierten Ostgebieten während des zweiten Weltkrieges unter besonderer Berücksichtigung der treuhänderischen Verwaltung von Unternehmungen und der Ostgesellschaften*. Tübingen: Institut für Besatzungsfragen, 1959.

Handrack, H.D. *Das Reichskommissariat Ostland. Die Kulturpolitik der deutschen Verwaltung zwischen Autonomie und Gleichschaltung 1941–1944*. Hann. Münden: Gauke Verlag, 1981.

Heike, Wolf-Dietrich. *Sie wollten die Freiheit: Die Geschichte der ukrainischen Division 1943–45*. Dorheim/H: Podzun-Verlag, 1974.

Herzog, Robert. *Grundzüge der deutschen Besatzungsverwaltung in den ost- und südosteuropäischen Ländern während des Zweiten Weltkrieges*. Tübingen: Institut für Besatzungsfragen, 1955.

Herzstein, Robert Edwin. *When Nazi Dreams Come True*. London: Abacus Books, 1982.

Hesse, Erich. *Der sowjetrussische Partisanenkrieg 1941 bis 1944 im Spiegel deutscher Kampfanweisungen und Befehle*. Göttingen: Musterschmidt Verlag, 1969.

Hilberg, Raul. *The Destruction of the European Jews*. Chicago: Quadrangle Books, 1961.

Hillgruber, Andreas. *Hitlers Strategie. Politik und Kriegführung 1940–41*. Frankfurt am Main: Bernard & Graefe Verlag für Wehrwesen, 1965.

———. *Germany and the Two World Wars*. Translated by William C. Kirby. Cambridge, MA: Harvard University Press, 1981.

Hirschfeld, Gerhard, and Kettenacker, Lothar, Eds. *Der "Führerstaat": Mythos und Realität. Studien zur Struktur und Politik des Dritten Reiches*. Introduction by Wolfgang J. Mommsen. Stuttgart: Klett-Cotta, 1981.

Höhne, Heinz. *The Order of the Death's Head: The Story of Hitler's SS*. Translated by Richard Barry. New York: Coward-McCann, 1970.

———. *Canaris*. Translated by J. Maxwell Brownjohn. Garden City, NY: Doubleday, 1979.

Höhne, Heinz, and Zolling, Hermann. *The General Was a Spy*. Introduction by H.R. Trevor-Roper and translated by Martin Secker and Warburg Limited. New York: Coward, McCann & Geoghegan, Inc., 1972.

Hoffmann, Joachim. *Deutsche und Kalmyken 1942 bis 1945*. Freiburg: Verlag Rombach, 1974.

———. *Die Ostlegionen 1941–1943: Turkotataren, Kaukasier und Wolgafinnen im deutschen Heer*. Freiburg: Verlag Rombach, 1976.

———. *Die Geschichte der Wlassow-Armee*. Freiburg: Verlag Rombach, 1984.

Hoffmann, Peter. *The History of the German Resistance 1933–1945*. Translated by Richard Barry. Cambridge, MA: The MIT Press, 1977.

Homze, Edward L. *Foreign Labor in Nazi Germany*. Princeton, NJ: Princeton University Press, 1967.

Hubatsch, Walther, *Kriegswende 1943*. Darmstadt: Wehr und Wissen Verlagsgesellschaft mbH, 1966.

Ilnytzkyj, Roman. *Deutschland und die Ukraine 1934–1945; Tatsachen europäischer Ostpolitik*. 2 vols. Munich: Osteuropa-Institut, 1955.

Institut Markisma-Leninizma Pri Tsk KPSS, Ed. *Istoriia Velikoi Otechestvennoi voiny Sovetskogo Soiuza, 1941–1945*. Moscow: Voenizdat, 1960–64.

————. *Nemetsko-Fashistskii okkupatsionnyi rezhim (1941–1944)*. Moscow: Izdatel'stvo politicheskoi literatury, 1965.

Irving, David. *Hitler's War*. New York: The Viking Press, 1977.

Jäger, Jörg-Johannes. *Die wirtschaftliche Abhängigkeit des Dritten Reiches vom Ausland*. Berlin: Berlin Verlag, 1969.

Kamenetsky, Ihor. *Hitler's Occupation of Ukraine, 1941–1944*. Milwaukee, WI: Marquette University Press, 1956.

————. *Secret Nazi Plans for Eastern Europe: A Study of Lebensraum Policies*. New Haven, CT: College and University Press, 1961.

Kern, Erich. *General von Pannwitz und seine Kosaken*. Oldendorf: Verlag K.W. Schütz KG, 1971.

Klink, Ernst. *Das Gesetz des Handelns: Die Operation "Zitadelle" 1943*. Stuttgart: Deutsche Verlags-Anstalt, 1966.

Kramarz, Joachim. *Stauffenberg: The Architect of the Famous July 20th Conspiracy to Assassinate Hitler*. Translated by R. H. Barry. New York: Macmillan, 1967.

Krausnick, Helmut, and Wilhelm, Hans-Heinrich. *Die Truppe des Weltanschauungskrieges. Die Einsatzgruppen der Sicherheitspolizei und des SD 1938–1942*. Stuttgart: Deutsche Verlags-Ansalt, 1981.

Laqueur, Walter. *Russia and Germany: A Century of Conflict*. Boston: Little, Brown, 1965.

Landwehr, Richard. *Fighting for Freedom: The Ukrainian Volunteer Division of the Waffen-SS*. Silver Spring, MD: Bibliophile Legion Books, 1985.

Lemkin, Raphael. *Axis Rule in Occupied Europe*. Washington, DC: Carnegie Endowment for International Peace, 1944.

Littlejohn, David. *The Patriotic Traitors: The History of Collaboration in German-occupied Europe. 1940–1945*. New York: Doubleday, 1972.

Lundin, C. Leonard. *Finland in the Second World War*. Bloomington, IN: Indiana University Press, 1957.

Militärgeschichtliches Forschungsamt. *Der Angriff auf die Sowjetunion*. Vol. 4 of *Das Deutsche Reich und der Zweite Weltkrieg*. Stuttgart: Deutsche Verlags-Anstalt, 1983.

Milward, Alan S. *The German Economy at War*. London: The Athlone Press of the University of London, 1965.

————. *The New Order and the French Economy*. London: Oxford University Press, 1970.

Moczarski, Kazimierz. *Conversations with an Executioner*. Edited by Mariana Fitzpatrick. Englewood Cliffs, NJ: Prentice-Hall, 1981.

von zur Mühlen, Patrik. *Zwischen Hakenkreuz und Sowjetstern. Der Nationalismus der sowjetischen Orientvölkern im Zweiten Weltkrieg.* Düsseldorf: Droste Verlag, 1971.

Müller-Hillebrand, Burckhart. *Der Zweifrontenkrieg.* Vol. III of *Das Heer 1939–1945.* 3 vols. Frankfurt am Main: E.S. Mittler & Sohn, 1969.

Müller, Norbert. *Wehrmacht und Okkupation 1941–1944. Zur Rolle der Wehrmacht und ihrer Führungsorgane im Okkupationsregime des faschistischen deutschen Imperialismus auf sowjetischen Territorium.* Berlin: Deutscher Militärverlag, 1971.

Myllyniemi, Seppo. *Die Neuordnung der baltischen Länder 1941–1944. Zum nationalsozialistischen Inhalt der deutschen Besatzungspolitik.* Helsinki: Vammalan Kirjapaino Oy, 1973.

Nekrich, Aleksandr M. *The Punished Peoples.* Translated by George Saunders. New York: W.W. Norton, 1978.

O'Neill, Robert J. *The German Army and the Nazi Party 1933–39.* London: Cassel & Company, Ltd., 1966.

Orlow, Dietrich. *The History of the Nazi Party: 1935–1945.* Pittsburgh, PA: University of Pittsburgh, 1973.

Orlowski, Slavomir. *Erich Koch pered polskim sudom.* Moscow: Institut Myezhdoonarodnikh Otnosheii, 1961.

Pfahlmann, Hans. *Fremdarbeiter und Kriegsgefangene in der deutschen Kriegswirtschaft 1939–1945.* Darmstadt: Wehr und Wissen Verlagsgesellschaft m.b.H., 1968.

Reitlinger, Gerald. *The House Built on Sand: The Conflicts of German Policy in Russia 1939–1945.* London: Weidenfeld & Nicolson, 1960.

Rich, Norman. *Hitler's War Aims.* 2 vols. New York: W.W. Norton, 1973–1974.

Riedel, Matthias. *Eisen und Kohle für das Dritte Reich.* Göttingen: Musterschmidt Verlag, 1973.

Scheurig, Bodo. *Henning von Tresckow: Eine Biographie.* Oldenberg: Stalling Verlag, 1973.

Smith, Woodruff O. *The Ideological Origins of Nazi Imperialism.* New York: Oxford University Press, 1986.

Speer, Albert. *Infiltration.* Translated by Joachim Neugroschel. New York: Macmillan, 1981.

Steenberg, Sven. *Vlasov.* Translated by Abe Farbstein. New York: Alfred A. Knopf, 1970.

Stein, George H. *The Waffen-SS: Hitler's Elite Guard at War 1939–1945.* Ithaca, NY: Cornell University Press, 1966.

Steinert, Marlis G. *Hitler's War and the Germans.* Edited and translated by Thomas E.J. Dewitt. Athens, OH: Ohio University Press, 1977.

Streit, Christian. *Keine Kameraden: Die Wehrmacht und die sowjetischen Kriegsgefangenen 1941–1945.* Stuttgart: Deutsche Verlags-Anstalt, 1978.

Thorwald, Jürgen. *The Illusion: Soviet Soldiers in Hitler's Armies.* Translated by Richard and Clara Winston. New York: Harcourt Brace Jovanovich, 1975.

———. *Wen sie verderben wollen. Bericht des grossen Verrats.* Stuttgart: Steingrüben-Verlag, 1952.

Tys-Krokhmaliuk, Yuriy. *UPA Warfare in Ukraine.* Translated by Walter Dushnyck. New York: Vantage Press, 1972.

Uustalu, Evald. *For Freedom Only: The Story of Estonian Volunteers in the Finnish Wars of 1920–1944.* Toronto: Northern Publications, 1977.

Vakar, Nicholas P. *Belorussia: The Making of a Nation*. Cambridge, MA: Harvard University Press, 1956.

Weinberg, Gerhard L. *The Foreign Policy of Hitler's Germany: Diplomatic Revolution in Europe, 1933–36*. Chicago: University of Chicago Press, 1970.

Zeller, Eberhard. *The Flame of Freedom: The German Struggle Against Hitler*. Translated by R.P. Heller and D.R. Masters. Coral Gables, FL: University of Miami Press, 1969.

Ziemke, Earl F. *Stalingrad to Berlin: The German Defeat in the East*. Washington, DC: Office of the Chief of Military History, 1968.

SECONDARY SOURCES: UNPUBLISHED MATERIALS

Theses and Dissertations

Blackstock, Paul W. "Covert Political Warfare: The Failure of German Political Warfare in Russia, 1941–45." Ph.D. dissertation, American University, 1954.

Burton, Robert B. "The Vlasov Movement of World War II: An Appraisal." Ph.D. dissertation, American University, 1963.

Gibbons, Robert J. "Soviet Industry and the German War Effort, 1939–1945." Ph.D. dissertation, Yale University, 1972.

Newland, Samuel J. "Cossacks in Field Grey: A History of the Recruitment of the Cossacks into the German Army, 1941–1945." Ph.D. dissertation, University of Kansas, 1982.

Pronin, Alexander. "Guerrilla Warfare in the German-occupied Soviet Territories 1941–44." Ph.D. dissertation, Georgetown University, 1965.

INDEX

ABOUT THE AUTHOR

TIMOTHY P. MULLIGAN was born in Baltimore, MD, on October 3, 1950. He received his B.A. and M.A. degrees from the University of Maryland, where he also received his Ph.D. in modern diplomatic history in 1985. Since 1979 he has served in the National Archives as a reference archivist specializing in captured German and related records. His articles on German military history and World War II have appeared in *The Historian, Military Affairs, Russian History* and the *Journal of Contemporary History*.